FOR LIMITED
REGISTRATION ONLY

This book is to be returned on or before
the last date stamped below

Forensic Psychotherapy

Crime, Psychodynamics and the Offender Patient

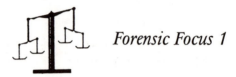 *Forensic Focus 1*

Forensic Psychotherapy

Crime, Psychodynamics and the Offender Patient

VOLUME I • MAINLY THEORY

Editors:

Christopher Cordess

*Consultant Forensic Psychiatrist, North West Thames
Forensic Psychiatry Service, London*

Murray Cox

Consultant Psychotherapist, Broadmoor Hospital

Forewords by

John Gunn, *Professor of Forensic Psychiatry, Institute of Psychiatry*
Richard Wells, *Chief Constable, South Yorkshire Police*

Jessica Kingsley Publishers
London and Bristol, Pennsylvania

First published in the United Kingdom in 1996 by
Jessica Kingsley Publishers Ltd
116 Pentonville Road
London N1 9JB, England
and
1900 Frost Road, Suite 101
Bristol, PA 19007, U S A

Copyright © 1996 Jessica Kingsley Publishers

'Murderous Guilt' by Nicholas Treurniet was first published in
The Dutch Annual of Psychoanalysis 1993 edited by H. Groen-Prakken and A. Ladan
(Swets and Zeitlinger, Lisse, 1993.) Reproduced by kind permission.

British Library Cataloguing in Publication Data
Forensic Psychotherapy:Crime,
Psychodynamics and the Offender Patient. -
(Forensic Focus Series; no.1)
I. Cordess, Christopher II. Cox, Murray
III. Series
614.1

Library of Congress Cataloging in Publication Data
A CIP catalogue record for this book is available from the Library of Congress

ISBN 1 85302 240 3
VOL I ISBN: 1 85302 371 X
VOL II ISBN: 1 85302 372 8

Printed and Bound in Great Britain by
Athenaeum Press, Gateshead and Tyne and Wear

Contents

Volume I • Mainly Theory

Volume II • Mainly Practice

Acknowledgements

One of the themes repeated in these pages is the fact that forensic psychotherapy always implies a corporate endeavour. No forensic psychotherapist can work in isolation. This applies, *a fortiori*, to those whose editorial task it has been to collate and integrate material from so many sources. First, our thanks are focused upon those patients and their therapists whose encounters furnish the substance of the numerous illustrative vignettes. Second, we are grateful to all who have written against the clock, and the constraints of space, to give us such a richly woven tapestry of theory and practice. Third, it is doubtful whether Jessica Kingsley and her colleagues could ever know the magnitude of the debt we owe them, although the very size of these volumes speaks volumes. Finally, mention must be made of Malcolm Smith of Karnac Books, who originally suggested that it was about time a book on Forensic Psychotherapy was written.

To all, our thanks.

That these final notes were written on Guy Fawkes Day may have some unconscious link to the possibility of threats to walled-off, closed institutions – no matter whether these are of the mind, of professional disciplines or of custodial establishments. On the other hand, Bonfire Night is also associated with the Catherine Wheel, and Saint Catherine is the patron saint of learning!

Christopher Cordess and Murray Cox
London
5 November 1994

Caveat

Substantial though this publication is, it has a relatively circumscribed frame of reference. This is not a text book embracing the wider field of forensic psychiatry. Thus it is taken for granted that, for the patients under discussion, forensic psychotherapy is one of the relevant treatments of choice. Important though forensic psychotherapy is in its own right, it only represents a fraction of an overall therapeutic policy which may legitimately apply to a forensic patient. When there are sound clinical indications, physical treatments, such as ECT, may be life-saving. For example, a patient may be so depressed that his psycho-motor retardation renders him inaccessible to dynamic psychotherapy, until appropriate medication has been prescribed for an adequate duration. Yet again, there are other general medical conditions, such as organic brain damage, hypertension or diabetes, which may have contributed to the pre-disposing/precipitating constellation of determinants originally leading to an individual entering the forensic field and becoming an 'offender patient'.

These introductory remarks are self-evident and patronizing to those who know the field well. Nevertheless, we hope that early establishment of such basic frames of reference will avoid subsequent misunderstanding and confusion.

By the same token, it will soon become apparent that our aim has been to present material which will be of relevance to those from a wide range of disciplines and at all levels of professional experience.

Before engaging with the first sentence of the book itself, it is to be stated unequivocally that any details which might render an individual patient recognizable or identifiable have been changed. We trust, however, that the psychodynamic significance of the clinical material and its illustrative potential are not thereby diminished.

Issues of confidentiality are of crucial importance in the forensic field. This cannot be emphasized too strongly, especially at a time when the communications explosion and the introduction of market forces into public health care systems threaten to blur the boundaries of who should know what about whom.

In the interest of gender presentation, brevity and cadence, as editors we have avoided the 'he/she', 'his/her' amalgam by using 'he' when individuals of either gender are implied. We would be equally happy writing 'she' to include 'he'. But, being male, this seems unnecessarily pedantic and absurd.

C.C. & M.C.

Foreword

John Gunn

It is a pleasure to me to welcome a book devoted to 'forensic psychotherapy'. As one of the editors says in one of his introductions, forensic psychotherapy is not a wholly felicitous term. Presumably this is because psychotherapy does not actually relate to the court of law ('the forum' of forensic). Presumably, too, it is because although psychiatry is getting specialized, is it not yet so specialized that it is legitimate to identify a special form of therapeutics called forensic psychotherapy. Nevertheless, the term is a useful one and many potential readers will rightly discern what they can expect between the covers of these volumes.

The treatment of mentally disordered people who offend has always and will always lean heavily on the talking treatments. Psychotherapy is an essential skill in any branch of psychiatry, and is particularly important for patients who have chronic problems and who are relating to the rest of society through unwelcome deeds, rather than through words. The term forensic psychotherapy also serves to remind mental health professionals that individuals with mental disorders who are offensive and prone to rejection need psychotherapy just as much as the better organized, better heeled members of society who traditionally make their way to the psychotherapist's chair or couch.

This book is written by professionals and enthusiasts with a wide range of skills, from psychoanalysis to occupational therapy, from law to social work, from psychology to dancing. One bias I have discerned is that most (but not all) writers seem to be talking about treatment within an institution. Perhaps this is inevitable as forensic psychiatry becomes the last repository of extended inpatient treatment, and furthermore there are groups of offender patients who can only be reached within an institution. Partly for that reason I want to highlight the few chapters that deal with offenders who live in the community. In many ways forensic psychiatry, with specialist hostels and sophisticated probation services has been a leader in community psychiatry, and pioneers such as Glover did most of their work in the outpatient clinic. It is important, therefore, to emphasize this aspect of psychotherapeutic potential, especially now that closer collaboration with police and probation services is becoming easier.

There is no danger in this book of an over-emphasis on what some people who work within the criminal justice system call 'the medical model'. This curious term, often used in a pejorative sense, seems to mean an over-emphasis on medical practitioners as therapists. This book acknowledges the obvious, that good treatment needs many skills (including exclusively medical ones such as pharmacotherapy) and these skills will always be delivered by a wide range of professionals. It is best that they work in harmony.

It is highly gratifying to see a chapter on research in this book. So often psychotherapy and research seem incompatible. As the authors of the chapter lament 'in an ideal world this chapter would review a large number of publications...but we do not yet live in that ideal world'. The chapter sets out many useful ideas for research in psychotherapy. Perhaps forensic psychotherapy can not only show that it is possible to treat the untreatable, but also that it is possible to research the unresearchable. Certainly a topic that tries to persist without a scientific basis is ultimately doomed to extinction.

There is another chapter which says it is a research chapter, but I found more difficulty with that one. Treurniet calls his detailed account of the psychoanalysis of a killer, scientific research. I wonder whether this is just a semantic problem, or whether there is something fundamental here which forensic psychotherapy needs to tackle. The chapter is interesting and the treatment enabled both the psychotherapist and the patient to acquire meaning for the killing; it seemed to provide a way for the patient to grow a little, perhaps become less guilt ridden, and thus find it easier when he was released. However, whilst this is a nice description of a piece of psychotherapy in action, it is not an example of scientific research. That is not to demean it or devalue it, it is simply to say that scientific research is a different enterprise with its own rules. Scientific research is not the only way we can understand the world, but it is a very powerful way and psychotherapy cannot afford to eschew it, nor, in my view, can it afford to make the error of thinking that all descriptive activities such as the careful recording of a psychoanalysis are necessarily the same thing as scientific research.

This book has something for everyone; a veritable bran tub. My hope is that it will make tongues wag, first in the clinic (that's what it is all about), but also in the corridors and in the committee rooms, so that the role of psychotherapy in forensic psychiatry can be more easily understood and appraised.

Foreword

Richard Wells

I am delighted to be able to offer a modest introduction to this seminal work edited by Christopher Cordess and Murray Cox, each in his own right a signal contributor to the corpus of knowledge and experience in forensic psychiatry.

Many readers in this specialist field may be provoked to ask: why on earth a foreword from a police officer?

The answer, for me, is fairly simple. Whereas once the world of psychiatry and psychotherapy was inward-looking and inclined to find its contentment and even verification in its own deliberations, these days this seems to be less and less the case. Perhaps it is because of the access to this specialist world provided by increasingly popular television documentary films; perhaps it is a result of society's becoming more questioning and challenging about itself; yet again, it may be in furtherance of a genuine spirit of partnership which appears to be growing in kindred professions, inspired by national strategies of trying to squeeze more product out of fewer resources.

Police officers encounter daily the world of the emotionally disturbed. Sometimes the degree of disturbance necessitates immediate care for and control of the patient, and officers, ill-equipped to make judgments on 'sectioning' despite the fact that the law suggests the opposite, call with relief upon the services of those who *are* so equipped.

Officers who are confronted, in their peace-keeping role or in their investigative role, with what to them are inexplicable horrors – either horrors of commission by individuals or horrors of omission by society – seek first practical assistance and then, often in the quiet of the aftermath, seek explanations, some sense of context in which their experience can be placed.

I do not suppose this to be a text book for police officers, for it is truly a specialist work, with a great deal of intricate and professional detail for the enrichment of each practitioner in the field of forensic psychotherapy. But it is a compendium which acknowledges, owes its origins to and complements the emergent spirit of partnership between parties within the criminal justice system.

There is something in this unique volume for all who are involved, whether at the core of forensic psychotherapy or, like me, at its periphery; whether interested in theory or practice, in understanding short of treatment or in understanding in order better to treat, there is an abundance of wisdom and experience captured in these pages.

In a hundred years, future practitioners – and, if they are so minded, social historians – will devour this text as offering a panoramic view of our contemporary society seen through the eyes of a wide variety of professional commentators.

One of the challenges for present readers will be to stand back sufficiently far to be able to glimpse that same broad perspective of our own communities, to ask ourselves what part we play, however small, in its betterment and to determine to widen that role through greater understanding and collaboration.

This work will provide both significantly greater appreciation of virtually every aspect of the field, and invaluable indicators to ways in which co-operative ventures might usefully be undertaken.

Preface
In and Out of the Mind

The Editors

'In and out of the mind' is a phrase which presented itself in early editorial discussions. It was intriguing because it had arisen simultaneously in separate settings. It occupies the key location which the opening words of a book always command for two reasons. First, in non-technical terms, it is in keeping with those vital polarities between inner and outer world phenomena, and between contents and container, which forensic psychotherapy ignores at its peril. This book is concerned with events in the inner world which destructively influence events in the outer world which, in turn, impinge upon the inner world of both assailant and victim. The forensic psychotherapist constantly weighs and re-weighs the impact of turbulence in one world as it precipitates turbulence in the other. This, subsequently, calls for the offender patient's tailor-made corrective emotional experience which it is hoped that psychotherapy can provide. With this end in view, the therapist's attention is never far from those energies and objects which are both 'in and out of the mind'.

It is important to underline the fact that the first paragraph refers to '*the* offender patient'. In other words, *individual* forensic psychotherapy pervades our subject and permeates both 'Mainly Theory' (Volume I) and 'Mainly Practice' (Volume II), to the extent that it seemed superfluous to include a separate chapter on Individual Psychotherapy.

The second source of 'In and out of the mind' is the title of a book by Ruth Padel (1992), a classicist, who is also at home in our field, her father, John Padel, being a psychoanalyst and Shakespeare scholar. The perspectival world of the classicist serves to re-frame current experience by setting it against earlier frames from history and larger frames from myth. Forensic therapeutic experience repeatedly testifies to the fact pointed out by Erikson (1959, p.13) that 'we cannot lift a case history out of history' – and forensic clinical histories are always embedded in the history, both 'in and out of the mind', of those who commit the criminal act and those who are their victims, whatever form this may take. Most psychotherapeutic processes can, with minor modifications, be regarded as ways of framing, de-framing and subsequently re-framing perception, emotion, experience and behaviour: the vicissitudes of transference development, differentiation and subsequent resolution can be thought of as the re-framing of affective location and attachment. We may link current preoccupation with clinical history, via trans-generational conflicts – and their resolution – to the ubiquitous and constant cosmos of myth. By way of illustration of this widest frame of reference, the first specific question posed in the present volumes is one which invites the reader to make an informed guess as to how many times the word *Oedipus* (or Oedipal) is likely to occur in a work of this size, without taking the short cut to the index pages! The very mention of *Oedipus* makes the point that timeless issues are also finely focused in the numerous clinical histories which forensic psychotherapy explores and these pages explicate. Padel (1992) writes as follows:

> '*When tragic poets write about what is inside people, they are also writing about what is outside,* as their culture represents it. *Outside explains inside, and vice versa.*' (p.11. Emphasis added)

It should come as no surprise that the second invited guest to join the theme of this preface is Sherlock Holmes, for the impact of myth and the work of the detective have close links to forensic dynamics. In *The Cardboard Box* (Conan Doyle 1893), Sherlock Holmes asks:

> 'What is the meaning of it, Watson?
> What object is served by this circle of misery and violence and fear?'
> (p.52)

Although there is a long tradition of the application of psychodynamic ideas to the understanding of the offender and his act, it is only in recent years that this body of experience and theory, and the treatments which have evolved from it, have been acknowledged as an essential ingredient within the hybrid speciality of Forensic Psychiatry. A main reason is the increasing recognition of the centrality of psychological trauma and victimization in the personal histories of offenders, together with recognition of the suffering of the victims of criminal acts and other traumata, and their psychological sequelae. Whether we are considering the individual offender or the offender within the context of the family, the group, the institution or broadly within society, forensic psychotherapy asks, along with Sherlock Holmes, 'What is the meaning of it... this circle of misery and violence and fear?' The answer may frequently be complex and is sometimes elusive. But, invariably, it contains elements of past neglect, or trauma – such as a major early loss (of parent or sibling, for example) – or of abuse and failures of parenting, with consequent failure to achieve full emotional and personality development. This may later be manifest in a restricted capacity for empathy, poor self-esteem and unusually disruptive attachments and relationships, which may all play a part in leading to offending behaviour. This is as true for the major mental illnesses as for the personality disorders and sexual deviations. Mental illness alone is rarely a sufficient explanation of later violent and offensive behaviour, since there is no clear association between mental illness, *per se*, and criminality, except in the case of the paranoid psychoses.

The work of the forensic psychotherapist is similar to that undertaken in generic psychotherapy but with the crucial additional task of understanding the psychological necessity and the meaning of the criminal act. Within the therapeutic relationship, psychotherapist and patient *together* seek to understand the whole situation – not only intellectually but also emotionally.

One of the turning points in man's view of his place in the world, and specifically a spur for future developments in theories of sexuality and aggression, was Darwin's publication of *The Origin of the Species* (1859) and later *The Descent of Man* (1871). Later in the century and around its turn there was a rapid development of the concept of the unconscious which had a considerable impact upon the dynamic understanding of deviant and criminal acts. Mention only has to be made of the dynamics of 'dissociative phenomena' to bring a range of clinical considerations into focus. Ellenberger (1970) shows how much Freud was indebted to numerous scientific and literary sources in the gradual elaboration of his theories of the unconscious and of the repression and expression of sexual (libidinal) and aggressive instincts.

The Freudian body of clinical and theoretical knowledge forms the basis from which contemporary forensic psychotherapy traces many of its origins. Although Freud wrote little specifically on criminality – the classic papers being 'Criminals from a sense of Guilt' (1916) and 'The Exceptions' (1916) – there are other texts of particular relevance, such as 'Three Essays on the Theory of Sexuality' (1905c), 'The Case of Schreber' (1911b), and 'Group Psychology and the Analysis of the Ego' (1921), to cite just a few.

Later, the development of 'object relations theory' provided a huge impetus to psychodynamic thinking in relation to the criminal and his act. It should be noted that in this technical sense as used here and throughout these volumes, 'object' refers to another person, an animal or a thing. In their different ways Klein, then Winnicott, Bowlby, Fairbairn and later Bion moved away from instinct theory and the *intra*-personal, and towards 'object' relatedness, that is, the *inter*-personal, inter-subjective and the social context. Some of the crucial theoretical concepts, which are fully addressed in this book, include those of 'internal objects' (or 'mental representations'), 'unconscious phantasy', the 'holding environment' and the 'container and contained'. Using these concepts, psychodynamic knowledge has been applied increasingly beyond the individual patient to the greater understanding of groups. Its relevance and application to both secure and open institutions has been a recent growth area (see 'Special Settings' in Volume II). The former includes regional secure units, prisons and Special Hospitals and the latter category embraces a wide range of different settings in addition to the Therapeutic Community.

Forensic psychotherapy consists of the adaptation and application of this psychoanalytic *corpus* of knowledge, in conjunction with related sister disciplines – such as the other psychotherapies, criminology, sociology, psychiatry and ethology. It necessarily contains elements of the interests of society and of an expectation of social adjustment. There is thus always the idea of a third party present. Moreover, a third party is usually present in fact, represented by one or more elements of the Criminal Justice System. The concretization of this third party, in terms of legal constraints, and its impact on the inherent dynamic processes, forms much of the substance of this work.

A cursory glance through these pages will immediately convey the impression of a wide variety of writing styles and modes of presentation. Not only was this inevitable, it was also encouraged. But lest we are accused of diminished editorial responsibility, it needs to be stated that each contributor was given free rein, within the minimum of inevitable editorial constraints, to write as he felt best. There is thus no enforced editorial imprint. When a book of over 1000 pages, with 66 chapters, has been written by an ensemble of more than 60 authors a certain degree of repetition and overlap is inevitable.

It is our hope and expectation that the confluence of diverse professional interests and theoretical positions has been allowed to begin to map out the boundaries surrounding the currently crystallizing discipline of forensic psychotherapy. The orchestration of the 'Mainly Theory' section is clear evidence that no single theoretical persuasion has a monopoly of explanatory truth. Critical eclecticism is of the essence. These pages also give clear evidence of the interdependence of theory and practice. 'Mainly Theory' invokes illustrative clinical vignettes, whilst 'Mainly Practice' is permeated by conceptual and theoretical issues.

There are certain axiomatic aspects of forensic psychotherapy which, although beyond question, still need to be made explicit. They could be regarded as 'ground-base' motifs which underlie the ensuing theme and its variations. We refer first to the relationship between the *criminal act* and the tantalizing search for an accurately fitting *therapeutic act*. Or should we speak of the *criminal process* to be reflected in a reversed yet isomorphic *therapeutic process*? Second, we underline the collaborative nature of forensic psychotherapy.

It is entirely fitting that the first chapter of Volume I should be devoted to the crucial issue of 'the criminal act and acting out'. Debate about the nature and duration of such an act is both heated and prolonged. Thus, in answer to the question 'How long does it take to commit a murder?' one patient replied 'A lifetime', although the lethal gunshot wound required increased pressure on the trigger for less than a second. But if the criminal act cannot easily be defined and isolated, how much more complicated is the endeavour to delineate the therapeutic act. Again, the self-positing question is 'does such a definable entity exist?' In these volumes the forensic therapeutic process is looked at by a wide range of experienced practitioners, who inevitably approach the theme from divergent vantage points.

The necessity for eclecticism is underscored by the fact that, despite the size of the present volumes, there is much that remains conjecture or rests upon the weight of 'clinical experience' which may be only slightly more reliable than hazardous. It is for this reason that, as editors, we attach such importance to the triple-authored chapter on research. We well understand that critics and reviewers will be searching for hard evidence as to the efficacy or otherwise of forensic psychotherapeutic practice. Even so, immediate existential imperatives also refuse to be silenced. When dealing with such awesome issues, frequently involving interpersonal violence, humane 'containment' and all that this implies can never be less than important: this ambiguous, bi-focal term refers both to the *concrete* containment within a secure environment and the *metaphorical* containment within a holding relationship. The offender patient often needs both at the same time.

The second ground-base of this theme and variations is the indubitable fact that forensic psychotherapy always implies a collaborative endeavour between a range of agencies and disciplines. Sometimes, it is involved in residential and/or custodial settings and sometimes it is practised in the wider community of the 'body politic'. No forensic psychotherapist can 'go it alone'. Ethical issues are inevitable and intrinsic to the whole field. Such topics as confidentiality, public safety, the dilemma between the premature release of a potentially dangerous offender, or the unnecessarily prolonged detention of a no-longer-dangerous detainee, are matters of daily deliberation.

However encompassing a text such as this may be, there are inevitably some areas which deserve more emphasis than they have received. These volumes are no exception. The significance of issues of gender, of the differential rate of criminality and the different responses of the criminal justice and healthcare systems to men and women are increasingly acknowledged. The social, political and psychological constructions which underlie such differences are complex. In Chapter II:15 Estela Welldon contrasts the male and female perversions, but forensic psychotherapy needs to address issues of gender more widely. Similarly, issues of race, of ethnic diversity, of refugees and exile, where they impinge upon criminality, are increasingly the focus for other related disciplines – forensic psychiatry, for example (Cope 1990; Department of Health 1992). This is another important area in forensic psychotherapy which requires greater exploration. We hope that both these themes will be the subjects of future volumes in the *Forensic Focus* series.

It was more by good fortune than deliberate foresight that the interesting dialectic emerged between the title of the first chapter, *The Criminal Act and Acting Out*, and that of the last, namely, *Dance Movement Therapy*. In psychodynamic circles mention is often made of 'movement' occurring during the session. This usually refers to intrapsychic movement. It is evidenced by a relinquishment of primitive defences and a growing capacity to enjoy creative living: this includes an augmented ability to be both self-critical and more self-controlled in some ways and less so in others. It is therefore something of a light relief to discover that movement therapy and the dance – literally that which involves whole body movement as well as an abandonment to creative body rhythms – invites us to 'take the floor' and see where the latent energy in the ideas presented in these pages may lead.

As editors, we hope that these volumes will suggest areas of expertise which should be the preserve of specialist forensic psychotherapists. A greater hope is that they will be a source of information and stimulus to those who work in related disciplines where society, the offender and particularly the victim try to come to terms with the implications of what Shakespeare described as 'the acting of a dreadful thing' (*Julius Caesar* II.1.63).

Sherlock Holmes and his question 'What is the meaning of it, Watson?' here join forces with those of antiquity in studying and attempting to modify issues which are 'in and out of the mind'.

Mainly Theory

Introduction

Christopher Cordess

'Forensic psychotherapy' is the not wholly felicitous term used to describe the psychodynamic treatment of offenders and victims. Offenders themselves have frequently been victims of earlier exploitation and trauma and, psychologically speaking, are commonly victims of their own criminal behaviour, whether they fully recognize it or not; victims and survivors may become offenders. The overlap is great and is increasingly recognized.

Crime statistics inform us that reported criminal activity increases year on year, and, for example, popular literature, film and the media attest to a preoccupation within our culture with the criminal, and especially with violence. Whilst crime *per se* is a man-made concept, its origins lie in such notions as transgression, evil, sin and wickedness (Midgely 1992) and are as old as history. Just as we largely define health by the absence of ill health, so it appears that we seek to define our experience of the 'good' by an absence of its negative; at least some of our interest in or fascination with crime can be attributed to this function.

The origins and evolution of the psychodynamic body of knowledge are part of the history of ideas. As such, psychodynamic ideas draw from a range of different sources; they change, develop and even now are moving on. Ellenberger (1970) describes the diverse ancestry of the concept of the 'unconscious' and of 'the first dynamic psychiatry' which grew rapidly during the nineteenth century. He further traces 'the dawn and rise of the *new* dynamic psychiatry' in this century, and the part played by its four great representatives – Janet, Freud, Adler and Jung.

This broad ancestry of psychodynamic theory in general is reflected in its contemporary application to the understanding of the criminal mind: it necessarily shares territory with many close and, one hopes, friendly neighbours. Thus, in Part I, alongside chapters on the central concepts of psychoanalytic theory and related forensic aspects, the reader will find contributions from many cognate and overlapping disciplines, and their incorporation and

9

application to evolving psychodynamic theories of offending behaviour and treatment. We take as our cue Freud's (1925b) own view that 'in the case of children and young delinquents, and as a rule, criminals dominated by their instincts, the psychoanalytic method must be adapted to meet the need' (p.vii).

Exploration of the inter-relation of criminology with early concepts of the unconscious mind were also common in the nineteenth century. For example Freud (1916a) in his brief and classic paper 'Criminals from a sense of Guilt', records that 'a friend has since called my attention to the fact that the "criminal from a sense of guilt" was known to Nietzsche, too. The pre-existence of the feeling of guilt, and the utilization of a deed in order to rationalize this feeling glimmer before us in Zarathustra's sayings "Of the Pale Criminal"' (p.333) – which Nietzsche wrote in 1883. Ellenberger (1970) describes, too, the pre-Freudian concept of self-deception of consciousness by the unconscious and by emotional thinking. He writes that, 'the vicissitudes of instincts (their combinations, conflicts, displacements, sublimations, regressions and turnings against oneself), the energy load of representations, the self-destructive drives in man' (p.543), as well as the origins of conscience, of guilt feelings and morals were typically Neitzschean, and common to much German Romantic philosophy of the nineteenth century. The reader will find much in the following chapters of these and other roots and their development in contemporary psychodynamic thinking.

There is one concept of particular interest which provides a forerunner to much which is central to forensic psychotherapy – and indeed any dynamic psychotherapy – and that is the theme of 'The Pathogenic Secret' (Ellenberger 1966). The idea of the pathogenic effect which a guilty secret may exert over its bearer has been common in different civilisations throughout history: so, too, have related ideas of the healing action of group or individual confession. The concept was brought into the psychotherapeutic sphere largely by Moritz Benedict (1835–1920): its development can be traced, through early dynamic psychiatry as a consciously held secret, into the theories of Janet and Freud who first conceptualized it as an *unconsciously* known secret. For Freud it was classically one consequence of repression and 'splitting' from consciousness of unacceptable events and phantasies. The concept of splitting – of both the ego and the object – and of fragmentation of the mind were much developed by Klein (1946) and by later theorists, and have become central to our subject. The theme of the pathogenic secret provides a strong link with contemporary theories of trauma – and specifically of the emotional and psychological consequences of early neglect and physical and sexual abuse – and the later effects if the traumatic event (the 'secret') cannot be worked through. These include abnormalities and impoverishment of personality, a range of psychiatric disorders, a propensity to 'dissociative' states of mind, and most pertinently, later offensive and criminal behaviour. The idea of the pathogenic secret is a forerunner, too, of the whole debate and furore which surrounds 'recovered memory syndrome'. The concept of 'the secret' and of the clandestine – both conscious and unconscious – have centrality in psychodynamic theories of offending and therapeutic practice, and are a primary theme which is explored in many different ways in the following pages.

The range of different viewpoints which exist within contemporary psychodynamic thinking is perhaps nowhere better illustrated than in the theories of aggression and hostility, which lie at the heart of forensic psychotherapy. They provide a direct focus for a number of these chapters, but are a prominent theme, indirectly, in others; for example, in the chapters on 'Psychotic and Borderline Processes', and in 'Defence Mechanisms'. The harnessing of aggression is described, too, in the chapter on 'Personality and Sexual Development'. The creative use and management of aggression within the transference–countertransference relationship brings us to the very core of our subject.

The Criminal Act and Acting Out

Christopher Cordess & Arthur Hyatt Williams

In law there are two requirements for a criminal act: the *actus reus* – that is, the overt act or offensive conduct (which may include an omission) – and a *mens rea* – or guilty state of mind. The exceptions are the so-called crimes of strict liability. For pragmatic reasons the law generally places greater emphasis upon the cognitive aspects of mental state rather than the emotional, although clearly the two elements are intimately entwined. Thus different offences may require a range of different mental elements, from intentionality, for example 'malice aforethought' as in murder, to recklessness or negligence. Other common terms which can be the source of legal dispute include questions of whether an act was 'voluntary', or whether it was 'knowingly' committed and whether the subject can be judged mentally responsible.

For the forensic psychotherapist such questions are central but viewed from a different standpoint. For the psychotherapist the criminal act is seen as a consequence of a state of mind in which unconscious processes and unconscious phantasy, as well as conscious thought, may also be major components. What is the meaning of the act? is the recurrent question. The therapeutic process aims to elucidate the frequently multiple conscious and unconscious meanings, and to lend to it greater affective as well as cognitive understanding. The offender may thereby no longer wish to repeat his criminal acts and may achieve greater powers to desist: he may also become able to make both psychic and actual reparation.

Crime is a man-made construct and is relative within different societies at different times. For the psychotherapist there is an assumption that all of us from our earliest years, as well as later, 'commit crimes' within our unconscious and conscious minds which we do not necessarily, however, enact. Thought,

fantasy (conscious) and phantasy (unconscious)[1] is free: the 'thought crime' of
George Orwell, or adultery 'in the heart' of the New Testament have had no
place, at least yet, within English law. Williams (1983) quotes Sir Edward Coke
'No man shall be examined upon secret thoughts of his heart, or of his secret
opinion: but something ought to be objected against him what he hath spoken
or done' (p.146).

The 'secret thoughts of his heart' and his emotional life are the primary
focus of all psychodynamic psychotherapy, but forensic psychotherapy takes
account also of past and future possible criminal acts. The personality of the
patient and his way of being are the subject of mutual investigation by patient
and therapist. The psychodynamic model assumes developmental continuities
through stages of life built upon inherent (constitutional) capacities of the new
born and dependent upon later progressive life experience ('object relations').
It places particular emphasis upon the developmental importance of the
experience of the first and early years, so that early failure by the primary carer
(usually the mother) or experience of trauma or abuse are predicted to have
significant psychological effects in later life. It joins with Socrates, in its own
particular way, in assuming that 'the unexamined life is not worth living' (Plato
1993, p.63). It is the theory of the unconscious and of the use of the
transference and counter-transference inter-action within therapeutic relationships which give it its particularity.

All psychodynamic psychotherapy provides some sort of narrative to a life
– as a particular type of biography or autobiography. There is debate (as in
biography) about the degree to which this is an historically true narrative and
the degree to which, instead, it can aspire only to be an emotionally true
re-construction (Spence 1983). Strict historical truth is not necessary for the
healing process to evolve. Forensic psychodynamic psychotherapy emphasises
the criminal act (or acts) as an important focus within this narrative. To borrow
from behavioural-cognitive terminology, the task is to examine as many as
possible of the 'antecedents' to the act, the 'act' itself, and its 'consequences'
in detail, both consciously, and for the psychodynamicist also in terms of
unconscious forces and phantasy.

There have been, it should be said, some strident objections to the use of
such narrative re-constructions in the understanding of the criminal mind and
the criminal act, and to the drawing of deterministic and causal inference from
the re-construction. Foucault (1979), for example, objects that (in his terminology) 'the *delinquent* is to be distinguished from the *offender* by the fact that
it is not so much his act as his life that is relevant in characterising him' (p.251,
emphasis added). This objection needs to be taken seriously; a variant of it is

---

1   The convention of the different spellings of fantasy/phantasy is used in this chapter to refer to
    conscious and unconscious representation respectively.

heard day-to-day, clinically, in the justifiable complaint of some offenders, as in, for example, 'I am not a rapist, but I am a man who committed a rape'. Foucault goes on to argue against a 'punitive technique...(which) reconstitutes all the sordid detail of a life in the form of biographical knowledge and a technique for correcting individual lives' (p.252). Actually it is the conjunction of criminology and psychiatric discourse which Foucault criticizes but the critique provides a significant counterpoint for the over-zealous, and to the coercive imposition of 'correctives' to offensive actions in the name of 'therapy' which may thereby follow. The Criminal Act – as other acts – is multi-determined, and is the consequence of many variables both in the external world and in the internal world of the mind.

Richman (1932, p.45) points us to some of the obvious but frequently neglected truths concerning some crime: first, the criminal cannot always give a reasonable explanation for his act: second, there is frequently a compulsive element to the behaviour, and third, criminals, when we meet them often do not, in fact, appear to be so aggressive as we expect and as they are commonly regarded by the general public, as a consequence of their act. For the forensic psychotherapist these are common observations which require investigation and understanding in each individual case.

How does the *actual* crime emerge from a conscious fantasy or unconscious phantasy? Does it directly short circuit into action or hesitate for a shorter or a longer time in a constellation of 'criminal impulses'? What psychic processes are involved in the different procedures? In an individual case, how much is the potential criminal consciously aware of what is going on inside his mind? And most important, from a therapeutic point of view, can the sequence be diverted into some less criminal outcome, or will it gather a more criminal nature (as in the mental 'rehearsal' of a crime) during the course of the progression from phantasy-to-impulse-to-action? Retrospectively, the pre-existing fantasy (or phantasy) is commonly found to have been present and to have crystallized in the mind long before the actual criminal act. Sometimes it is quite simple, like the children's story about Burglar Bill and Burglar Betty whose behaviour was based upon a greedy wish and need to get what they wanted by simply taking it. Sometimes it is recognized by the conscience of the subject as being wrong and while his reality sense battles with the impulse to act it out, the impulsive part of his mind demands that he should 'do it', whatever it is.

Freud (1911a) describes the interplay and opposition of the *pleasure principle* – that is, the desire for the direct discharge of impulses – and the *reality principle* – which may oppose such discharge. Translated into our own terms the question becomes: can this conflict – which may be conscious or unconscious – be kept in the mind, so that some 'mellowing in cask', so to speak, can occur whereby the outcome may be modified and the action (in this case the criminal act) not therefore necessarily follow? In certain circumstances, the conflict 'to be or not to be' is pre-loaded by earlier experiences and the way they have been handled in the mind. Commonly, traumatic sensitizing experience, repressed in the unconscious, may be reawakened and detonated by a subsequent similar experience. Unworked-through anger and resentment, for example, may explode in a way which is quite out of proportion to the contemporaneous provocation. There may be triggering factors such as alcohol or drug intoxication: or intoxicating substances may be taken intentionally – to give 'Dutch courage' – in order to make the commission of the criminal act possible. An opportunity for violence may be sought or provoked. In forensic practice one frequently meets people who routinely carry a lethal weapon, which is rationalized as 'for the purposes of self defence': underlying such rationalization there may be the thought or phantasy: 'if I am threatened, I can and I will kill'.

A prisoner patient in psychotherapy with one of the authors (HW), said, 'It all happens in my mind and I feel that I can contain it no longer, so I go out and do it: after that I feel better, and I can be kind to my victim, and I can face the consequences' (of the action). The action was the serial assault of pre-pubertal girls. It consisted of a token constriction of the throat with her scarf, then quickly releasing it, then touching, but never penetrating, her genitals with his penis. In this sequence, as it became understood during therapy, he reversed and re-enacted what had happened to him as a young boy at the hands of a pre-pubertal girl. Although the fantasy is partially enacted in this repeated sequence, shame, guilt and reparative wishes had so far intervened before the ultimate tragedy ensued. A similar – albeit more terrible – pattern may be seen in the case of a type of serial murderer. In those instances in which the victim does not die immediately as the perpetrator intended, then, when, for example, the victim recovers consciousness, the later actions may be basically reparative (Masters 1985). The surge of murderous intent has by then diminished for the time being.

Of course, some criminal acts are planned in full conscious awareness, and may be motivated, for example, by greed, revenge, envy or perverse sexual desire. Nevertheless, they will all, also, have less conscious elements. The elucidation of these elements and the opportunity to talk about them may enable the individual to have the luxury of prior consideration and a capacity for thinking about what he has a mind to do, and may thereby offer him the possibility of not having to carry it out.

The aim of helping the potential offender talk about his emotional state is captured, at its very simplest, by William Blake (1794)

'I was angry with my friend:
I told my wrath, my wrath did end.
I was angry with my foe:
I told it not, my wrath did grow.'

As already described, a previous, emotionally unbearable traumatic experience may erupt into offensive action if it has remained 'split off' and, psychologically speaking, has remained 'undigested' or 'unmetabolised'. When there are later psychological stresses – either external, like the loss of a loved one, or intrapsychic, such as depression or a paranoid illness – then the previously stable, internal dynamic situation may explode, so that the individual feels 'taken over'. Such a situation was described first in the psychiatric literature by Wertham (1949) as the 'Catathymic Crisis', which for the perpetrator at that moment appears to be 'the only way out'.

Such eruptions into action are sometimes loosely referred to as 'acting out', by an analogy to the specific use of the term 'acting out' (German: 'agieren') as used by Freud (1905a, 1914b). 'Acting out' referred originally to a clinical, psychoanalytic concept which was confined quite specifically to the psycho-analytic, treatment relationship. It was seen as a transference reaction, as a manifestation of resistance to it, and as a substitute for a failure of 'remember-ing', and being able to think within the analytic relationship. In the case of Dora (S. Freud, 1905a), the patient left treatment, according to Freud, as a way of taking her revenge on him transferentially, in a way that she felt that she had been deserted by a figure in her past. Later, Freud (1914b) writes of this phenomenon as '...the patient does not remember anything of what he has forgotten and repressed but acts it out. He reproduces it not as a memory but as an action; he repeats it, without, of course, knowing that he is repeating it...for instance, the patient does not say that he remembers that he used to be defiant and critical towards his parents' authority; instead he behaves that way to the doctor (therapist)' (p.150).

Premature departures from treatment are particularly familiar in the treat-ment of offender patients, and acting out may well be an accurate description of such occurrences. However, many authors have commented upon the imprecision and over-generalization which have accrued to the term: for example Blos (1966, quoted by Sandler et al. 1973, p.94) writes that the concept 'has by now been expanded to accommodate delinquent behaviour and all kinds of...pathology and impulsive actions'. The term 'acting out' has even been applied on the one hand to the actions of creative artists, and on the other to the whole range of offending behaviour, the addictions, to the conversion symptoms of hysteria, to the rituals of the obsessional and to psychotic states. When a term is used so widely it becomes devalued.

Put another way, if the term 'acting out' is to be used, there is a necessary subsidiary question to be asked 'an acting out of what?'. As applied to the criminal act committed by a person who is not in a therapeutic relationship, it is being used in its widest sense and refers to a motor action associated with conscious or unconscious fantasy or memory. When applied to the action – whether criminal or not – of a patient who is already in a therapeutic relationship, its specific meaning is that of the *actualization* of unconscious memory (for example, of a trauma) or phantasy which is not being contained within the transference. Rycroft (1979a) puts the matter characteristically simply, 'Since psychoanalysis is a "talking cure" carried out in a state of reflection, acting out is anti-therapeutic. Acting out is characteristic of psycho-pathy and behaviour disorders and reduces the accessibility of these conditions to psychoanalysis' (p.1). It is for this reason that forensic psychotherapy – although it traces its origins predominantly to the psychoanalytic body of experience and knowledge – is an applied discipline, which necessitates the incorporation of the points of view of many other related disciplines and the application of techniques of 'management', when acting out threatens to become unacceptably dangerous.

In addition, although a pejorative sense is not intrinsic to the concept, its usage has often amounted to a description of actions which others (frequently the therapist) condemn, and it has come to imply too great a judgmental quality. Whilst this may have a 'feel good' factor in it for the therapist, it is useless to the patient unless the meaning of the action can be understood by the therapist, and communicated to the patient so that he feels understood.

Freud made the distinction between acting out *within* the analytic (thera-peutic) relationship, and acting out *outside* of it, but 'both forms are regarded as a consequence of the analytic work and the treatment situation' (Sandler *et al.* 1973, p.96). An obvious example of the former is that of a patient repeatedly missing his sessions or turning up late: an example of the latter is when a form of idealized relationship is preserved with the therapist, but the patient behaves dismissively and aggressively in his relationships with others, as a consequence of unconscious rejection of, and anger with, the therapist.

Extrapolating from the concepts of Klein, and Bion (1970), 'acting out' may encompass a 'breaking in' of the self as a container into psychosis or suicide, or alternatively 'breaking out' into offending behaviour.

Two other terms should be mentioned, for the sake of completeness. 'Acting in' is a term which has been coined to refer to non verbal enactment within the therapeutic session, for example psychosomatic manifestations of anxiety or aggression. It is a disputed and specialized concept and need not detain us here.

More important is that of 'acting out' in the countertransference – or, alternatively 'acting out *of* the countertransference'. This is a constant and ubiquitous danger in forensic psychotherapy. Put starkly, the patient may induce in the therapist – by projective identification – a range, for example, of antagonistic or seductive feelings which the therapist may act upon without conscious realization. Acting out of the countertransference – in fact, acting out *for* the patient – may merely repeat for the patient what he sadly already knows from past experience only too well. An obvious example is that the therapist may feel that he wishes to reject the patient who has had a lifetime of rejection: the patient repeatedly induces an impulse or desire to dismiss him and thereby, as it were, to fulfil his expectation. Alternatively, the feelings engendered by the patient may be more than the therapist can hold and the therapist may act out outside of the relationship with the patient, or he may himself break down. Alternatively, he may cut off emotionally from the patient, and, thereby, behave in an emotionally ruthless way. Put another way, the therapist may become 'blind' and 'deaf' to the criminal past and potential for the future. The task of finding a way of talking to the patient using the countertransferential experience, without succumbing to these alternatives, is part of the essence of forensic psychotherapy. The subject is more fully discussed in Chapter I:2.

The Criminal Act can tell us much about aspects of the internal (mental) world of the perpetrator, which frequently have remained unconscious and unknown to him consciously – until, that is, he is faced with the fact and the consequences of his act. The internal 'state of affairs' – to use a phrase of Fairbairn's (1951, p.170) – may be denied by the perpetrator in many different ways, both conscious and unconscious, but all with the common goal of 'not wishing to know'. For example, in the sexual perversions, say in the actions of paedophiles, there may be an *exquisite* requirement for replicated detail, with evidence of planning, but remarkably little conscious fantasy. Denial may be conscious and stark as in: 'I didn't do it', or it may be that there are a range of different levels of partly conscious or unconscious self-deception. Typically, the paedophile may maintain 'I really do love children' – a denial and reversal of hate and of his wish to damage; or, 'they wanted me to do it' – a clear projection of desire and responsibility. A very literal example of desperate (and only partial) self-deception was that of a patient treated by one of the authors (CC), who not only effectively emptied his mind of any thought or other form of mentation whilst he sexually abused his step-daughters, but also covered his eyes with a pillow during the act – for fear of seeing what he was doing. In fact the acts were ritualized, elaborate and unvarying.

Alternatively, denial may take the form of a genuine amnesia. For example, in something like a half of all murders and some other major violence (at least in Britain) there will be partial or total amnesia for the fateful act, as if the mind could not bear the stark and emotionally traumatic experience of it: in other cases there may be memory but little or no feeling. Part of the task of the psychotherapist will be to try to help the perpetrator know more, both cognitively and affectively, about his action.

Some criminal acts may be considered analogous to the dream in which the 'manifest' content (S. Freud 1900, 1901) is either a representation of the internal unconscious state of mind, or the consequence of a compromise between 'latent' content and defensive censoring. For example, one psychotic patient spoke of his act of murder not as something that had, tragically, *actually* happened, but rather as 'a dream' (more like a day-dream): upon being asked to tell the dream, he related the narrative sequence of his act in minute and (so far as corroboration allowed one to judge) exact detail.

Stoller (1979) makes a related but more general point when he writes that, 'In an episode of erotic excitement is packed an individual's life history, the resultant character structure, and the more varied and movable defences we call neurosis…a fine way to understand someone is by that person's typical erotic daydream (p.293). Later he says 'Daydreams – all, not just the erotic – are terribly revealing as their owners know' (p.294); it is the tragedy of the criminal that he may only know his possible 'day dreams' by his acts, as it were, after the fact.

Another analogy is that of 'play'. Klein (1927) writes of her experience in the analysis of children using her (then) very original play technique. By the use of tiny dolls, animals, cars, trains and so on, she could, she writes, 'enable the child to represent various persons – (for example,) mother, father, brothers and sisters – and by means of the toys to act all its most repressed unconscious material' (p.174). She describes the very violent, murderous – biting, cutting and mutilating – phantasies of the normal child revealed by this technique, as well as the feelings of guilt and the consequent reparative wishes which are engendered by them. Klein herself draws attention to the analogy between this evidence of children's unconscious phantasies and some 'very horrible crimes', enacted by adults: she cites Jack the Ripper and serial killers known indirectly to her from contemporary reports.

In this chapter we have placed the criminal act centre stage. The psychotherapist allows himself to forget the past, or current, criminal acts of his patients at his peril: 'I've put it all behind me, doctor', and 'I've turned over a new leaf'; or 'I'm starting a new life', are tempting but frequently omnipotent fantasies with which we can all sympathize. If based on denial, they can be catastrophic as a way of dealing with a traumatized and traumatizing history. However, it also needs to be said that the past criminal act should not be allowed to occupy the whole of the arena of the therapeutic relationship all of the time, and there are some patients at some stages of their treatment who invite the therapist to do this. A patient may feel a consuming guilt for his act(s) – for example, the killing of a child or a spouse, *or* an objectively relatively minor transgression but one which he feels is unforgivable and puts him beyond redemption or recovery. In these cases the therapeutic task will be to help the patient to gain perspective, to help him hold on to a feeling of hope, and to the possibility of making some form of reparation.

It is within the psychotherapeutic relationship and the interplay of transference and countertransference reaction that the 'criminal act' and offensive behaviour needs to be experienced for it to be understood, jointly, by therapist and patient.

Transference and Countertransference
General and Forensic Aspects

Nicholas Temple

INTRODUCTION

In this chapter I will outline how the concepts of transference and counter-transference are used in psychotherapy. These concepts provide a framework which allows us to understand the therapeutic relationship and its complex interaction with the patient's subjective conscious and unconscious mind (the 'internal world'). In the forensic field this framework is essential to understand the often very disturbed aspects of the internal world which are acted out in criminal behaviour. These disturbed aspects become part of the transference relationship and present the therapist with special difficulties in tolerating his responses.

In psychodynamic psychotherapy transference and countertransference are the main therapeutic tools and the most important means of making contact with the patient's unconscious mental life. This type of psychotherapy is defined by the use of the relationship with the therapist as a focus of the work and distinguishes it from other forms of therapy.

Transference not only occurs in therapeutic relationships but also appears in many human relationships, when a way of relating to a figure from the past is repeated in the present, with a person who may trigger the old pattern of relating to be re-enacted. It is essential for all psychiatrists to be aware of this tendency and to be able to recognize and understand it, even when it is inappropriate to take it up with the patient. This understanding can prevent the psychiatrist from re-enacting with the patient an unhelpful pattern of behaviour derived from the past. The psychiatrist's countertransference feelings may draw him more deeply into acting out with the patient or can be the means by which he can begin to understand what is happening.

Transference is part of everyday life, because we all live out scenarios from our own inner world. We repeat our own internal unresolved dialogues with the people we come across. Frequently, this enactment will involve the other party in a similar repetition of a past relationship. This is why people find they repeat the same pattern of relationship, for example in a marriage, even with a different partner. The power of the internal world and its tendency to repetition is greater than is commonly recognized. The re-enactment of relationships with internal figures will be accompanied by emotional qualities and anxieties which are characteristic of the past relationship.

The internal relationships reflect relationships with early and important figures which have been transformed into the inner objects. These figures are found again in the present and repetitive attempts are made to resolve the difficulties of the past in the present. All too often these attempts at resolution are based on a sense of grievance derived from experiences of neglect, which involve the preoccupation with justified revenge and the conviction that revenge can bring about a resolution. The preoccupation with revenge is rooted in a wish to punish the figure that has failed and will involve sadism towards that figure, who is felt to deserve cruelty. This form of transference can be the explanation for many crimes in which a chance victim becomes the focus for revengeful and cruel acting out.

Forensic psychotherapy presents many difficult therapeutic tasks. One of the central problems is the powerful countertransference that is set up as a response to the patient's transference. The predominance of sado-masochistic pathology makes this particularly difficult. In forensic psychotherapy a good understanding of transference and countertransference phenomena is vitally important. Anyone undertaking this work should have supervision from senior colleagues and peers and will need to have had personal therapy as part of their training.

TRANSFERENCE

Freud (1895) first noted the phenomenon of transference in Breuer's treatment of Anna O. The patient's intense erotic attachment led Breuer to discontinue the treatment with some alarm. Freud first gave the process the name 'Transference' in 'The interpretation of dreams' (1900). He began by regarding it as an instance of the displacement of affect from one idea to another and did not see it as a useful part of the therapeutic relationship, but rather as an obstacle to treatment. He thought it was a manifestation of resistance to the therapeutic process of making the unconscious conscious. Emotional events and relationships are repeated in the transference without their being remembered. He identified the transference as being based on the repetition compulsion, in which old patterns of conflict and relationships are repeated in an attempt to find a solution, where separation from the primary object does not occur. Later, he discovered that the transference was an essential tool of the analytical process, a valuable means of gaining access to an understanding of the patient's unconscious inner world. The patient's relationships to his original objects were recreated and brought to life with all their richness in the analytic relationship, and transferred onto the person of the analyst.

Strachey (1934), in examining the therapeutic action of psychoanalysis, showed that what is being transferred is not the real relationships of the child's past but the internal objects which are built up by projection and introjection and represent a psychic reality which is different from the historical truth of the individual's past.

Klein (1952) helped to extend understanding of the nature of transference and the processes which create it, particularly projective identification. She emphasized that total situations are transferred from the past. She also made it clear that many aspects of everyday life reported by the patient gave clues to the unconscious anxieties provoked by the transference situation. This view of the transference as having wide repercussions in the whole relationship with the analyst and in the patient's everyday life was further developed by Joseph (1985, p.47) who describes how the patient unconsciously acts on the analyst to feel things and to become drawn into acting out with them in order to communicate the inner world. She emphasizes how many of these experiences are beyond the use of words and they can only be discovered through the feelings aroused in the analyst through the experience of the countertransference. The countertransference, like the transference, was originally seen by Freud as an obstacle to analytic work. Its discovery led to Freud's requirement for personal therapy in training, on the grounds that the analyst's own emotional difficulties would have a distorting effect on his response to the transference. The countertransference can now be seen as essential to the analytic process – the analyst's feelings in the countertransference provide a powerful means of understanding the patient and of monitoring the changing state of the transference.

In the analytic and psychotherapeutic relationship the transference is intensified by the encouragement to regression. The offer of emotional help alone may be an invitation to regress. This has certainly been noted at the Cassel Hospital where admission for in-patient psychotherapy causes some patients to regress severely and destructively. Some of the techniques of psychoanalytical treatment such as the analyst's neutrality and the use of free association and the couch will reinforce regression. The transference is itself a form of regression. The projective processes involved are a primitive means of communication, which are of great importance in infancy and will be a major means of communication in a regressed patient. In criminal acts projective processes are central to the acting out and will give rise to strong emotional responses in those who are on the receiving end of the projections.

In the transference, early experiences are brought to life with a strong sense of immediacy. Freud observed that in psychoanalytic treatment the transference could reach a great intensity and become the focus of the patient's emotional life, creating the transference neurosis. Then the transference became the basis of a new set of symptoms focused on the relationship with the analyst. This neurosis intensifies with the deepening of the therapeutic work. The intense experience of the transference facilitates the therapeutic effect of interpretation because of the emotional involvement with the therapist.

When the transference becomes dominated by deluded or paranoid ideas and the therapist is viewed in a fixed and unchanging way for example as a persecutory figure, a psychotic transference has been formed. This can be a persistent and unchanging state which may make further psychotherapy impossible. There is a preoccupation with the therapist's neglect and lack of care and a determination to seek revenge. Sometimes this state will be preceded by an idealization of the psychotherapist. The patient loses contact with any benign aspect of his internal objects and negates the existence of good aspects of the therapeutic relationship. He becomes stuck in what Klein described as the paranoid schizoid position, where good and bad objects (internal representations) are totally split from each other.

The implication for all transference work is that the therapist becomes the subject of powerful emotional attitudes in the patient. The transference is brought about by active projective processes. The patient will project parts of his internal world onto the psychotherapist in a way that causes the psychotherapist to feel as if he were one of those internal figures. Introjection will also occur when the patient identifies strongly with the psychotherapist and internalizes aspects of his personality, rather as children identify with parents and adopt aspects of their character.

Melanie Klein's concept of projective identification is basic to understanding how the therapist can feel taken over by an aspect of the patient. Projective identification causes the therapist to feel invaded by experiences which belong to the patient's internal world. Klein (1932a) describes phantasies of attacking the inside of the mother's body and invading it. She developed the term Projective Identification to define this process. It is closely associated with the paranoid schizoid position, where there is a phantasy of the projection of split off parts of the subject's own self or even of his whole self into the mother's body. The split off parts of the self are seen as having been put into and having become part of the other person. Projective identification is a type of projection – the ejection of something bad into the outside world which the subject cannot tolerate in himself, with the result that part of the subject's self is projected. A danger of this process is that the patient's ego can be impoverished because projective identification deprives it of parts of itself, both good and bad, which are lost and cannot contribute to the ego's function.

The psychotherapist on the receiving end of projective identification is liable to experience complex countertransference feelings, which may appear in his mind without an immediate sense of where they originated from.

B, a professional man, was consciously unaware of guilt about his destructive sexual behaviour and delinquency. He was calm but concerned at the unfairness of the proceedings being taken against him. His psychotherapist, on the other hand, experienced a sense of intense moral disapproval about his behaviour. His own harsh, critical super ego seemed to have been projected into the psychotherapist, while he remained unaware of it, with the danger that the psychotherapist would become morally disapproving and unable to understand the patient's split off superego. The patient had frequently acted as if he was in defiance of an unfair authority and sometimes had set up cruel punishment for himself by having accidents or being passive in the face of danger, as if his severe conscience was an active force in him which remained unconscious or was projected into the external authorities against whom he had rebelled.

In working with a forensic patient where sado-masochism is often present, the therapist can have the experience through projective identification of feeling himself to be a sadistic figure, representing a cruel internal figure of the patient. The cruel figure will be a manifestation of the patient's own harsh superego, an internal conscience figure inclined to cruel judgment rather than fairness. This type of transference and its retaliatory countertransference response may explain the cruel treatment of sexual offenders and the inherent sadism of the culture of some penal institutions, where the cruel superego may be acted out by the authorities and the other prisoners. The transference can also involve the projection of a submissive, masochistic part of the patient, so that the therapist may, in identifying with this projection, become the victim of the patient's sadism. This can occur when a psychotherapist finds himself colluding with unreasonable demands, or placating criticism.

The transference involves the therapist deeply in the patient's projections and can easily become an overwhelming experience. In forensic work where the patient has a disturbed internal world, the bad early experiences in the distorted form which they now exist in the internal world will be recreated in the transference relationship and, by projection, experienced directly in the countertransference, sometimes by feelings which are difficult to contain. It can prove to be difficult for the therapist not to be drawn into acting out a retaliatory response to the transference and so to create a repetition of the patient's experience of primary relationships. The psychotherapist needs to be closely in touch with his countertransference to enable him to monitor the transference and to improve his understanding of the patient and his own reactions.

THE COUNTERTRANSFERENCE

Freud (1910b) described the countertransference as resulting from the patient's influence on the physician's unconscious feelings and he stressed the fact that no psychoanalyst goes further than his own complexes and internal resistances permit, emphasizing the psychoanalyst's part in creating the countertransference. It is from this conclusion that he developed the principle that all psychoanalysts must have personal analysis as part of their training. Freud's own self-analysis must have played a part in his understanding of this. Personal therapy or training analysis is essential to enable the psychoanalyst or psychotherapist to be able to understand his own unconscious difficulties and make allowance for them in studying his countertransference responses. The therapist must maintain constant attention to his self-analysis.

Carpy (1989) has pointed out that although Freud changed his views about the therapeutic value of the transference, he never realized the therapeutic value of countertransference. In fact, Carpy points out that Freud's use of the term (S. Freud 1910b) referred to the analyst's unconscious resistance against dealing with areas of the patient's psychopathology that the analyst found difficult. This is quite distinct from the present day use of the term where it is applied to all the conscious, pre-conscious and unconscious feelings which the analyst has towards the patient.

Heimann (1950) was the first to clarify this view when she defined countertransference as 'all the feelings which the analyst has towards the patient' and includes the unconscious in this, concluding that there is an important communication of the patient's unconscious to the analyst's unconscious in the transference–countertransference relationship.

Carpy underlines the point that modern usage can neglect these unconscious aspects of countertransference, yet if one of the main vehicles of the transference–countertransference interaction is projective identification, then a significant part of the countertransference is unconscious and this only becomes conscious as a result of the analyst's or psychotherapist's analytic work on his countertransference feelings.

Carpy has helpfully pointed out that although the countertransference may lead to an understanding of the transference which could be the basis of an interpretation, this may often be counter-productive, creating in the patient the feeling that the analyst is trying to force something at him. Since transference experiences are often completely split off and projected, the attempt to create the link again may be disturbing to the patient. Carpy describes the therapeutic value of a capacity to tolerate the countertransference, until such time as it may be possible to take it up interpretatively. The timing of the interpretation derived from the therapist's countertransference will depend on the patient's capacity to reintegrate something split off and projected. This is an important principle in forensic psychotherapy, where too early attempts to interpret or too intensive forms of psychotherapy can intensify paranoid feelings, with the breakdown of treatment. This has long been recognized at the Portman Clinic where most treatment is based on a once weekly approach.

The countertransference will be the means by which the transference can be understood and experienced by the therapist and is therefore an equally important therapeutic tool. If the countertransference experience too closely corresponds to the transference and the therapist consequently acts it out, it may not be possible for the interaction to be understood at a conscious level. Rather, there will be a re-enactment of the unconscious relationship, with neither patient nor therapist being able to be consciously aware of what is happening. There may well be a motive for the psychotherapist to join in the resistance against understanding which, as Strachey (1934) points out, can be painful and difficult for the analyst as well as the patient.

The significance of countertransference depends on the function of the psychotherapist in the treatment. The psychotherapist or psychoanalyst has two functions. First, he is the object of the unconscious processes and second, he observes and interprets these processes (Racker 1968). As Carpy points out, a third function is the capacity to contain or tolerate the countertransference. The countertransference can help or hinder the perception of unconscious processes. The psychotherapist's countertransference experience sheds light on the unconscious processes of the transference but it will also provoke emotional reactions which impair the psychotherapist's understanding and interpretative capacity. The countertransference may affect the psychotherapist's manner and behaviour which will in turn affect the patient's perception of him. Thus the countertransference by affecting the psychotherapist's understanding and behaviour influences the patient's further transference and affects the therapeutic process. This emphasizes the dynamic and changing nature of the transference–countertransference interaction despite its capacity to remain very stable over long periods.

The much greater understanding of projection and projective identification which has resulted from the work of Klein and others has led to a greater emphasis on the countertransference as a field in which the therapist can experience and understand the patient's internal world. Internal objects can be understood much more thoroughly through having been directly projected, when the therapist experiences them as if they were part of his own feelings or attitudes, although he subsequently understands them as originating in the patient.

The countertransference becomes an important method of understanding the patient's unconscious experience, which may be quite different from what he is aware of. The therapist can have powerful emotional experiences which derive directly from the countertransference and seem at odds with the patient's conscious presentation. A middle aged man described being left in hospital for a long period as a child. He described this without emotion, as an interesting historical event and he made an effort to remember what had happened. His psychotherapist felt overwhelmed by sadness and had difficulty in controlling tears. This part of the patient's emotional experience had been located in the psychotherapist.

There has been disagreement about the extension of the concept of countertransference. Some authors take the countertransference to include everything in the analyst's reaction liable to affect the treatment, while others restrict it to the more unconscious processes brought about in the analyst by the patient's transference. A broad definition of countertransference allows the total situation in the transference to be better understood since any reaction in the therapist is liable to have a bearing on the unconscious relationship between patient and analyst.

The countertransference can usefully be divided into two categories: first of all into reactions which relate to the analyst's own internal figures which may be projected onto the patient, for example when the patient becomes a conscience figure for the psychotherapist. This can be described as the analyst's transference to the patient, when the patient becomes a transference figure for the therapist and the patient represents a figure from the therapist's own internal world. This can become a source of difficulty in psychotherapy and can cause confusion, particularly if the therapist acts out and is unaware of his unconscious interaction with the patient. Second, when the psychotherapist experiences emotions or attitudes which he is aware derive from the patient's transference and do not belong to him. Frequently there will be a situation in which the therapist's own internal world does interact with the transference projections but the therapist is sufficiently aware of his difficulties to identify the interaction.

If the psychotherapist's countertransference is reinforced by his transference to the patient, a confusion develops which can become overwhelming. This can always occur because of the tendency of the patient's transference to find areas in the psychotherapist's unconscious which resonate to the projections.

At times the patient may have a transference attitude that does not powerfully affect the therapist, leaving him emotionally uninvolved but aware of a misperception on the part of the patient. This is more likely to occur when the psychotherapist has understood what is taking place.

The psychotherapist's own training therapy should help him to be more aware of these areas and more able to distinguish between projections from the patient and his own internal objects. The countertransference work will need to be maintained by continued self-analysis by the psychotherapist. Brenman Pick (1985) described the importance of carefully monitoring the countertransference and the need for the analyst to work through its interaction with the analyst's own defences and vulnerabilities. Helpful interpretative work would grow out of this process of working through, in which the analyst can begin to distinguish his own areas of disturbance from that which is projected by the patient and to see how the two may interact. One of the dangers for those undertaking psychotherapy who have had no personal therapy is that they are not well equipped to be able to study their own inner world, including areas of disturbance in themselves. They are thus handicapped in using countertransference experiences.

A young psychiatrist, who had had no personal therapy, had taken on a difficult patient in regular psychotherapy. The patient was demanding and critical of the ward staff. The psychiatrist had rather positive views of his therapeutic capacity, which he thought would be enhanced by his special understanding of the patient. He became over-involved with the patient, giving her sessions at her demand. Despite the increasing strain he remained convinced that he would make her better because of his conscious desire to help her. A situation developed which was similar to that described by Main (1957). The psychiatrist concealed his anxiety and incapacity to cope with the patient's hostility by placating her and regarding himself as an ideal caring figure, while allowing all the criticism to be directed at other members of the staff team.

The patient's tendency to split can be seen to match closely the psychiatrist's own tendency to avoid hostility and criticism by seeing himself as an ideal therapist. The patient's and the psychiatrist's defences and transference matched one another quite closely. It was observed that this patient had a powerful tendency to affect staff by getting them over-involved. Other staff were inclined to be dismissive and critical of the patient. As a consequence of the interaction with the psychiatrist, the patient's hostility could not be tackled in the psychotherapy. The patient became troubled when the psychiatrist wished to bring the treatment to an end because he was moving to another job. He considered taking the patient to his next job but was advised against this because of anxieties about his over-involvement. The patient was quite unprepared for the collapse of the ideal relationship and regressed, became disturbed and made a suicide attempt. Some of this reaction was rage at the disillusion with the therapist but it is likely that the patient experienced the psychotherapist as having retaliated against her hostility which was split off in their relationship and not able to be dealt with openly.

The patient's projections into the therapist will lead the therapist to feel strong emotions, derived from these projections, either directly from them or from the emotional reactions caused by them. If they do not strongly link to the analyst's own internal figures they will not create such a difficult unconscious reaction in the analyst. He may become aware that these reactions do not really belong in him and are the result of a projection from the patient. It will necessarily be a complex task for the analyst to sort out his own internal feelings and reactions to the patient from that which has been projected into him. For this reason he will need to examine his countertransference carefully (Pick 1985; Carpy 1989).

This capacity to accept and understand countertransference reactions lends strength to the therapist's therapeutic understanding and is of importance as a way of tolerating the patient's internal world. It is also a valuable therapeutic tool that allows the analyst both to experience and empathize with the patient's internal state. It is the basis for the beginning of accurate interpretive work.

Before an effective interpretation can be made the process of working through the countertransference experience will need to take place. Sometimes this is an unconscious process when the analyst suddenly feels he knows what is happening or knows what to say without having thought it through at a conscious level. On other occasions it requires a period of reflection before it is possible to make sense of the countertransference experience. Supervision and clinical discussion are important sources of help to enable the psychotherapist to identify and understand the countertransference experience.

Vignette

L was a volatile young woman who had sought help for homosexuality, delinquency and phobic states. When she was agitated she relieved herself of the overwhelming anxiety by making another person agitated and upset. She would often choose a minor official such as a ticket collector, a policeman or a taxi driver and proceed to make this individual feel angry, humiliated and confused. This had been the pattern of her relationship with her father whom she had always provoked in this way. When she achieved this she gained relief and felt calm and triumphant, feeling superior to the other person who was now agitated and aggressive, even though she was at risk of being physically attacked.

She was often anxious and uncertain on Monday after a weekend break. She started the session by being highly critical of the analyst and the work that had taken place. She impugned the analyst's ability and claimed a general weakness in the whole theoretical basis of psychoanalysis. It appeared that she had felt anxious about her dependency on the analyst and was made more aware of it by the break and needed to protect herself from this vulnerable state. Despite the predictability of this attack the analyst felt provoked and inclined to retaliate by strongly refuting what the patient was saying or even, when the pressure became very great, felt like kicking the patient out. It was necessary for the analyst to remain silent and not to attempt to interpret what was going on until he had regained a capacity to examine his countertransference response and to note what was being projected, including the strong irrational wish to counter-attack and kick out the persecuting, humiliating experience.

In the midst of an intense countertransference experience it may not be possible to respond until the pressure to act has been contained. After a period of reflection it becomes possible to recognize the projection and to understand what has happened. This requires a knowledge of the patient's experience; in the case of L, needing to rid herself of an overwhelming experience of anxiety and humiliation by a critical internal figure. The patient triumphantly identified with the critical superego and projected the vulnerable attacked version of herself into the psychotherapist. The psychotherapist can learn how intolerable this experience is for the patient, leading to its expulsion into the therapist. The therapist's countertransference experience helps to throw light on the superego's relationship with the self in this patient.

This pattern of transference projection can underlie the delinquent individual's relationship with the victim of his crime. The psychic function of the criminal act enables the criminal to free himself of persecution and humiliation and project this into the victim, while he has a sense of omnipotence and triumph, because he has rid himself of intolerable feelings.

The psychic relief obtained by projection is reinforced by the material gain which results from the crime. In sexual crimes such as rape, the sadistic excitement associated with that which is disturbing and humiliating to the victim is profoundly important to the perpetrator of the crime. It allows him to rid himself of a very disturbing internal experience. Sado-masochism is closely connected with this defensive mechanism and the sexual excitement involved. Sadism allows the projection of what is disturbing and upsetting into the victim and allows the sadistic person to feel omnipotent and sexually excited by the triumph.

The treatment of adolescent offenders demonstrates how common these defences are. The psychotherapist will often first encounter the projective defences in his experience of the countertransference during the assessment.

In violent individuals it is evident that the violent murderous attack occurs at a time when the patient is feeling intolerably persecuted and identified with the victim by projection of the persecuting figure. The attack on the victim would reverse the situation to the extent that the persecuting experience becomes located in the victim and the attacker becomes identified with the aggressive internal object.

Vignette

D, an eighteen-year-old boy, was walking home with a rather sexually provocative adolescent girl who lived next door to him and to whom he felt attracted. She insulted him sexually by using a word for the female genitalia when he tripped over in the gutter. This humiliation led to an explosive reaction in which he stabbed her many times, leaving her bleeding and near to death. In subsequent psychotherapy with this patient, it became clear that it was easy for D to experience ordinary comments or questions as being critical and persecuting, whereupon he became agitated and aggressive. He also experienced his forceful mother as mocking his sexuality. On several occasions it felt as if a violent incident could occur in the consulting room, after an interpretation from the psychotherapist which the patient experienced as an intrusive criticism which humiliated him and made him feel small.

The projective mechanisms that are involved in criminal offences are more extreme versions of the same processes which take place in any transference relationship between patient and therapist. The forensic psychotherapist needs to be skilled at understanding his countertransference reactions to be able to cope with encountering the internal world of the offender and to be able to contain the projections without acting out or retaliation, which can be liable to lead to an explosive situation.

The most difficult kind of countertransference reaction is that which remains unconscious, so that the therapist is not aware of his reaction to the transference, nor properly of the nature of transference itself. This may occur when the therapist feels satisfied or pleased with what is happening. A patient who creates a pleasant, conforming atmosphere and a good response to the therapy may be creating a false, compliant atmosphere, setting up a relationship which is supportive and avoids conflict. The seductiveness of this situation can result in a therapy which does not progress, or where perverse or destructive behaviour is hidden and not dealt with. When this occurs it is likely that the analyst is unconsciously involved in a collusion with the patient. An intense sense of anxiety about destructiveness can lead to this collusion. The therapist may wish to avoid dealing with an angry, disappointed, or paranoid patient. This can make the pleasure of a conforming, positive patient very rewarding, as an avoidance of these difficulties. The therapist's own capacity to cope with persecutory anxiety and criticism and to be able to make a judgment about what is a valid criticism and what is an accusation will be necessary if a collusive situation is to be avoided.

Where perverse sexual fantasies in the patient are involved it may be difficult to examine the analyst's own involvement and perverse excitement. The psychotherapist's unconscious interest in perversion can result in collusion with the patient's perverse excitement. As Chasseguet-Smirgel (1985) points out, we are all capable of perverse excitement and sadism. This can include the subtle perversion of the therapeutic relationship itself.

It is possible for the psychotherapist to become unconsciously the masochistic victim of a bullying or sadistic and perverse situation in the therapy. A perversion involves a sadistic attitude towards the object, who can respond in a retaliatory fashion, and so be sadistic in return to the patient or become masochistic and accept the role of victim. It is possible for the psychotherapist to act out in either of these ways. The talion principle is fundamental to the sado-masochistic state, where the principle of 'an eye for an eye and a tooth for a tooth' is dominant, as if only by full retaliation can the injury be undone.

One of the greatest difficulties is to intervene in the sado-masochistic relationship between the superego and the patient's self in a way which allows some form of mediation and fairness in this cruel exchange.

SOME PROBLEM AREAS IN THE TRANSFERENCE–COUNTERTRANSFERENCE INTERACTION FOR THE FORENSIC PSYCHOTHERAPIST

Many of the problems encountered in managing the transference–countertransference relationship and in using it constructively to further therapeutic work are common to forensic psychotherapy and all psychodynamic psychotherapy, but there are a number of areas in which the forensic psychotherapist is presented with particular difficulties because of the intensity of disturbance which is encountered in forensic patients and because of the particular type of primitive defences which are encountered. It may be helpful to consider some of these areas separately to clarify the problems which can be encountered in forensic work.

Severe Disturbance and Primitive Defences

The high degree of underlying disturbance which is defended against in delinquent and perverse acting out will inevitably be drawn into the therapeutic relationship and will be projected in the transference. There will be a tendency for more paranoid processes to be evident which will test the therapist's capacity to contain and understand this in the countertransference. The therapist is likely to be treated as a dangerous and persecuting figure who will need to be controlled. Inexperienced therapists find this difficult when their conscious intention is to be helpful. A recognition of this state will allow the therapist to be cautious in not interpreting too quickly or forcefully and not demanding too great an intensity of contact which may provoke uncontrolled reactions. The capacity to tolerate the countertransference as described by Carpy will be important, particularly in the early stages of the treatment, when a treatment alliance is being established. The treatment alliance will have to become sufficiently strong to contain the negative disturbed aspects of the transference.

Sadism and Masochism and Sexually Perverse Defences

The importance of the sadistic dynamic has already been emphasized. As Chasseguet-Smirgel (1985) has pointed out, perversions are 'temptation in the mind common to us all'. The perversion is based on sadism which, apart from triumphant and erotically exciting cruelty, aims to destroy the order and structure of differentiation. Differences are abolished and feelings of helplessness, smallness, inadequacy as well as absence, castration, death and loss are abolished. It is possible to see how effective an omnipotent defence sadism can be against a sense of loss or psychic pain. This is even more clear when it is organized into a sexual perversion so that the destruction of differentiation, the projection of weakness into another and sexual excitement are combined to avoid the individual's sense of vulnerability. When the psychotherapist enters into this situation and a transference relationship develops, he will feel the consequence of these primitive defensive structures; initially he may feel the victim of them, and then become identified with a wish to retaliate, thus acting out the countertransference. The therapist's experience of vulnerability in the countertransference can make the pressure to retaliate sadistically very strong, although to do this is to enter into the sado-masochistic exchange and to act out with the patient.

Vignette

P, a sixteen-year-old boy who had a strong sense of vulnerability about his masculinity, developed a paedophiliac perversion. He had a compulsion to control girls aged seven or eight to prevent them urinating and then finally to hold them when they became desperate and did urinate. He had imprisoned girls for this purpose. The control and sadistic excitement gave him great relief from his own sense of weakness. The fear engendered in the girls was essential to his excitement. He engendered a vicious retaliation from the police and parents, including castration threats which indicated the degree to which he projected an internal attacker while he was excited to identify with the same attacker in the perverse behaviour. In psychotherapy the same dynamic was recreated. The therapist felt controlled by the patient and yet to break free of the control seemed like an attack on the patient. It became clear that P's experience was of the therapist being a dangerous figure who had to be controlled in this way.

Acting Out

Patients in forensic psychotherapy are by definition strongly prone to dealing with conflict by acting out. Action is substituted for thinking or feeling because this would involve contact with painful experiences of humiliation, vulnerability or persecution. In acting out, the internal world and its internal objects are projected into the outside world, in such a way that others are forcibly recruited to play the parts of internal figures. One of the effects of acting out on the countertransference is for the therapist to be under pressure to join in the acting out and to take the part of one of the internal figures. This can result in a situation in which the therapist finds it very hard to contain his responses long enough to be able to understand the projective processes that are involved.

There are times when acting out in forensic patients needs to be contained by external structures such as institutional care, the police or probation officer. Inevitably prison is a container for acting out which becomes so dangerous as to force a containing reaction, even if an extreme one.

In the countertransference the therapist will need to be able to take acting out seriously, including the dangers of it, while avoiding retaliation. The therapist must take care that he is not drawn in to the cruel relationship between the patient's super ego and a more vulnerable part of the patient's self. Often acting out represents a defiant attack upon the threatening superego figure which is provoked to a punishing retaliation, as was the case with the patient P whose acting out led to such threatening retaliation. Acting-out has been addressed elsewhere, and specifically in Chapter I:1.

Rigid Defences and Resistance

The nature of the disturbance and the primitive internal world mean that there is a fear of a catastrophic reaction if the system of defences comes under threat. There may be the phantasy that the breakdown of defences will lead to an explosive state of extreme persecution, murder, violence or psychosis. The therapy can therefore be experienced as a dangerous threat to the psychic equilibrium.

The resistance will represent the forces which oppose change or understanding. It will certainly be present in the patient and the therapist as a pressure against understanding the transference–countertransference relationship.

Resistance is important in that it will protect the patient against the catastrophic breakdown of defences. The resistance will be directed against the therapeutic endeavour and will maintain the status quo. In depressed patients there can be an intense attachment to a sadistic superego figure which cannot be abandoned at any cost. The therapist will need to be able to cope with countertransference reactions to destructive blocking of the resistance, which can be seen as purely negative and it is easy to lose sight of the protective function of the resistance.

Negative Therapeutic Reaction

The negative therapeutic reaction is a particular example of a resistance against therapeutic progress which protects against the catastrophic risks of change. Phobic anxiety about contact with the therapist is a common situation in the delinquent and perverse patient. This leads to a state of affairs in which good contact established with the patient can itself lead to further worsening of the patient's state and acting out. The negative therapeutic reaction occurs where good progress leads to disturbance in defences and a violent worsening of the patient's state, restoring the equilibrium of the patient's defences. A negative therapeutic reaction can lead to a very confused countertransference experience for the psychotherapist, when progress and real contact with the patient lead to a worsening in the symptoms, implying a failure of the treatment. The negative therapeutic reaction can take the form of a new set of symptoms which block the progress of the therapeutic relationship.

Vignette

A borderline young woman, who entered psychoanalysis with a male analyst and began to engage in the treatment, developed an intense homosexual affair within a few months of beginning, which directed her away from the developing work in the analysis. During this period of sexual acting out, which included sado-masochistic behaviour with her partner, it was not possible for much work to be done in the analysis. She had once before had a homosexual affair in her life, when she left home to go to university and felt guilty about leaving her ill mother.

Timing of Interpretative Work

In considering the patient's reaction to involvement with the therapist, it has been observed that too rapid interpretation and involvement can lead the patient to become persecuted and to break off treatment. This will be because the analyst's involvement and interpretation are experienced as if they were an attempt to push something persecuting back into the patient. By this means the psychotherapist becomes an actively persecuting internal figure and this will lead to more forceful acting out, as if in an attempt to rid the individual of this disturbing experience.

Thus it will be important for the therapist to be able to judge rather carefully, by examining the patient's reactions, how much involvement and interpretation the patient can take on at that time. It will be a difficult judgment since it will be important to be able to interpret these persecutory anxieties, but in such a way that the patient feels that something is being contained rather than being forced at him.

Defence Mechanisms
General and Forensic Aspects

Anthony Bateman

INTRODUCTION

A central theme of psychotherapy is of division and conflict between internal wishes and external reality, producing inner tension and anxiety, which in turn necessitate adaptation and compromise to both internal need and external demand. Adaptation is made possible by defences – psychological configurations which minimize conflict, reduce tension, maintain intrapsychic equilibrium, regulate self-esteem and play a central role in dealing with anxiety whether arising from internal or external sources. If used inappropriately or excessively they distort perception, increase vulnerability, and may lead to incongruous or dangerous behaviour. This traditional view of defence as an internal moderator has been complemented by other formulations such as relational models in which defences are considered to operate between a vital experience of the self on the one hand and an insufficiently responsive environment on the other. The subjective sense of oneself is viewed as authentic and protected by defences rather than distorted; defences form part of an attempt to facilitate the development of a 'true' (Winnicott 1965) or 'nuclear' (Kohut 1984) self in balance with relational needs. Alvarez (1992) has taken this point further and sees some uses of defence as developmentally necessary. The boasting of a little boy becomes a powerful force in overcoming inferiority and attaining manhood; omnipotent and paranoid defences rather than being protective against inherent destructiveness or innate division and conflict are desperate but necessary attempts to overcome and recover from states of terror and despair.

By contrast Klein (1946) extended the psychopathological aspects of defence in her concepts of splitting of the object, projective identification, omnipotent control over objects, idealization and devaluation; her followers have extended these ideas further and now consider defences not so much as transient psychological processes but as combinations of psychological configurations that coalesce to form a rigid and inflexible system. These defence systems of the personality have been variously known as narcissistic organizations (Rosenfeld 1964), defence organizations (O'Shaugnessy 1981) and pathological organizations (Steiner 1982) and are invariably associated with powerful, controlling internal objects. Meltzer (1968) described a patient dominated by a 'foxy part' of the self that continually persuaded him of the attractions of grandiose and destructive aspects of relationships; Rosenfeld (1971) an internal 'mafia gang' that demanded emotional protection money from the good parts of the personality which then had to collude with the idealization of destructiveness and devaluation of love and law and order; Sohn (1985) the omnipotent self, formed by identification with an external object, which takes over the whole personality and splits off the weak and needy parts which are then incorporated as an omnipotent 'satellite' self or 'identificate', a composite of the arrogant parts of the self and those of the external object. One difficulty that needs working out with regard to these ideas of defence systems or styles is the limited number of defences involved, namely projection, projective and introjective identifications, idealization and devaluation, which contrasts with the distinct differences of the patients described and the complexity of their individual psychological functioning.

Bowlby reframed defences in terms of attachment theory and saw them not so much as reducing internal distress and disruption but as different patterns of attachment (Hamilton 1985). Secure attachment provides a positive primary defence whilst secondary or pathological defences retain closeness to rejecting or unreliable attachment figures. These 'avoidant' and 'ambivalent' strategies respectively can also be formulated as dilemmas (Ryle 1991) or in terms of intrapsychic processes. In avoidance the aggression may be seen as split off and the individual has no conscious knowledge of the need to be near the attachment figure, appearing aloof and distant, whilst in ambivalence, omnipotence and denial lead to clinging and uncontrolled demands.

The use of defensive structures as part of functioning social systems is well recognized and forms a major aspect of interventions in the organization of business as well as the Health Service (Jaques 1955; Trist and Bamforth 1951; Menzies Lyth 1988b; Hinshelwood 1987, 1994), and Prison Service (Hinshelwood 1993). The work of Bion has also been influential in the understanding of defensive systems in groups (Pines 1985a).

A further theoretical aspect of defences is their relationship to levels of development with some mechanisms being appropriate to earlier development and others to later stages. The excessive use of stage inappropriate mechanisms through regression, or their persistence to a later stage in an unmodified form may lead to the formation of psychiatric symptoms and a propensity to anti-social behaviour. Such ideas stem from Freud (S. Freud 1894b, 1896b, 1926) and although there is little confirmatory evidence to link particular defences with specific psychiatric diagnoses, there is empirical evidence to suggest a relationship with psychological adjustment and maturity. Vaillant (1971, 1977) has shown that there is a continuum of defences from normal or mature through to the distinctly pathological and that the use of theoretically more mature defences is correlated with successful life adjustments in work, relationships and medical history. The differentiation of defences into psychotic/immature, neurotic, and mature, functioning along a continuum from pathological to normal, forms a powerful theme within contempory psychodynamic theory linking specific aspects of childhood psychological functioning to emotional difficulties in adulthood if immature mechanisms persist or are used inappropriately. However, the use of immature or psychotic mechanisms is not in itself pathological, as under stress we may all resort to earlier tried and tested ways of dealing with anxiety and distress; it is their persistent use that is maladaptive.

In summary, there are five aspects of defence phenomena that need to be taken into account when formulating personality and character. These are:

(1) Defence as a way of deflecting and adapting to internal desires, feelings, and phantasies.

(2) Defence as part of a stable defensive style.

(3) Defensive interactions with the environment.

(4) Defence in the context of attachment patterns.

(5) Defence as primitive or mature developmental phenomena.

Turning now to forensic aspects of defence mechanisms, we can see that all the formulations of defence enumerated above are necessary in understanding criminal behaviour. Offenders are often unable to account for their criminal actions, feeling at the mercy of their emotions, which they experience as irrational and frightening. As emotional turmoil increases, phantasies become compelling, and pressure for action builds up; internal attempts at defensive adaptation occur; defences against intolerable emotion lead to stable defensive configurations forming a fixed part of character – a 'foxy' or 'mafia gang' controlling the personality and leading to sudden and dangerous behaviour; delinquent behaviour suggests the individual is trying to obtain a particular response from his environment which is perceived as hostile and threatening to his underlying self; violence is often encountered in the context of ambivalent attachments; and the presence of immature/psychotic mechanisms is pervasive.

Implicit in these formulations is the presence of innate, underlying emotional impulses causing anxiety which have to be controlled either by internal defence or by acting on the environment. Defences are seen as operating against the expression of aggressive instinct. The belief that humans are innately dangerous, tamed by up-bringing and social pressure, is a popular one in psychodynamic theory as well as in literature and religion. Melanie Klein especially emphasized the role of destructiveness in shaping the psychological development of the child. However, there has also been emphasis on the astonishing capacity of humans to be socially orientated (Montagu 1979) or object related (Fairbairn 1952b). In essence, there is conflict between unconscious aggression and destructive phantasy of an individual and his relational needs and experience of social pressures. In mental health an individual's internal needs and phantasies are in equilibrium with external pressures and social mores whereas in criminal behaviour the balance is lost. When internal defences fail the individual is only left with action. Criminal behaviour itself becomes a defence, often trying to stabilize a mind in emotional turmoil. What then are the ways in which an individual utilizes defences to maintain intrapsychic equilibrium?

Repression, the pushing back of unacceptable wishes from consciousness, is the primary mechanism of defence, ensuring that wishes incompatible with reality remain unconscious or disguised. The intrinsic tendency of repressed wishes and impulses to return to consciousness – the return of the repressed – means that tension and anxiety remain and an array of other defences are mobilized to alleviate the resulting conflict, reduce tension and stabilize the personality, but at the cost of distorting internal reality. Repression is best seen as primarily dealing with the internal world, whereas many of the defences mobilized as a result of its failure are interactional, for example projection, splitting and projective identification. All operate outside the realm of consciousness. To complicate matters further, those that are primarily related to external experience, such as denial, are sometimes conceived of differently, especially within experimental and social psychology, and are conceptualized as coping mechanisms (Lazarus, Averill and Opton 1974). In contrast to the unconscious nature of defence mechanisms, coping mechanisms are supposedly conscious, but this distinction has also been questioned (Murphy 1962; Haan 1963). First, a number of everyday coping activities occur automatically, much like a reflex, whilst a refusal to listen to something or the denial of particular feelings may be conscious. Second, changes in the external world may evoke unacceptable affects which are dealt with through the mobilization of the mechanisms of defence. Third, the perceived danger of an external threat requires internal assessment, which is itself dependent on unconscious antecedents, and so there can be no clear distinction between internal and external conflict, with the two interacting in a complex way (Bond 1992). Coping strategies can be taught and further developed into cognitive-behavioural strategies as well as operationally defined. Unconscious defence phenomena can also be operationally defined, although this is not an easy task (see Vaillant 1992 for summary). Horowitz *et al.* (1990) have attempted to link up mechanisms of defence with cognitive psychology; they see defences as the outcome of cognitive control processes which sequence ideas and join meanings together. Thus too rigorous a distinction between mechanisms of defence and coping strategies or too great an emphasis on either aspect, misses elements of the whole picture. Defence and coping mechanisms are related phenomena and yet exemplify the great but unnecessary divide between psychodynamic psychiatry and experimental psychology.

TYPES OF DEFENCE

Immature Mechanisms

In forensic psychotherapy an understanding of immature mechanisms is essential if treatment is to be informed and appropriate. the most important are splitting, projection, projective identification, manic denial and omnipotence.

Splitting

Splitting is most often used to refer to a division of the object into good and bad. A child, in her mind, will split her mother into two separate persons, the bad, frustrating mother whom she hates and the good, idealized mother whom she loves. By mentally keeping the good and bad mother strictly separate, the ambivalent conflict between loving and hating her mother who is, in reality one and the same person, and a mixture of good and bad, can be avoided. This developmental aspect to splitting persists throughout life in the widespread tendency to split the world into good and bad, right and wrong, black and white, heaven and hell and profoundly affects our attitudes not only to individuals but also to social institutions and political, religious and other organizations. It enables an individual to regard others as being one-dimensional rather than characterized by a myriad of human characteristics.

Vignette

A 25-year-old man, living at home with his parents, violently attacked his father with a carving knife, stabbing him in the groin. When interviewed, it transpired that following puberty he had become withdrawn, self-contained, and shy, and rarely went out. He looked after his disabled mother, seeing her as an 'angel' who was ill-treated by his father who seemed to embody all that was bad – 'someone who gets in the way'. In fact the stabbing had occurred at a moment when his father had been showing some tenderness to his wife and their son had come into the room telling him to 'take his dirty hands off her'. The son's love for his mother had been sexualized, split off within his mind and represented as a black and white view of his mother and father. His father came to represent the sexual split of parts of himself and it was these aspects that he attacked in trying to castrate his father.

Splitting is often associated with projection and projective identification.

Projection and Projective Identification

We commonly attribute our more difficult and unacceptable feelings to others, sometimes blaming those who are close to us for our own short-comings. This externalization, the outward limb of projection, allows us to disown responsibility and to see problems as belongings to others rather than ourselves; but if our unwanted impulses and feelings boomerang back and result in a feeling of being under constant attack, the projection has gone full circle and leads to anxiety or, if extreme, paranoid delusions.

Identification is the process by which our self-representation is built up and modified during development and is distinct from imitation, which is a conscious process of copying. The little boy who copies his father is simply imitating, but if his internal image of himself is then changed and this later becomes transformed into a personality characteristic identification has occurred. Piaget (1954) referred to these aspects of learning as accommodation and assimilation respectively.

Projective identification combines aspects of projection and identification thereby emphasizing a dynamic process. It is often considered to be a concept that has developed in three stages (Sandler 1987, p.20):

(1) It was originally cast in terms of a one body system taking place in phantasy within the intra-psychic realm (Klein 1946), the projection and identification taking place within the individual's mind.

(2) In the second phase of development, the concept became a phenomenon with an interactional or two-body context with the phantasy being enacted with someone else.

Vignette

A patient with a borderline personality disorder cared for her new-born baby in an exemplary fashion. However, as her baby grew, she began to feel that he needed more and more affection and care, and was looking at her resentfully whenever she tried to do something for herself. She started to punish him and became so frightened by her wish to hurt him that she left him on the steps of a hospital. The love that she herself desired was projected into her baby who was then cared for in the way she wished to be cared for herself. As this process faltered she felt increasingly threatened by her child and envious of all he had received seeing him only as emphasizing her deprivation.

Heimann (1950), Grinberg (1962) and Racker (1968) developed this second stage concept of projective identification within the treatment situation to involve the helper's identification with the self or object representations in the patient's unconscious phantasies thereby linking it with countertransference.

(3) In the third stage of the evolution of the concept, parts of the self are actually conceived of as being put into the external object (Bion 1955). In this form of projective identification, whole aspects of the ego are split off and projected into another person, animal or inanimate object who then represents and becomes identified with the split off parts; attempts are then made to control these split off parts of the self by asserting control over the other person. Sandler (1987) takes the view that control over the object is important – 'what one wants to get rid of in oneself can be disposed of by projective identification, and through controlling the object one can then gain the unconscious illusion that one is controlling the unwanted and projected aspect of the self' (p.5). He sees the process as one of 'role responsiveness' in which there is a creation and actualization of a phantasy in which each individual has a particular role. This gives projective identification a communicative component as it may evoke unspoken feelings in the recipient who may process them and give them back in a modified, less persecuting form – a process known as introjective identification. Inevitably, processing may fail and instead of the interactional element being positive, the relationship becomes a vehicle through which aggressive, sadistic, violent, or other phantasies are acted out. This is in contrast to projection, in which the recipient of the unacceptable feelings may be unaware of his role; the paranoid individual may project malevolent intentions onto all sorts of people with whom he never comes in contact, such as KGB, Freemasons and politicians. In projective identification the projections go 'into' the object, whilst projection only takes them 'onto' the object – the 'into' versus 'onto' debate.

Vignette

Two young men, one of whom was sexually experienced with both men and women, spent most evenings together trying to 'pull' women. Neither individual went 'prowling', as they called it, alone. One evening, following rejection by a woman in a local pub, they lay in wait. As she left, they bundled her into a car, took her to a warehouse and tied her up. Whilst one raped her, the other masturbated. Afterwards, the boasting of the rapist led to their arrest and subsequent imprisonment. The joint activity was the result of a mutually satisfying projective system. The rapist carried in him the aggressive sexual needs of the other. In phantasy his accomplice identified with the victim, wishing to be aggressively dominated by his friend. Indeed his friend taunted him as a sexual weakling. The rapist had projected his own underlying feelings of sexual inadequacy into his friend.

Recently there has been much discussion as to whether the term projective identification should be used for all those instances described above or restricted to those occasions when the recipient is himself emotionally affected. A restricted use of the term would have the advantage of precision and clarity but it would gently limit its usefulness, and projective identification is best seen as an umbrella term. Spillius (1994) suggests the use of adjectives such as 'evocatory' to describe the type in which the recipient is put under pressure to respond according to the projector's phantasy. In the example above each young man evoked a particular role for the other. A further sub-type may be normal projective identification which, like splitting, has useful developmental aspects and forms part of the basis of human empathy. It is wrong to see it as solely a primitive mental mechanism representing severe underlying pathology.

It has already been mentioned that when mechanisms coalesce they form defensive styles. Of particular importance in forensic psychotherapy are the manic defences in which omnipotence, projective identification, denial, idealization, and splitting come together. They specifically attack reality and are characterized by a triad of feelings – triumph, control and contempt. These feelings aim to diminish need of and dependency on someone who is valued in order to avoid the experience of loss, yearning and guilt. Sometimes the need is projected and seen outside the self. This may be the case in some paedophiles who believe they are showing necessary paternal affection to the children with whom they become involved. In phantasy the paedophile omnipotently 'becomes' the child and through his phantasy during masturbation magically repairs his own earlier trauma. He idealizes the relationship, believing it to be beneficial to the child, feeling safe in dependency which can be controlled.

Other individuals enter a grandiose world through their omnipotence in which they believe their wishes are others' commands.

Vignette

One such patient was referred via a magistrates court where he had been charged with theft of pornographic magazines. At assessment he outlined his own conditions of treatment which included being seen in a specific hospital. When this was questioned he became angry and dismissed the psychiatrist as a fool. Later he contacted the Purchasing Authority demanding to be referred to the hospital of his own choice even though they had no department of psychiatry or psychotherapy. His sole reason for being seen in the hospital was that he liked the style of the building. He expected his psychiatrist to see him in surroundings that befitted his importance. The reasons behind his odd request became clearer when he eventually relented and came into treatment in a day hospital setting. His father, said to be an Hungarian soldier, had left home before he was born and he was brought up by his mother with whom he shared a bed until he was fifteen. His relationship with his mother was infused with ambivalence. On the one hand he wished to be free of her and had moved into a bedsit nearby but, on the other, he found himself needing her – he neglected himself enough for her to have to visit him every day to bring food. On occasions he had attacked her by throwing the food at her. His brittle compromise was to buy pornographic magazines of older women, and masturbate whilst spitting onto the pages. He also visited prostitutes who humiliated him whilst dancing in front of him naked until he threw them onto the floor, triumphing over their control, and buggering them.

This man was as much a victim as a victimizer. His overly close relationship with his mother, in the absence of a father who could intervene, had left him with an omnipotent structure in which either he controlled or was controlled. The sexualization, resulting from a simultaneous arousal and abhorrence of incestuous wishes, became encapsulated in enactments with prostitutes and the use of pornography. He was enraptured and tempted by their seductions before taking recourse to identification with a powerful fantasy father who saved him from their control. Inevitably, he brought this to treatment, experiencing the refusal of being seen at a hospital of his choice as a humiliation. He tried to sabotage treatment many times, complaining to the hospital managers and threatening to sue. Need and dependency were experienced as annihilatory, a final surrender. Tolerance on the part of the staff, along with an understanding of his fight to avoid dependency led to some improvement.

It is not only immature mechanisms that are important in the understanding of offenders. Other mechanisms may play a part and one aim of treatment is to help an individual move from the use of immature mechanisms to more mature ways of dealing with underlying turmoil.

Neurotic and Mature Mechanisms

Neurotic mechanisms are common in healthy individuals as well as those with neurotic disorders, and in persons dealing with stressful situations. They may appear as quirks to the observer, for example the individual who persistently approaches things from an intellectual point of view, rationalizing life and his actions. Offenders may use particular neurotic mechanisms such as 'reaction formation' and 'identification with the aggressor', to stabilize themselves in relation to someone else and it is only when the relationship is threatened, usually by a loss, impending separation, or rejection, that breakdown may occur. The possibility of a sudden criminal act should not be overlooked in these individuals as it may range from a petty crime to a sudden outburst of violence. Mature mechanisms, such as sublimation and humour, integrate reality, interpersonal relationships and private feelings. In general, the use of mature mechanisms is absent in criminality since the offender finds a solution in more immature ways of reacting.

Reaction Formation and Identification with the Aggressor

If an individual takes a psychological attitude which is diametrically opposed to his wish or desire it is known as a reaction formation. Reaction formations develop during latency and bridge to more mature defences such as sublimation which make up whole aspects of character. Reaction formations may be highly specific, such as loving someone whom one hates, despising someone one feels dependent on, or caring for someone else when one wishes to be cared for oneself, or more generalized, in which case they form part of a character trait. The personality traits of conscientiousness, shame and self-distrust may be examples of this when they are associated with obsessional personality and obsessional neurosis. Reaction formations alter the structure of the ego in a permanent way so that the defence is not simply used when the danger threatens but is used as if the danger is always present.

Vignette

A quietly spoken and timid patient was a successful lawyer who argued his cases in court forcefully and intelligently but often used fraudulent tactics to obtain information and to win. He justified his activities on the basis that he was looking after his clients, which was in part a rationalization as he enjoyed seeing his adversaries squirm. It became apparent that his sadistic wishes were covered by a successful professional attitude and a quiet, unassuming manner. Inevitably, this clouded his marital and social life. The psychodynamic background to this defence is described below.

Although Freud (1920) had alluded to identification with the aggressor, and Ferenczi (1932) had used the term to describe the behaviour of a child to an adult in which there was a total submission of the child to the adult's aggression and a resulting internalization of profound feelings of guilt, it was Anna Freud (1936) who described the mechanism in detail and linked it to the early formation of the superego. Identification with the aggressor has links with both reaction formation, in that there is a reversal of affects, and identification.

Vignette

Returning to the lawyer, we can see an example of an identification with the aggressor. When he was a small boy his father used to dominate the household and often threaten, humiliate and beat him. Prior to being beaten he would run away to his room whilst his increasingly angry father chased him. After the chase the little boy would suddenly go quiet and bend over and his father would then beat him, whilst he remained completely silent and entered a dissociated state. At this moment, the boy had dis-identified with his self-representation and identified with his father (the aggressor) who was going to beat his naughty bad body. In adult life, he himself continued the identification with the abusive father by taking illegal drugs and cutting himself, thereby allowing both the abuser and the abused to continue living out their interaction through his mind and body and through his behaviour in court. He also challenged authority, often breaking the law himself, and continually risked being caught.

Identification with the aggressor is particularly important in theories of child abuse in which there may be a cross-generational cycle with the abused in one generation becoming the abuser in the next.

The mature mechanisms of defence, namely sublimation and humour, allow partial expression of underlying wishes and desires in a socially acceptable way whilst simultaneously enriching society. In sublimation, wishes are channelled rather than dammed or diverted; aggressive urges may find expression in games and sport; feelings are acknowledged, modified and directed towards significant goals; narcissistic needs may be fulfilled by becoming a successful stage actor. Our basest and deepest desires as well as our aspirations and ambitions are contained within our culture and gain expression through carnival, drama, music, poetry and within societies' highest ideals. Humour allows us to share emotion without discomfort, to regress without embarrassment, to play games with freedom, to laugh with impunity and relax with pleasure; it is involving rather than excluding and may at times allow what it too terrible to be borne.

Vaillant and Drake (1985) and Vaillant, Bond and Vaillant (1986) have demonstrated that mature defences have a higher adaptive value than all others and Perry and Cooper (1989) have shown how immature mechanisms of defence are associated with psychological symptoms, personal distress, poor social functioning, and delinquent behaviour. Psychotherapy encourages psychological development and therefore a shift from the use of immature or neurotic mechanisms to those of maturity. Psychotherapeutic treatment may allow the offender to move from distress to psychological health and to develop more mature ways of coping with turmoil and expressing his need.

I · 4

Related Disciplines

Introduction

Christopher Cordess

It is emphasized throughout these volumes that forensic psychotherapy, whilst having a basis in applied psychoanalysis, also shares ground with many related and overlapping disciplines.

It is in the tension *between* the similarities and the differences that much of the stimulus to thinking lies. Thus, for example, as cognitive science comes increasingly to acknowledge a form of *the unconscious* (albeit different from the 'systematic unconscious' and the 'descriptive' and 'dynamic' unconscious of classical Freud (see Power and Brewin 1991)) so *some* cognitive–behavioural approaches (section (ii)) come to share *some* common ground with dynamic psychotherapy. Also, the development of cognitive–analytic therapy (Ryle 1991) offers new points of view, at the same time as psychoanalytic ideas of the unconscious, for example of the place of repression, are modifying.

Similarly, the comparatively young science of ethology (section (iv)) offers psychodynamic theories challenging new data and ideas which have been taken up for example, in attachment theory, and in the understanding of aggression and violence.

Hermeneutics (section (iii)) is defined by the OED as 'the art or science of interpretation', which definition itself raises that old but significant chestnut of where to place dynamic psychotherapy within the contemporary 'arts' and 'science' divide. That debate is for another place but is touched on here: 'interpretation' in its many manifestations, and 'communication, speech and language' (section (vi)) are clearly central to much of the content of this volume.

Dynamic psychotherapy began with an emphasis upon the psychology of the individual, with a predominantly intra-subjective focus; later developments have stressed and incorporated the inter-personal, and have been applied to the wider family, group and corporative perspective. Systems theory (vii) and contemporary sociology and criminology (v), start as it were from the other end, from a social rather than an individual standpoint. These two latter sections describe the possible interactions at the interface of these different emphases.

In this chapter only a selection of related disciplines can be represented. We believe, however, that they provide a broad and stimulating canvas in which the reader will be able to find his own preferred landmarks and points of interest.

The Cognitive–Behavioural Approach

Derek Perkins

INTRODUCTION

Cognitive–behavioural psychotherapy (CBP) is a branch of psychotherapy which has its origins in the phenomena of classical and operant conditioning which were first studied in Russia and the USA respectively.

In what follows the terms 'therapist' and 'patient' will be used to cover the range of other variations commonly used in the psychotherapy literature.

LEARNING THEORY

In classical conditioning, the repeated presentation of a conditioned stimulus (e.g. a bell) at the same time as an unconditioned stimulus (e.g. food) eventually elicits a conditioned response (salivation) to the bell (conditioned stimulus) just as the unconditioned stimulus (food) elicits an unconditioned response (salivation).

In operant conditioning, an action (e.g. asking a question) which is followed by a rewarding consequence (e.g. interest and praise) makes the action more likely to occur in the future (positive reinforcement). When the action is not followed by positive reinforcement, its repetition is less likely (extinction). When the action is followed by an unpleasant consequence such as ridicule its future occurrence is likely to be suppressed (punishment).

Behavioural science expressions such as reinforcement, extinction and punishment are technical terms with precise definitions. It is important to be clear in clinical discourse whether these and other terms (e.g. negative reinforcement, shaping and generalization) are being used in their (precise) scientific sense or in their non-scientific (imprecise) sense.

The term 'punishment', for example, is often used in its unscientific sense to mean something which the therapist presumes will be unpleasant for the patient, for example verbal confrontation. In the scientific sense, it can only be ascertained that punishment is operating if repeated use of the supposed punishing stimulus actually reduces the behaviour it follows.

BEHAVIOUR THERAPY

Early therapeutic uses of these principles in behaviour therapy, for irrational fears and avoidance of situations, drew from what was known as the two factor model of fear. If avoidance of a situation had developed through previously experienced pain in that situation (classical conditioning) and, subsequently, if avoidance of similar situations was then reinforced by anxiety relief at avoiding the situation (operant conditioning), a maladaptive or neurotic pattern of behaviour could develop.

Clinical applications of behaviour therapy seek to break these learned maladaptive behaviour patterns (e.g. fear of social situations) by a process of deconditioning the conditioned response of fear and avoidance. For example, in the method of systematic desensitization the patient gradually learns within therapy sessions to associate calmness and relaxation with a hierarchy of potentially anxiety-arousing images (systematic desensitization in imagination) or real life situations (systematic desensitization *in vivo*).

Relaxation is achieved and the patient thinks about meeting one close friend whilst remaining calm, and then moves on to the next level of the hierarchy whilst maintaining this relaxation. Eventually, the patient would be able to tolerate the top of the hierarchy (e.g. entering a social situation comprising friends and strangers) whilst maintaining relaxation, which would be incompatible with the previously experienced fear and avoidance.

Other methods of deconditioning were developed by behaviour therapists, such as flooding treatment for phobias, exposure treatment for obsessional disorders, and aversive treatment for dangerous maladaptive behaviours.

COGNITIVE–BEHAVIOURAL PSYCHOTHERAPY

Progress in behaviour therapy suggested that analyses confined only to behaviour patterns in their environmental context was inadequate to achieve successful results for some problems, and that the cognitive, emotional and physiological responses of the patient would also need to be taken into account.

Techniques such as self-efficacy and self-control were developed, based on the finding of Bandura (1977, 1986) that patients' perceptions of their ability to handle situations can help bring about behaviour change. Seligman (1975), Meichenbaum (1977) and Beck (1970, 1976) developed other cognitive techniques for treating patients' negative automatic thoughts, often rooted in childhood, and which can be associated with behaviour problems such as depression, dysfunctional sexual relationships and criminal behaviour.

The main features of cognitive behavioural psychotherapy (CBP) are:

(1) an agreed contract with the patient on the problem behaviours to be reduced or eliminated and the desired behaviours to be strengthened or established

(2) an historical analysis of the development or non-development of these behaviours

(3) a functional analysis of the patient's current problems, including a comprehensive description of the antecedents ('triggers') of the problem behaviour and its consequences for the client ('reinforcers')

(4) the design of a programme of intervention for the specific features of the patient's maladaptive learning, informed by the above functional analysis, aimed at achieving the patient's legitimate goals, and

(5) a recognition that the therapeutic process is itself a social learning situation subject to reinforcement contingencies within therapy sessions and within the patient's legal and social circumstances.

In this work the therapist's own *mores* will play a part: most therapists will not, for example, work towards goals aimed at the patient continuing to perpetrate child abuse. However, these *mores* are explicit and negotiated at the contract stage.

It is also inherent in this approach that, although therapy goals are specified and progress toward them monitored, the patient's initial appraisal of what he or she wishes to achieve may change as a result of therapy and this review and redirection needs to be accommodated. The patient who begins with a goal of stopping child sexual abuse and establishing an adult heterosexual relationship may come to view as more appropriate a goal of achieving adult homosexual relationships.

The clinical practice of CBP requires an overview of the patient in his or her total context. This means the context of personal history, the context of the environment(s) within which problem behaviours have arisen, the context of his or her current circumstances and the context of the therapeutic relationship.

All forms of psychotherapy recognize that problems of human behaviour do not just spontaneously arise. They are the product of a personal history of family, peer group and other social relationships, through which developments or failures to develop occur within the educational, occupational, social and sexual spheres of life.

CBP views these developments within a learning framework, in which personal assets, deficits and problems, first elicited by early environment, are then shaped or extinguished by subsequent events. The interaction between classical and operant conditioning is seen as the mechanism whereby these developments occur.

FORENSIC COGNITIVE–BEHAVIOURAL PSYCHOTHERAPY

In the context of anti-social behaviour, research has shown that certain features of early environment such as disrupted early relationships, inconsistency of care and general poverty can predispose to subsequent anti-social behaviour. These features are, however, not uncommon and it is also not uncommon for young persons to pass through a phase of anti-social behaviour, peaking in the mid teens, which subsequently diminishes or disappears (see Feldman 1977).

Persistent delinquency is less common, and less common still is persistent anti-social behaviour which has its expression in physical aggression towards other people. It is this kind of behaviour which is typically the focus of forensic psychotherapy.

At a global level, researchers have shown that persistent interpersonal aggression has a number of markers in childhood and adolescence. For example, Burgess *et al.* (1986) found that the perpetrators of sexual homicide tended to have childhoods characterized by low levels of adult supervision or inappropriately high demands placed upon them.

The significance of this finding seemed to be that this early social context set the scene for traumatic or abusive events, which in turn set in motion maladaptive learning and hostile acting out. Personality traits such as interpersonal hostility or secretive introversion gradually became established, which increased the likelihood of fixed and aggressive behaviour patterns.

For the individual aggressor, a process of personal development might arise thus: inadequate early social environment and lack of social competence results in inappropriate approaches to other children which are ridiculed (punishment), making such approaches less likely to recur. Aggressive responses terminate the ridicule temporarily (negative reinforcement), making the use of aggressive retaliation more likely in the future. Ruminations about revenge lead the individual to feel powerful (positive reinforcement) and to wish to repeat the experience in imagination or perhaps in reality.

Later, in adolescence, masturbation to distorted media images of women leads to an association between these images of women and orgasm (classical conditioning). Inappropriate approaches to girls or women results in rebuff (punishment) but watching, and then following women leads to the reactivation of ideas about revenge and feeling powerful (positive reinforcement) and provides imagery for future masturbation (positive reinforcement).

As opportunities for pro-social behaviour and sexual relationships diminish, the individual's repertoire of thinking, feeling and behaving becomes progressively more fixed on ruminating about being different, of having 'the right for pleasure', of anticipating sexual pleasure from following and assaulting women, and from the sense of power that this creates. A feedback loop is set in place in which the individual's repertoire results in negative reactions from others, a decrease in self-esteem and/or an increase in self-justifying thoughts, with further escalation in dangerousness.

This kind of analysis, originally confined just to observable behaviour, was subsequently extended in forensic CBP to include 'internal behaviours' such as thoughts, feelings and physiological responses, about which the patient's self-report (supported by such other data that may be available) then becomes of major importance. The way in which a patient's 'chains' of cognitions, feelings and behaviours link together and interact with the environment to produce aggression vary from individual to individual.

For example, some people feel angry over one event and then ruminate upon other similar events before acting aggressively. Others begin ruminating about a situation, then feel depressed and hopeless and then seek compensation in the thrill of aggression. Knowledge of these individualized chains of reactions is helpful in structuring the sequence and intensity of therapy with the patient.

Assessment

Where the therapist is dealing with patient problems for which the patient is highly motivated to receive help and to cooperate with the therapist, self-reports (systematically recorded in interviews, diaries and rating sheets etc.) will prove helpful in understanding how problem behaviours are being triggered off and maintained, as well as monitoring how therapy is progressing.

However, where the patient may be experiencing mixed motivation about cooperating in treatment, as is often the case in forensic settings, there may be greater need for caution in the use of self-reported information. This is not to minimize the importance of such data, but to underline the fact that greater sophistication is required in addressing the questions of reliability and validity for such unobservable behaviour.

This can be achieved by checking the reliability of information provided on different occasions (and under different conditions) and by different sources (e.g. the patient, friends or relatives, and other professionals). Psychometric assessments with norms for different populations and with built in detection of 'faking good' or 'faking bad' can also help clarify the picture. So, too, can methods of assessment which are difficult to fake such as role play assessments of social skills or psychophysiological assessments of sexual interest.

Inherent in this process is the fact that patient disclosures can themselves been seen as pieces of behaviour which are subject to the influence of conditioning principles. Hence, those who work with offenders soon come to realize that client disclosures about aggressive impulses or deviant sexual interests will soon dry up if the client is 'punished' but anxiety-provoking or anger-provoking confrontations about his or her behaviour.

THERAPY

Clearly, important therapeutic goals for forensic patients are likely to be to work with the therapist on reducing or eliminating antisocial propensities and achieving other related goals such as enhanced self-esteem, a successful job and a satisfactory sexual relationship. Within the CBP paradigm this needs to be carefully structured so as to facilitate an experience of gradual progress towards agreed goals.

Gratifying as dramatic bursts of therapeutic progress can be for both patient and therapist, CBP accepts that progress will often be a gradual process. The patient will typically achieve change in one area of functioning (e.g. improved social skills) before moving on to the next (e.g. overcoming fear of rejection) and then another (e.g. managing anger non-aggressively).

The sequencing of these interventions tends to be determined by some compromise between the logical course of action suggested by the functional analysis (e.g. work on victim empathy before social/sexual relationship skills) and the patient's own wishes and insights (e.g. the patient may see the need for, and be motivated to gain sexual relationship skills but be unmotivated to work on victim empathy, which he or she may not yet see as a problem). In community-based treatment, the tackling of issues in this patient-directed way can be more of a problem than in secure settings: social/sexual skills without victim empathy is a greater potential danger in the community than in a secure hospital.

The Therapy Process

Since many forensic patients have not actively chosen therapy, there can be considerable potential for change in the fact that external contingencies are operating on the patient, such as a forthcoming court appearance or consideration for eligibility for parole. However, for the therapist to wield these contingencies at the patient in a threatening way can be punishing and counterproductive.

Equally, though, to collude with the patient in suggesting that these contingencies are unimportant or unreal is equally counterproductive. A calm recognition that the contingencies are present and that the therapist and patient can work together to create the best outcome for the patient within the legal and social influences that are acting upon him or her is a good starting point.

Theoretically, a dilemma can arise where the patient reacts in a way which prevents him achieving his own objectives, for example ruminating over past misfortunes (which the patient might maintain is an acceptable thing to do) where evidence exists that such ruminations tend to result in an escalation to aggressive urges (which the patient accepts are in need of change).

This dilemma can perhaps be best expressed as 'how to help the patient do what is best for himself despite himself?' Within the principle of working towards the patient's own goals, the therapist has several possible strategies. One is to use rational argument and persuasion with the patient about what he should be doing in order to meet his therapy goals: this is a simple idea but one which patients often say has not been used.

Within this process, conditioning principles will continue to operate. Patients are more likely to change their own ideas if these changes are positively reinforced. Setting out the advantages for the patient that the change will bring about and the disadvantage that not changing will create can help. Encouraging the patient to come up with his own suggestions and then reinforcing those for which most evidence exists of their likely efficacy is more likely to be effective than arguing with the patient that the therapist knows best. Reducing the tension in the situation by allowing the patient to make decisions at his own pace (but in recognition of the external contingencies which are operating) can be a powerful influence for the patient to move through self-imposed barriers to his own progress.

Specific Interventions

Within this therapist–patient interaction specific interventions are devised to address each aspect of the patient's problem. For example, a patient who is violent partly through a lack of skill in dealing with confrontations might receive a structured programme of training in which increasingly difficult interpersonal situations are role played and discussed. Feedback might include videotape replay, discussions with the therapist or the comments of others if in a group therapy situation.

There may also be skills or responses which the patient exhibits which contribute to his violence and which may usefully be redirected. For example, the patient who derives a sense of power partly from the planning and physical exertion inherent in his nocturnal prowling in search of a victim may learn to redirect this pleasurable side of his offending into a legitimate channel, such as sport.

For other problem behaviours, there may need to be an elimination or suppression of a particular repertoire. It is difficult to envisage, for example, a legitimate means of redirecting the sadistic sexual arousal of a serial rapist in a way which will not leave the risk of reoffending still present. For such repertoires, aversive conditioning techniques may be helpful. Contrary to what is sometimes supposed, the level of aversive stimulation required should not be high as this will interfere with the patient's learning process. It is sufficient for the unwanted behaviour to be followed by stimulation which is just sufficiently unpleasant that the patient would wish it to stop.

A good example of this is the technique of satiation used with sex offenders (see Marshall, Laws and Barbaree 1990). In this technique the offender masturbates to orgasm but then, unlike his usual practice, he continues to masturbate to his deviant imagery beyond the point of orgasm. The frustration and boredom which results is a punishing outcome, which eventually contaminates the arousing properties of the deviant imagery and makes the use of this deviant imagery less probable in the future. Despite the somewhat contra-intuitive feel to this procedure, follow up data does suggest that it is one of the most effective means of reducing deviant sexual arousability and helping sex offenders avoid relapse.

CONCLUSION

The key features of cognitive behavioural psychotherapy (CBP) with forensic patients are:

- the explicit nature of the contract with the patient on behaviours for reduction or strengthening

- a comprehensive assessment of the patient's history

- a comprehensive analysis of the antecedents and consequences of the patient's problem behaviour and desired alternatives

- the importance of a collaborative and positive relationship between therapist and patient in which the undesirability of his/her problem behaviour is recognized

- recognition of, and working with the legal and societal contingencies operating on the patient

○ the use of conditioning principles to maintain and extend the patient's motivation for change and cooperation with the process of uncovering the facts necessary to understand and modify his or her behaviour, and

○ the construction of specific therapy programmes to bring about the necessary changes in behaviour, thinking and feelings necessary to achieve the patient's therapy goals.

Hermeneutics

Anton Mooij

In a general sense, the primary aim of forensic psychotherapy is to treat the mental or personality disorder of a criminal by psychotherapeutic means, in order to diminish the chance of his or her reoffending as a result of that disorder. When put like that, forensic psychotherapy seems to be a category of psychotherapy: psychotherapy in so far as it is applied to a certain well-defined group of clients, namely criminals.

PRIMACY OF THE ACT

The above representation is not, of course, in fact wrong, but in principle it is. Forensic psychotherapy is not merely a sub-division of general psychotherapy – although it is that too; its forensic emphasis lends the psychotherapy a character of its own that results from the central position of the act. Indeed, the criminal act forms the basis of forensic psychotherapy the aim of which, as we have seen, is to prevent a repetition of this or a similar act. This means that not only a certain type of act, namely a criminal act, lies at the heart of forensic psychotherapy, but the concept of action itself. This may, however, be interpreted in several ways. Within the context of forensic psychotherapy we are not concerned with the appearance of the act, but with what it says or expresses. This double aspect distinguishes forensic psychotherapy – in this sense – from behavioural therapy on the one hand and experiential therapy on the other (Rogers 1961). In behavioural therapy, the primary emphasis is on externally observable behaviour, while experiential psychotherapy emphasizes experience or emotion. Forensic psychotherapy may look to both approaches, but will always have an emphasis of its own. For it is concerned with neither external behaviour nor with introspective, internal experience, but with the way in which behaviour expresses meaning. The emphasis lies both on behaviour and on meaning.

The central position of the act and its expressive nature forms a specific characteristic of forensic psychotherapy, but does not constitute its exclusive domain. Rather the opposite: an emphasis on the expressive nature of action places forensic psychotherapy within the broad field of hermeneutics, a wide philosophical school of thought that originated with such thinkers as Schleiermacher and Dilthey and was further developed by, for example, Heidegger and Gadamer. Initially, Dilthey was concerned with the interpretation of texts, but widened his field to include the interpretation of action and non-textual, cultural products. Heidegger broadened the field even further to include not only texts, acts and cultural products, but human existence itself, regarding it as a form of understanding, a form of designing possibilities from within a given situation. Finally, Gadamer narrowed the focus further by pointing to the historicity of understanding, resulting in a specific concept of experience as something that occurs within a context of prejudices. We shall take a closer look at Dilthey, Heidegger and Gadamer in the following paragraphs.

THE INNER AND THE OUTER: DILTHEY

From a general point of view, hermeneutics occupies a position somewhere between positivism on the one hand and phenomenology on the other. Hermeneutics is concerned neither with the outer nature of things, as is positivism, nor with the inner nature as is phenomenology. Rather, there is a third, hermeneutic, perspective that lies between the objectivism of positivism and the concern with the subjective of phenomenology. The specific hermeneutic approach concerns the way in which the inner is expressed in the outer: the importance that is attached to the outer links hermeneutics with positive science, the emphasis on the inner forms a protection against far-reaching positivism and a link with phenomenology.

The inner itself can be divided into different types. The early Dilthey was concerned with the inner, mental state of an actor. He maintained that we cannot observe the pure mental state of another – anger or anxiety, for example – but we can observe their expression in gestures, attitude and so forth. Moreover, we have experienced ourselves what it is to be angry or anxious and therefore we can determine anger or anxiety from their expression because we know from experience what they are. The early Dilthey regards this subjective state of, for example, anger or despair, as the inner factor. In his later work there is a shift from the inner factor conceived as a subjective state, to a general entity such as the mind, the state of an era, a culture. There is a shift in emphasis from the 'subjective' to the 'objective' mind (Hodges 1952). This is the mind or mentality that is expressed in a certain culture or in a cultural product, society or group behaviour. This change with regard to determining the inner factor does not mean that there is a change in scheme. Indeed, the same scheme can also be found among philosophers who do not advertise themselves as hermeneuticists, but nevertheless can be so regarded on the basis of this general theme, such as Wittgenstein and the representatives of the Anglo-Saxon philosophy of action (Wittgenstein 1953; Melden 1961). The knowledge of the inner through the outer, and the mutual dependency of both, is also one of Wittgenstein's central themes. The theme of the outer that expresses the inner and of the inner that is expressed in the outer was, however, first expounded by Dilthey as a specifically hermeneutic theme.

THE NATURE OF HERMENEUTIC RELATIONSHIPS

Unravelling such relationships is neither purely descriptive nor explanatory. To qualify behaviour as an expression of anger or anxiety is more than simply to describe that behaviour, it is to add something: the behaviour is placed in a broader context. This contextual addition, however, does not concern causal, but expressive relationships. There is no causal relationship because the inner state (anger, intent) cannot be seen as a causal antecedent of the outer consequences. Exactly because the act cannot be seen as the external result of intent or meaning, the relationship between the act (the outer) and intent, meaning or mental condition (the inner) must be regarded as an internal relationship. Such internal, hermeneutic relationships therefore differ essentially from external, causal relationships. As a result, a basic strategy of hermeneutics is to regard relationships that are presented externally as being nevertheless internal relationships. The primacy of the expressive relationship within the hermeneutic perspective therefore leads to a strategy of internalization (Mooij 1991, pp.50, 60–62).

In its turn, this hermeneutic strategy is important to forensic psychotherapy, because it is here that patients are so often inclined to externalize the determination of their behaviour. The neurotic is inclined to internalize the determination of his behaviour – seen as guilt – and to localize it within himself as a subject. The criminal (whose structure might be narcissistic, antisocial or borderline), however, is inclined to externalize phenomena – although this does not rule out the possibility of free-floating feelings of guilt. Appropriation therefore, is a central concept of hermeneutics; it is also central to forensic psychotherapy (Schafer 1983, pp.241–9).

THROWNNESS AND PROJECTION: HEIDEGGER

Appropriation in operation does not concern the sphere of incidental action alone. What happens in appropriation is that what is apparently external and experienced as alien, is recognized as internal. In general, this refers to the situation in which we find ourselves, that we have not chosen and in which we have, therefore, to use one of Heiddeger's expressions, been thrown (Heidegger 1962, p.135). Thrownness means that there is an element of contingency in the fact that we are where we are. It also means that the situation in which we find ourselves but did not choose to be in makes us what we are because we can never be without any situation. Lacan, who has elaborated on Heidegger here, gives a specific meaning to thrownness by seeing the situation in which we find ourselves from birth as a part of a symbolic order (Lacan 1977, pp.65–68). The symbolic order is made up of the language and its structure, the narrative network, the symbolic system of rules and norms that makes speaking, telling and acting possible. The symbolic order surrounds us as alien, but also offers markers for building our own identity.

Existence is not only thrown, a thrownness that we may or may not appropriate, it is also a projection (Heidegger 1962, p.145). Man is not simply determined by a given situation and cultural order, he is not pinned down by it: man is able to transcend the given order. Therefore human existence can be described, again in Heidegger's terms, as a potentiality for 'being in itself' (p.143). We are in a given situation, but there is always the possibility of somehow interpreting it. From this perspective, we are never completely knocked out by a situation, but always somehow able to look at it, think about it, process it emotionally and therefore transcend it, precisely because human existence is a thrown potentiality for being (p.144).

The final question here is that of responsibility. In the projection of one's own life, one is in charge because certain possibilities are realized while others are not and one can be called to account for that choice and that realization. However, this responsibility is already present at the level of appropriation of thrownness, namely the possibility of accepting as one's own the situation into which one has been thrown. This even refers to one's own past, in so far as it is disturbed. This is congruent with what Freud (1909) calls 'choice of neurosis', according to which a subject may choose and agree with his own neurosis or disturbance, however intangible this may be (pp.153–250). This is a moment of choice – although it need not occur within a moment and may be prolonged over a certain period of time – in which a person may choose a certain disturbance, rather than another which, considering the given situation, would also have been possible, allowing for a certain degree of health.

The emphasis on the idea of appropriation, and on one's own responsibility, within the hermeneutic perspective, give it special importance for forensic psychotherapy, because the criminal is more inclined than the average neurotic patient to refuse responsibility not only for incidental acts but for his life as a whole. This may form a trap for the psychotherapist, who could be tempted to go along with the patient's story in which the situation into which the patient is thrown (parents, environment, culture, society) will be blamed for shortcomings in his own life.

In the sense of countertransference, the therapist's reaction here may also be one of adopting a contradictory attitude: drawing the patient's attention to missed opportunities and generally approaching him in an aggressive manner. Psychotherapeutic discourse has scope for both approaches: identifying with the patient by pointing an accusing finger at the situation or another person; or identifying with another person and pointing an accusing finger at the patient because he failed to make use of opportunities. The hermeneutic perspective may serve as a corrective by neither excusing nor accusing, but by posing the question of the patient's responsibility for his own problem.

EXPERIENCE: GADAMER

An emphasis on appropriation and responsibility, however, does not give an activist tinge to hermeneutics; rather this is linked to their antithesis: experience. This point was already raised by Dilthey. The outer expresses the inner, that is experienced itself. The dimension of experience is therefore essentially linked to the hermeneutic project. As hermeneutics developed further, Gadamer in particular drew attention to this aspect. It is partly concerned with the interpreter (or psychotherapist), who must approach the experiences that the patient evokes with an open mind. He will not achieve understanding by leaving his own experiences behind, but he will achieve objectivity by introducing his own subjectivity and prejudice (Gadamer 1985, pp.245–67). By introducing these, the therapist becomes vulnerable and relinquishes the position in which he knows all, in which he is the all-knowing teller of the patient's life-story (Lacan 1986, pp.230–43).[1] By correlation, the status of what the client says is raised because he is afforded a hermeneutic 'right' in accordance with which he is regarded as an intentional subject, responsible for what he says, to whom no one can attribute anything without his permission. The other must open his mind to whatever the text (or expression) expresses as the truth (Gadamer 1985, pp.333–45).

However, if it is not only the psychotherapist but also the patient who is able to introduce his own prejudices, thereby rendering his own horizon debatable, there will be scope for what Gadamer has called a 'fusing of horizons'. Both horizons come together partially: the patient takes over (part

---

1 Lacan's concept of a 'subject who is supposed to know.'

of) the psychotherapist's perspective, while the psychotherapist adjusts his view of the patient. This gives hermeneutics its own concept of experience that emphasizes its dynamic nature. Experience is not something one possesses, rather it is a specific attitude: that of openness (Gadamer 1985, pp.323–4). This concept of experience seems to have special significance for forensic psychotherapy. In the forensic context, decisions about the patient are often taken in which the other appears as the almighty other with no shortcomings. In the life histories of such patients, others are often almighty figures who have no respect for the patient's ownness. A therapeutic situation in which the other in the figure of the psychotherapist is emphatically not an all-knowing figure, but a person who is willing to be instructed by the patient's experiences, is of special significance in a forensic setting.

FINITENESS

The dialectics of experience, however, both in and outside of therapy, never end in comprehensive knowledge. In part experiences complement each other, for example because they are confirmed by others (the other). But life also provides what one may call negative experiences that cannot be integrated or placed within a framework (Gadamer 1985, p.320). If all goes well, such negative, traumatic experiences will lead to acceptance of the limits to human planning and looking ahead, and therefore also to acceptance of the ever continuing situatedness of human existence and of experience itself. According to Gadamer, such negative experiences lead to the ultimate hermeneutic experience: the experience of finiteness. This means that in the end the hermeneutic experience is not the appropriation of ever new points of view, but rather a disappropriation, in the sense of relinquishing one's own perspectives and desires and accepting one's own limitations and, as a result, the acquisition of radical openness (pp.148–9).

In so far as current hermeneutics are the hermeneutics of finiteness, this aspect too appears to be of special significance for psychotherapy, because its eventual aim is, as far as possible, the acceptance of one's own limitations, limits and finiteness. In so far as crime is concerned with a failure to recognize one's own limits, and therefore also those of the other (the victim), the theme of finiteness in the modern hermeneutics of finiteness, is of special significance for the whole of forensic psychiatry. The direct practical significance of the hermeneutic approach is, of course limited: it does not offer technical rules but rather it offers a framework within which it makes sense to place forensic psychotherapy in all of its aspects. And it does offer a specific framework for that form of psychotherapy that concerns itself with the problems that the limitations and finiteness of man present to everyone, and certainly to the criminal.

CONCLUSION

The central themes of hermeneutics are the mutual involvement of the inner and the outer with the internal link between them, a view of human existence as a thrown projection, a dynamic concept of experience, and openness towards the negative experiences of finiteness and death. Transposed within the framework of forensic psychotherapy, this leads to an emphasis on a strategy of internalization, on appropriation and responsibility. Activism, however, is avoided by stressing the limitations of the psychotherapist who is led and restricted by his own horizon or prejudices, and by stressing the significance of negative experiences and therefore also the significance of the finiteness and limitations of human existence as such.

Ethology

Digby Tantam

Ethology, the science of animal behaviour, has demonstrated a previously unsuspected complexity of behavioural organization throughout the animal kingdom. Behavioural patterns are, like organs, subject to evolutionary forces and are sufficiently stable to be traced from one species to another, in much the same way that anatomical features such as wing shape or pectoral bones can be traced. This suggests a close link between behaviour and heritability. Experimental evidence suggests that what is inherited is a population of neurones with receptors to one or more transmitters in common. Thus fight–flight behaviour is elicited by stimulation of the amygdala and the septum, which are receptive to gamma-aminobutyric acid (GABA) and benzodiazepines, and modulated by neuropeptides such as cholecystokinin (CCK). Comparable effects are elicited by stimulating these neurones in rats, monkeys, and probably all other mammals. The use of characteristic animal behaviours to model human states, and the manipulation of these models by novel drugs is one of the growth areas of ethology and psychiatry.

Desmond Morris' (1969) *The Naked Ape* remains a remarkable *tour de force* of primatology but I suspect that remarkably few psychiatrists would have it on their reading list. It no longer seems as likely as it once did that ethology will be a key to human behaviour. There may be two reasons for this attitude. The first is that it has always proved easy to underestimate the complexity of animal behaviour, and it has been equally hard to resist the temptation to apply simplified animal models to human behaviour. Thus Lorenz, one of the founders of scientific ethology, in his excellent book *On Aggression* (1966) reminds readers that aggression towards conspecifics serves important functions, not least the dispersal of territorial animals across a wide range. Elsewhere in the book he says that carnivorous animals have strong inhibitions against attacking conspecifics and bemoans the fact that man, as an omnivore, lacks these inhibitions. Lorenz cites the big cats specifically. These are, however, a particularly difficult species to study in the wild and Lorenz may have based his observations on captive animals, always an unreliable source of evidence. In fact, a recent study of Indian tigers has shown that juvenile tigers do disperse beyond the territory of the parents but in the process acquire wounds which indicate that dispersal is attended by fighting, presumably with their parents and siblings. *Homo sapiens* is neither the worst nor the best of animal species.

Ethology may also have been brought down by the fall in behaviourism and the rise in cognitivism. It is true that attempts to introduce cognition into animal studies have largely been a failure (Ristau 1991). However ethology is not inimical to cognitive science. Nor is it deterministic like behaviourism. It is recognized that the elementary behavioural sequences ('displays') which ethologists describe are rarely exhibited in pure culture in natural settings. Animal – and human – behaviour is always the result of the activation of several motivational systems simultaneously. These may produce conflicting behaviours, or behaviours which alternate according to the intensity of the evoking stimulus or the arousal of the animal (a typical example of this is approach–avoidance behaviour, in which an animal first approaches and then flees a strange or threatening object or animal). Ethology is not therefore concerned with 'instincts' – the fixed action patterns of the instinct psychology – but with dispositions to engage in particular action sequences, dispositions which rarely if ever manifest themselves fully in the intact animal and in a normal environment. In man, and probably in the higher primates, behaviour is also influenced by cognitive factors. Psychoanalysts will note that this distinction between cognition and behavioural disposition is comparable to that between conscious and unconscious motivation.

AGGRESSION AND SUBMISSION

Predators have developed behavioural sequences that culminate in a lethal attack on a prey animal. Prey have developed behavioural repertoires designed first to elude and, if this fails, to respond to an attack by a predator. The behaviour of the predator towards the prey is not associated with marked expressive display or signs of emotional arousal, and is therefore unlike the behaviour of conspecifics engaged in violent conflict. The terms 'aggression' or 'agonistic display' are therefore usually restricted to conspecific conflict and that is how I shall use them.

Aggression is bound up with three motivational systems: dominance; response to threat; and sexuality.

Dominance

Dominance is a means of structuring social groups of animals. Dominance ranks are also apparent in human groups, and are often institutionalized, as in some occupational titles. Animal species differ in the extent and importance of ranks, and that is also true of human societies. Primates have distinct, albeit overlapping, male and female rank orders. Male ranks are heavily influenced by success in conflicts, but this is less true of female rankings. Human dominance differs from the primate situation in that there are multiple criteria for ranking. A duke may be a major, and a commoner a general, and both may have lower status than a pop-star. Human ranks may be informal ('power'), legitimated but obtained through individual effort ('status'), or legitimated and hereditary ('class'). Moreover, dominance in one behaviour setting may not hold good in another. The person who dominates in the boardroom may not be dominant in the bedroom.

Dominance is a means of peaceably allocating scarce resources. High ranking individuals (known by primatologists as 'alphas') have their choice of food, water, or sexual partner and subdominant animals wait. Dominance is established and maintained by aggression, or by the threat of it, but the normal state of affairs is that dominance is not challenged. In a group with a stable rank order, competition for scarce resources can be managed without conflict. Dominant animals may, in fact, be less overtly aggressive than subdominant primates. Rank in primate groups changes as dominant animals age or become incapable for other reasons, or when newcomers arrive. They may also change as a result of the development of coalitions between subdominant animals, or with the dominant animal of the other sex. Kin animals may be more likely to form coalitions with each other. Coalitions may make subdominant animals strong enough to attack, and replace, a dominant animal. Observations of chimpanzees in the wild and observations of large chimpanzee and bonobo colonies show that *coups* of this kind may be the cause of severe violence or even killing (Waal 1989).

Raleigh, McGuire, Brammer and Yuwiler (1984) have shown that dominant rhesus monkeys are biochemically different from non-dominant primates, having lower levels of circulating cortisol and higher levels of brain serotonin. Animals which have ceased to be dominant, or which are removed from the social group, show a fall in brain serotonin. This is of particular interest because depression, a state which some say is associated with depleted serotonin, and impulsive aggression or self-harm, for which there is also evidence of serotonin influence, have been linked with social disintegration or social marginalization. Price (1992) has speculated that the function of depression is to minimize intra-group tension as a result of dominance changes. Depression, he suggests, incapacitates the humbled animal, and therefore stabilizes the *status quo*.

Fight–Flight

Aggression is also a response to threat, part of what Cannon (1927) famously called the fight/flight system. Whether or not threat produces aggression is likely to depend on the level of threat, and whether escape is possible. Kalin (1993) has performed a series of experiments examining the response of rhesus monkeys to a combination of separation anxiety – a young animal being moved to a cage on its own – and danger – an experimenter standing outside the cage. Kalin *et al.* (1991) showed that if the experimenter did not look at the monkey, the monkey adopted an inhibited fear response of immobility and concealment. However, if the experimenter stared at the monkey, this triggered an attack response in which there was a blend of fear displays, aggressive vocalizations, rushes towards the experimenter and shaking the bars of the cage. Since these animals were caged, escape was impossible but it was possible for the animal to avoid drawing attention to itself by 'freezing' (a common behavioural response to fear). Attack followed, Kalin suggests, because the animal could neither hide nor escape.

Animals may be unable to escape for social as well as physical reasons. Mother animals may refuse to separate from their young and so, if both are attacked and the young are unable to escape, may attack the attacker.

Sexuality

In many animal species overt sexual activity is a blend of mating and aggression. Sexual activity may also be a powerful inhibitor of aggression. Waal (1989) argues that primate species vary on the rigidity of their dominance hierarchies, and on the extent of their sexual expression. Pygmy chimpanzees, or bonobos, are highly sexually active, both heterosexually and homosexually. Sex in bonobos appears to act as a tension reliever, and is used to inhibit aggression by more dominant animals, being used along with other submission gestures. Acceptance of sexual invitation terminates hostilities

PREDATION

Although the distinction between predation and aggressive killing is well established in primate groups, primates of other species may be preyed upon and conspecifics belonging to other groups may also be attacked. In other species the recognition of in-group and out-group may be much less clear cut. Carnivorous rodents, for example, prey on the young of their own species and may eat their own young. Certain monkeys will also kill their young, although this may be a population control mechanism. Chimpanzees will attack and kill members of another chimpanzee group and strange monkeys introduced in a group will also attack and kill group members. Examples of 'child abuse' in primate colonies that have been studied suggest that monkey infants are at particular risk of attack, although probably not of predation from other monkeys within their group. It is not clear what motivates these attacks, but it may lie in infant monkeys' ignorance of the dominance hierarchy and unwitting challenges to it. Infant monkey abuse is more likely to occur when their parent is less watchful. It has also been shown that mothers who become more anxious at their separation from their infant are less likely to have children that come to harm.

THREAT AND APPEASEMENT

Management of Aggression in Animals

In order to avoid physical fights many animal species have evolved threat displays in which the possibility of aggression is signalled. The angry facial expression is one such threatening display. Other signals include intention movements – the first few movements in a behavioural sequence which are repeated without the whole behavioural sequence being activated. Chopping movements with the hands, or clenching the fist are examples of intention movements. Animals initiating a behavioural sequence may also show redirected behaviour in which the behaviour is directed away from the current target to another more neutral one. Banging the table is an example. Aggression may also be diverted into displacement behaviours. Drumming one's fingers on the table, brushing lint off one's coat or shuffling papers are all examples.

Many primate species have combined these *formes frustes* of aggression into specialized threat displays, and have developed appeasement displays alongside them. A major element of most appeasement displays is a display which is in some obvious way the opposite of the aggression display. Appeasing animals make themselves small by crouching down and by allowing their feathers or fur to lie flat. Threatening animals stare. Appeasing animals drop their gaze. The bow or the curtsey are both appeasing gestures. In the angry face brows come together and knit, nostrils become clenched, brows come down and 'knit', the lips thin and, if the person is very angry, part to reveal the teeth. The sad face – the eyebrows elevated, mouth turned down at the corners and tightly shut is in some ways the opposite of the angry face.

The possibility of agonistic encounters is increased by crowding but, when rhesus monkeys are deliberately crowded, aggression does not much increase. There is, however, a marked increase in the use of appeasement gestures, suggesting that appeasement serves an important function in stabilizing primate groups.

THE IMPLICATIONS FOR HUMAN ETHOLOGY

As animals are more exhaustively studied, it becomes apparent that their behaviour is always a blend of elementary behavioural types and that this blend allows for complex motivation. In social primates at least, animal behaviour cannot be understood without evoking concepts such as peacemaking, reconciliation, and appeasement which have previously seemed to be exclusively human. Similarly identification of the in- and the out-group, and therefore who is prey and who is not, has similarities to the type of identification which underpins human relationships. It may be time to rediscover ethology as a valid source of insights into the human condition.

Criminology
A Cautious Neighbour

Elaine Player

Contemporary British criminology incorporates a wide range of academic disciplines and a diverse subject matter. Historically it has claimed to be an empirical and scientific undertaking which yields a specific type of discourse about crime and criminality that can be distinguished from those produced by moral philosophers, theologians and lawyers. It has recently been argued that modern criminology has developed by combining two quite separate fields of inquiry: first, the 'Lombrosian project' which has attempted to create a scientific explanation of the causes of crime, unswervingly abiding by the positivist assumption that criminals possess discernibly different characteristics from non-criminals; and second, the 'governmental project' which has focused inquiry upon the administration of criminal justice and the development of penal policy (Garland 1994). According to David Garland, criminology is 'orientated towards a scientific goal but also towards an institutional field, towards a theoretical project but also towards an administrative task' (p.27). Yet, regardless of whether criminology is wearing its administrative or theoretical hat, it retains an empirical interest in forensic psychotherapy and, more generally, in the psychological treatment of crime and criminality. For the theoretician the practice of psychotherapy potentially unearths clinical information from which broader characterizations or typologies might be constructed. For those concerned with the administration of the criminal process, forensic psychotherapy offers treatment as part of a wide array of diversionary and sentencing strategies designed to manage and control crime in society. It is perhaps curious, therefore, that the level of communication between the disciplines, and the extent of joint enterprise, is so limited.

HISTORICAL LINKS

The distant relationship which now exists between criminology and psychotherapy has not always prevailed. During the first half of the twentieth century
criminology was dominated by psychological and psychiatric investigations
into the causes of crime, all of which emphasized the need to understand the
individual character of the offender and develop specialized programmes of
treatment. Much of the early research was undertaken by prison doctors, since
during the first two decades of the century there were no specialized research
units either in the Home Office or in the universities. Hamblin Smith, a
psychiatrically trained prison doctor, was an early proponent of psychoanalysis,
which he used both to assess the personality of the offender and as a means
of treatment (Smith 1922). Similarly, Dr Grace Pailethorpe, who had previously
worked with Smith in psychoanalytically investigating female offenders in
Birmingham, published a study of female prisoners in Holloway in which she
advocated psychoanalytic treatment as a means of correcting the women's
behaviour (Pailethorpe 1932). At this time interest in psychological treatments
was growing amongst the medical profession generally, and new out-patient
clinics such as the Tavistock and the Maudsley were established. In 1932 the
Institute for the Scientific Treatment of Delinquency (renamed the Institute for
the Study and Treatment of Delinquency (ISTD) in 1948) was founded and
the following year it opened its own clinic, which subsequently became the
Portman Clinic (Saville and Rumney 1992). The involvement of practitioners
working outside the penal system was important in that it introduced a new
emphasis into criminological theory. Although research continued to rely upon
the clinical exploration of individual psycho-pathology, it introduced a new
concern with crime *prevention*, whereby individuals could be treated before
their mental conflict led them into criminal activities.

Psychoanalytic approaches to the treatment of criminal behaviour were
perhaps too radical and esoteric to appeal to the pragmatic conservatism of
British politicians and civil servants of the 1930s. Instead, the work of W.
Norwood East, another prison doctor and subsequently a Prison Commis-
sioner, reflected the psychological approach to crime which proved most
influential in shaping official policy up to World War II (East 1936; East and
Hubert 1939). East was particularly concerned with the mundane problems of
the criminal justice practitioner and advocated a more cautious policy of
intervention, which acknowledged that only a minority of offenders were
psychologically abnormal and that research and experimentation were needed
to determine the parameters of this population and to identify effective
programmes of treatment. The influential legacy of this period of psychological
thought is evidenced by the continued existence of HMP Grendon, a therapeutic prison established in 1962 to give effect to East and Hubert's recommendation, made some 23 years previously, that an experimental institution

should be set up to offer psychological treatment to specific groups of abnormal offenders within the prison population (see Genders and Player 1995).

Up until World War II criminology in Britain was dominated by a medico-psychological model which concentrated upon the pathology of the individual offender and was specifically directed towards the development of a correctionalist penal policy. Garland notes that this is hardly surprising given that the key authors of criminological research had been 'virtually without exception, practitioners working in the state penal system or else in the network of clinics and hospitals which had grown up around it' (Garland 1994, p.54). The development of criminology as an academic discipline and its migration into the university began in the mid-1930s. Intellectual influences from abroad started to take hold, in particular the emergent sociological perspectives of American criminology. These progressively challenged biological and psychological theories and emphasized the need to explain the causes of crime in terms of social, rather than individual, pathology. Indeed, some sociologists disputed the concept of pathology altogether, arguing that crime can serve positive functions for society and that criminal behaviour may be a 'normal' response to certain situations (Davis 1937; Miller 1958). The importance of the social environment in determining who commits offences, and where and why offences are committed, came to dominate criminological debates and was variously explained in terms of 'social disorganisation' (Shaw and McKay 1942), 'anomie' (Merton 1938), 'differential association' (Sutherland and Cressey 1960) and 'sub-cultural conflict' (Cohen 1955). In common with the earlier medico-psychological perspectives, however, these theories upheld the basic principles of positivism: namely, that criminals could be differentiated from non-criminals by scientific means, and that these differentiating factors determined a person's criminality and placed it beyond their control. Social positivism thus established that crime is a result of flawed social conditions, caused by poverty, inequality and deprivation. Its policy agenda has thus focused upon the need to tackle these 'root causes' by social welfare interventions that largely address educational provision, employment opportunities, housing conditions and urban planning.

In the second half of the twentieth century British criminology has mounted a critical attack upon its positivist heritage. Modern political concerns about rising crime rates, and the apparent failure of social welfare programmes to rehabilitate offenders, has led to a resurgence of interest in eighteenth and early nineteenth century classical theories (Beccaria 1764; Bentham 1838) which portrayed the criminal as a rational and moral actor, freely choosing crime in pursuit of his or her own interests. Yet positivism is far from dead; the basic tenets of a positivist science have survived and remain a major component of contemporary criminology. Young (1994) has argued that the modern discipline of criminology essentially embodies the incessant competition between two equally abstract images of humanity: on one side, the individual who is granted 'free will, rationality and unfettered moral choice'; on the other, the non-rational actor who is determined by internal or external forces over which he or she has no control (p.69). Young characterizes criminology in the 1990s as encompassing four major paradigms: 'left idealism; the new administrative criminology; and realism of the right and of the left' (p.80). Each of these are rooted within distinct theoretical traditions and each points to contrasting strategies of criminal justice. More specifically, each of these approaches has implications for the nature of the relationship which can currently exist between criminology and forensic psychotherapy.

LEFT IDEALISM

For the left idealists crime is caused by the material inequalities of a class-based society. Within such a society, individual consciousness is structured by a series of institutions which, by means of persuasion and coercion, uphold and promote a dominant ideology that perpetuates certain conceptions of what is 'normal' and 'abnormal', 'good' and 'bad', 'desirable' and 'undesirable'. Far from reflecting an absolute natural order, these definitions are socially constructed and function to perpetuate the existing social order. Thus, from this perspective, the criminal justice system serves those who are in dominant and powerful positions in society by criminalizing, and thereby repressing, those who are poor and dispossesed. In so doing it diverts attention from the 'crimes of the powerful' and from the irrationalities and injustices of the existing social institutions (Reiman 1979). In short, the role of the criminal justice system is to maintain order – a specific type of order – rather than to control crime, and the task of the left idealist criminologist is to expose this duplicity and lay bare the true purpose and functioning of the criminal justice agencies.

This strand of criminological thinking has little room to accommodate forensic psychotherapy, locating it within the ideological machine of state control: the velvet glove of treatment concealing the iron fist of repression. The introduction of therapeutic programmes, staffed by the 'caring professions', which individualize and pathologize the causes of crime and promote solutions which address the dysfunctioning of the individual, are seen as a potent means by which attention is diverted from the true dynamics of criminal behaviour and the inevitable failure of the state to control crime. Only by transforming the economic and social institutions which destine specific groups in society to poverty and criminalization can the problem of crime be addressed. The correctionalist role of psychotherapy is, at best, limited to an unspecified, yet inevitably small, number of mentally disordered offenders. However, within the left idealist perspective it is possible to envisage a more radical role for forensic psychotherapy. This would be to provide offenders with insight into their own behaviour, and how it relates to their position in the social order, and thereby serve as a conciousness raising exercise which would foment political pressure for social change.

LEFT REALIST CRIMINOLOGY

The left realists criticize their idealist colleagues for failing to take adequate account of the lived realities of crime. The realists do not deny that the causes of crime are rooted within the structural inequalities of society, but they challenge the mechanistic notion that absolute levels of poverty and deprivation automatically lead to criminal behaviour. Crime is not simply created by powerful interest groups labelling as criminal the collective protest of those who are surplus to the needs of the capitalist enterprise. This type of analysis, they argue, contradicts reality in at least two important respects. First, it fails to recognize the degree of consensus and cooperation which exists across class lines in defining and policing the moral and legal boundaries of society. Although the majority of people in prison are working class, so too are their victims, who turn to the state to uphold the law and punish those who offend against them. The condemnation of murder, rape and other violent and sexual assaults is not restricted to any particular sector of society. Second, the left realists claim that the idealist approach distorts reality by overstating the collective nature of crime:

> 'The truth is that the majority of crime is an individualistic response: it does not have to be individualised by the powers that be.' (Young 1994, p.86)

They are criticized for their myopic tendency to focus on relatively rare instances of collective protest, such as the inner city riots of the 1980s, and to ignore the ways in which social conditions can foster individual, anti-social outcomes.

For the left realists the social context of crime must be understood as extending beyond a static analysis of the overarching social structure, to encompass an understanding of how individuals actually experience their structural location. Crime is thus conceived not as an inevitable consequence of an *absolute* level of material impoverishment but as a response to a sense of *relative* deprivation. Left realism thus emphasizes the subjective as well as the objective realities of the social context. The major cause of crime is 'when people experience a level of unfairness in their allocation of resources and turn to individualistic means to attempt to right this condition. It is an unjust reaction to the experience of injustice' (Young 1994, p.108). Certain social circumstances, such as unemployment and poor housing conditions, are seen as facilitating criminal behaviour not in a mechanistic way, which determines human action and denies the individual moral choice, but in a way which objectively restricts the options an individual actually has and shapes his or her subjective perception of what are available and appropriate courses of action. Emphasis upon the subjective experience of the offender, and the individualistic nature of the 'solution' that he or she chooses, thus enables crime to be seen as a category of conduct which occurs across all sectors of society rather than being the sole preserve of the poor and underprivileged.

The correlations that have been identified between crime and certain biological factors have not been ignored by the left realists, although they unconditionally reject the notion that crime is physiologically determined. Instead, they argue that it is the cultural meanings that attach to particular biological facts, rather than the facts themselves, which are the important predictors of criminal behaviour. For example, the significance of sex and age derive from the way in which gender and youth are conceptualized in given social situations, and not from a biological predisposition which is fixed and independent of time and place.

The intellectual foundations of left realism are not antithetical to psychotherapeutic analyses that attempt to understand how and why particular individuals behave as they do in particular circumstances. Similarly, although psychotherapeutic programmes are not a central plank of the left realist policy agenda, they are not necessarily inimical to its purpose. Left realists recognize that the control of crime requires a multi-faceted programme of social change that attacks, at a macro and micro level, the underlying causes of social injustice. Innovations to develop employment opportunities and decent housing conditions must aim not only to redistribute material wealth and power, but to build a sense of social cohesion and communal identity that undermine selfish individualism and foster a regard for community interests. Psychotherapeutic interventions that enable offenders to understand how they have arrived at the situation they are in, and which facilitate an awareness of the consequences of their anti-social behaviour for their victims, can be compatibly accommodated within the left realist perspective. It is, however, an accommodation hedged by conditions. The first is that psychotherapeutic programmes can only operate in conjunction with broader strategies of social transformation. Psychotherapy which aims to persuade offenders to reappraise their behaviour in the absence of major structural change is guilty of the charge levelled against it by the left idealists. This alleges that forensic psychotherapy enforces a particular conception of social reality and advocates a rehabilitative programme for the offender which protects and perpetuates the injustices of the existing social order. The second condition is that psychotherapeutic interventions must explicitly acknowledge that psychological characteristics do not single-handedly determine criminal behaviour, but are themselves created, at least in part, by material conditions which combine to shape individuals' perceptions of their situation and inform their behavioural choices.

ADMINISTRATIVE CRIMINOLOGY

This is arguably the dominant paradigm in modern British criminology (Rock 1988; Young 1988). Much of the research within this tradition has emanated from the Home Office's own research and planning unit and from academic criminologists who have been funded directly by the Home Office to carry out specific 'external' projects. The major emphasis of this work has been to address immediate policy questions concerning the control of crime and the cost effectiveness of the criminal justice process. Little, if any, effort has been devoted to exploring the root motivational causes of offending, since these are deemed to be of limited value in providing practical solutions to the 'crime problem' (Clarke 1980). Criminal behaviour is perceived not as reflecting an 'abnormal' predisposition on the part of the offender but as a 'normal' opportunistic response to certain situations which present possibilities for crime. The theoretical foundations of this approach are to be found in Travis Hirschi's control theory, which argues that the key question for criminologists is not why certain people offend, but why certain people refrain from doing so: it is conformity, not deviance, that requires explanation. He postulates that crime is caused where there is an absence of controlling factors which impose constraints upon an individual's behaviour and where certain courses of action are promoted over others. In other words, criminal conduct is likely to arise where an opportunity for crime exists and where there is a lack of controls which restrain and limit an individual's behaviour.

The approach to criminal justice policy which has been adopted by administrative criminologists has largely focused upon situational crime pre-vention schemes, which aim to control crime by reducing the structural opportunities for criminal activities. For example, the development of Neigh-bourhood Watch and the introduction of video cameras into public places are designed to deter offenders by increasing surveillance, and the installation of more sophisticated security devices in the home and on vehicles provide physical barriers which make crime more difficult to commit. From this perspective, social conditions are deemed to be of significance in understanding the causes of crime to the extent that they create the situational opportunities for crime to occur. The offender is depicted as a rational actor, making decisions based upon his or her perceptions of the available options. The positivist assumption that certain social factors predispose or motivate individuals to commit crime is largely rejected, as is the idea that a clear distinction can be drawn between the social or personal characteristics of criminals and non-criminals.

Within the administrative paradigm criminology is at its most empirical and pragmatic. Its purpose is to find answers, or at least temporary solutions, to pressing problems of crime control. The flawed nature of the earlier positivist approaches is seen to be demonstrated by the failure of their assumptions to be supported by empirical evidence and by the inability of their criminal justice policies to reduce the level of crime in society. Social utilitarian policies which attempt to control crime by means of deterrent, rehabilitative and incapacitative sentencing strategies have also failed to be proven effective (Martinson 1974; Tarling 1979). The feasibility of the criminal justice system effectively controlling the levels of crime in society has also been thrown into doubt by the evidence revealed in successive sweeps of the British Crime Survey which shows that only a small proportion of criminal offences come to official recognition and that, of these, only a minority result in prosecution and conviction (Mayhew, Maung and Mirlees-Black 1993). The Home Office cohort study has also revealed that criminal behaviour is far more widespread than previously imagined (Home Office 1989), and growing awareness of 'white collar crime' and, in particular, the crimes of powerful organizations in relation to health and safety in the workplace, environmental pollution and fraudulent business practices, indicate still further the inadequacy of conceiving of crime as an activity engaged in by a narrow and 'abnormal' sector of society.

Alongside these empirical and pragmatic criticisms are a series of moral and ethical arguments which claim that utilitarian criminal justice policies not only fail to achieve their own stated objectives, but also violate individual rights and basic principles of justice. The high degree of discretion accorded to criminal justice decision makers and the wide variation and inconsistency in the sentences meted out to persons found guilty of similar types of offence, have been denounced as fundamentally unjust. Individual offenders, it is argued, must be protected against the subjugation of their rights to broader social purposes. State punishment should be limited by the concept of 'just deserts', that is, guided by retributivist principles which ensure that individuals are treated in accordance with the seriousness of their offence.

The methodology of forensic psychotherapy, with its traditional emphasis upon clinical evaluation and case studies, contrasts sharply with the uncompromising empiricism of the administrative paradigm. However, it would be misleading to suggest that it is impossible for administrative criminology to accommodate forensic psychotherapy within its criminal justice framework. The administrative perspective does not deny the existence of individual pathology as a cause of criminal behaviour. Rather, it argues that this has been greatly exaggerated and extended beyond the limits of empirical validity. It is recognized that, aside from those crimes which are manifestly irrational and represent symptoms of a diagnosable mental disorder, there are other forms of criminal behaviour which demonstrate careful planning and execution but which are informed or driven by distorted patterns of reasoning. Cornish and Clark (1986), for example, acknowledge 'the operation of pathological motives acting in concert with rational means to secure irrational ends' (p.3). Similarly, proponents of a 'just deserts' approach to sentencing recognize the need to 'fine tune' sentences to accommodate the needs of individual offenders (Ashworth 1989, von Hirsch 1976). Rehabilitative and therapeutic programmes are viewed as having a definite, even if somewhat limited, role to play, so long as their degree of intervention is in proportion to the seriousness of the offence committed. However, the ways in which administrative criminology contributes to the development of criminal justice policy make it likely that any development or continuation of therapeutic initiatives would be subject to rigorous empirical evaluation in relation to their effectiveness and efficiency in achieving prescribed objectives. As mentioned earlier, the methodological foundations of psychotherapy do not fit comfortably within a paradigm which relies so heavily upon empirical measurements to establish validity.

RIGHT REALIST CRIMINOLOGY

Right realism has flourished in American criminology but has arguably gained little hold amongst British academics (see Rock 1994). Its influence in relation to debates about criminal justice policy, however, has not been so inconsequential. For the right realist the core task of criminology is to consider how the level of crime in society could most effectively be controlled. Its leading exponent is the American criminologist James Q Wilson, who has attacked the bedrock of liberal penal policies by repudiating the simplistic equation between poverty and crime. He points out (1985) that in the 1960s crime rates in the United States soared, despite unprecedented levels of prosperity and the initiation of a vast range of expensive welfare programmes designed to strike at the heart of social inequality and deprivation. Wilson acknowledges that the causes of crime may be many and varied, but he suggests that the long-term, upward trend in crime rates can be accounted for by three primary factors. First, demographic changes which increase the numbers of young males in society, in other words those 'most likely to be temperamentally aggressive and to have short time horizons' (Wilson and Herrnstein 1985, p.437). Second, variations occurring over time in the benefits and costs associated with criminal behaviour, in particular the increased opportunities for crime and the decreased risks of getting caught and suffering severe penalties. And finally, cultural changes which reduce the 'level and intensity of society's investment (via families, schools, churches and the mass media) in inculcating an internalized commitment to self-control', deferred gratification and a willingness to conform to social rules (p.437). Wilson (1985, p.253) acknowledges that much of what encourages crime in the United States reflects the competitive and individualistic culture of American society and that 'marginal improvements' in crime control, rather than the utopian goals of liberal criminal justice policies, are the realistic targets. Formal criminal justice policies, however, have only a limited role to play. Of far greater significance are the informal mechanisms of social control and, in particular, methods of child rearing, which inculcate a commitment to the social order. According to Wilson and Herrnstein, the early conditioning a child receives from his or her family enables certain rules to be internalized, facilitating the development of self-control, which can be reinforced and developed in the school, the work place and the local community. High crime areas are, by definition, those in which informal processes of social control have broken down, hence the primary role of the police and other criminal justice agencies must be to resuscitate effective methods of control by the community. However, the 'realism' of this perspective insists that there are some high crime neighbourhoods, typically those accommodating members of the 'underclass', that have deteriorated beyond repair. Police resources must, therefore, be concentrated 'where public order is deteriorating but not unreclaimable' (Wilson and Kelling 1982, p.38). Social utility becomes the guiding principle when dealing with high risk repeat offenders, who are to be targeted by the police and given disproportionately long incapacitative sentences in order to inhibit the spread of social malaise and protect the *status quo*. Priority is thus awarded to the maintenance of order and social control rather than to liberal concepts of justice. The protection of the public against crime and, by definition, the conservation of the social order, is given greater importance than the rules of due process and equal protection of individual rights.

In order for therapeutic programmes to be incorporated into a right realist policy agenda certain conditions would have to be met. The primary requirement would be that the programme promoted conformity to established values and codes of behaviour and directly inhibited conduct which deviated from this path. Given the aetiological assumptions of right realism, and the priority accorded to social utility over individual rights, therapy could be orientated toward preventive as well as curative goals, embracing those individuals considered to be in high risk categories who have yet to become involved in criminal activities. Obvious targets would be children deemed to be suffering from 'defective parenting' who require compensatory interventions to enable appropriate forms of social learning to take place. However, it is unlikely that psychotherapeutic methods would play a major role in the delivery of these therapeutic goals. Rehabilitative approaches which rely upon methods of behavioural conditioning would be more consistent with the ambition of right realism to foster a commitment to specific social rules and conformity to particular codes of conduct. Psychotherapeutic approaches tend to be considerably less prescriptive, striving principally to enable the individual to understand and appreciate the rich tapestry of life's choices, rather than imposing a specific and predetermined 'solution'. Regardless of methodology, however, the survival of any therapeutic endeavour within the right realist perspective would depend upon its ability to demonstrate at least a 'marginal gain' in the control of crime.

CONCLUSION

Criminology is a broad church, incorporating a wide range of different schools and disciplines. Its distillation here into four separate sociological paradigms is not the only way in which it can be depicted, but it does provide a conceptualization that acknowledges the diversity of criminological theory and practice whilst still enabling a generalized analysis of its relationship with psychotherapy. It has been noted that, despite an overlap of subject matter, criminology and forensic psychotherapy have tended to keep a respectful distance from one another. The previous discussion has endeavoured to explain how criminology variously approaches its field of study and how this can shape the contours of its relationship with psychotherapy. In this concluding section it is perhaps time to attempt a general synthesis of the major stumbling blocks criminology faces in bridging the gap which exists between itself and forensic psychotherapy.

Modern criminology is wary of positivist analyses and is particularly uncomfortable with those that individualize the causes of crime and associate criminal behaviour with personal pathology. Recent research has consistently emphasized the ubiquitous nature of criminality and has presented the criminal as a rational actor who has made a series of 'normal' adaptations to particular social environments. Few, if any, criminologists would dispute that there are some offenders whose anti-social behaviour is directly related to their psychopathology, and that psychotherapeutic and other psychological treatments might be appropriate and beneficial in these cases. The question is whether forensic psychotherapy has any theoretical or practical relevance for those who fall outside of this narrow band.

If it is accepted that the theory and practice of psychotherapy does not assume in all cases that the offender is acting irrationally, or is entirely determined by distorted psychological processes, then a second problem confronts the criminologist. This refers to the dilemmas of incorporating psychotherapeutic treatments within criminal justice policy. The criminal justice system coordinates a range of state punishments which are, by definition, coercive and non-negotiable. Is it possible, then, for psychotherapy to operate in this context whilst still enabling voluntary participation in treatment? In principle, the criminal justice system should not force offenders to receive or cooperate with treatment, unless they have been dealt with under specific conditions of the Mental Health Act 1983 and have thus passed into the care of the health services. Therapeutic programmes within the criminal justice system can only operate ethically with the consent of the offender. But, in a setting where the state arrogates power to itself and disenfranchises the offender, can such consent be regarded as voluntary? What pressures are offenders under to conform to a recommendation that they receive treatment? In a custodial setting these questions are particularly pertinent, especially in a system, such as the British, which incorporates indeterminate sentences and discretionary parole. But even in a non-custodial setting an offender's consent to treatment may be circumscribed by the real or imagined threat of more severe penalties being imposed in the event of his or her refusal to cooperate.

If therapeutic programmes were removed from the arena of state punishment then issues of consent would undoubtedly become less problematic. However, if all opportunities for treatment were to become totally separate from the formal process of punishment, and thereby located outside of the criminal justice system, a rather different set of problems might arise. These would focus largely upon definitions of eligibility. In particular, who should be the recipients of such opportunities: those whose psychological state is deemed to be most in need of treatment; those defined as most likely to benefit from any such intervention; or those assessed as representing the greatest risk of serious harm to the public? If it is the latter, then should treatment be extended to those whose behaviour has yet to constitute a criminal offence? A question is also raised about who should be responsible for making each of these assessments and what system of public accountability should exist to oversee such decision making.

The role of the state and the legitimate extent of its power to control and manage its citizenry has been a focus of concern in contemporary criminological debates. Evolving from the work of Michel Foucault (1979) it has been argued that the net of state control has spread insidiously across the population as methods of supervision and surveillance have increasingly superseded other more visible forms of punishment (Cohen 1979). The development of psychotherapeutic measures within the criminal justice system may be seen to epitomize the growth and intensification of such regulation by the state. Their control is described as potentially more intrusive and complete than traditional 'techniques' of restraint, embracing the ways in which individuals think as well as the ways in which they act. Yet their coercive nature has been shrouded by the identification of such programmes with the welfare of offenders and the humanitarian endeavours of the caring professions. Such invisibility, it is suggested, masks their true identity and purpose and thus places them beyond public scrutiny and accountability.

Finally, from the point of view of public policy, criminology can be seen to have played a role in exposing aspects of social 'malaise' which contribute to and encourage delinquent and criminal behaviour. Criminal justice programmes that start from the perspective of correcting individual pathologies are suspect, irrespective of their benefit to the persons concerned, because of their potential to divert attention and resources away from necessary social reform. Thus, it can be seen that, for criminology, there are a series of pitfalls which inhibit its relationship with forensic psychotherapy. A pre-requisite for bridging the gap that currently exists must be a less rigid adherence on the part of criminology to its distrust of the individualism inherent in forensic psychotherapy. But, in turn, there must be a corresponding flexibility on the part of forensic psychotherapy to acknowledge social, economic and political factors as relevant criteria in understanding the why, where and how of criminal behaviour.

Communication, Speech and Language

Jennifer France

COMMUNICATION

Disorders of communication, speech, language and hearing greatly reduce intelligibility of communication and limit communicative exchanges of thoughts and feelings. This is often met with intolerance, ridicule and rejection leading to isolation, hostility and anger, engendering feelings of low self-esteem and self-confidence, worthlessness and uselessness. Successful communication is the setting up and maintainance of full interactions of utterance and response which achieves mutually acceptable outcomes. People communicate in varied ways – for example, a look can kill, vocal tone can mean the opposite of what is being said and a touch can sometimes say more than a look or words – and effective communication can be more how something is said rather than what is said. We know that people are different when alone and when in groups and have different standards of approach according to the setting and those who are present.

There are a great number of human activities that cannot be avoided, according to Phillips (1984); just as there are few people who can avoid talking during the course of a day, there is no way to avoid being evaluated on the way we talk. Phillips believes that it is through talk that way we convey our personalities and that speaking well is usually associated with effective living as speech connects us with other human beings whom we try to influence in order that our daily lives are improved. People who are not able to communicate well experience a number of problems; communication can therefore be both the cause and cure of many emotional impairments.

Speech is the central component from which people may develop satisfactory social relationships as a result of effective communication. Many people believe that they need no training or education in an activity that they assume they perform quite well every day, but a variety of indicators reveal that our communicating needs are not always necessarily being met. It seems that seven per cent of the normal adult population experience serious difficulties in social behaviour (Argyle 1981) and therefore skill in communicating is not something that should be taken for granted. With all the communication devices available, it is almost impossible not to communicate. If you tried not to communicate, your accompanying behaviour alone would communicate your negative choice (Gleason 1992).

As good communication skills are a pre-condition for successful participation in most forms of psychotherapy it is important to understand the impact of disorders of communication, speech and language, by studying the complexities of their development and use in the normal context of every day life.

SPEECH

Speech is a complex physiological act which results in the production of sound waves involving the integration of neurological, physiological and anatomical systems (Grundy 1989). Speech is unique to man and its individuality manifests in several ways: for example, it requires only one person, a choice can be made whether to speak or not, what to say and how to say it. The speaker's assessment of the listener's state has a lot to do with what he says; just as speakers are free to ignore their listener, so too can others speak to destroy a conversation, as for example in some schizophrenic exchanges in which we know that conversational goals are not always being shared.

Speech has been defined as a system of communication in which thoughts are expressed and understood by using acoustic symbols (Espir and Rose 1976). These acoustic symbols are produced by the vibrations of the vocal cords situated in the larynx (which produces the vocal note), from which the vowels are formed (phonation). This is caused by the flow of air (respiration) and given final form by movement of the lips, tongue, alveolar ridge, hard and soft palates and pharynx, producing the consonants (articulation). The study of this sound system of language is phonology. Otswald (1963) states that normal human speech consists of two simultaneous sets of cues, the articulated sound patterns that convey semantically meaningful material, that is, words, phrases and sentences, and the discriminable qualitative features of the voice itself. As we listen to a person produce connected discourse Alpert (1981) states that we can make valid assessment as to the certain fixed or adherent characteristics of the speaker such as sex, age and education and a number of other factors. The experienced ear helps us to make remarkably skilful subjective evaluations of speakers from the speech they produce. The pragmatic criterion for communication competence is the appropriateness of speech used in context and this requires co-operation and emphasizes the usefulness and effectiveness of form and the accountability procedures practised by speakers in negotiating their different scenes. The analytical criteria for evaluating linguistic competence can be based on a sentence's grammatical structure (syntax), its semantic content and the pragmatics or appropriateness of speech in context (Dore 1986).

VOICE

The voice is an expression of who we are and how we feel and this includes both its tone and timbre. Newham (1993) also observes that there are vocal changes in therapy such as regression from adult to child's voice, as when describing childhood experiences and the child's ability to assume a mature adult voice when reflecting adult words. The voice can be an important indicator of both physiological and psychological well being or ill health.

As previously described, voice is the result of breath under pressure from the lungs causing the approximated vocal cords to perform the rhythmic excursions of separation and closure. The alternate expression and rarefaction of the stream of air particles thus created is responsible for the sound waves which determine the fundamental pitch of the vocal note produced (Greene 1975). Scherer and Scherer (1981) are of the opinion that voice can be affected by personality variables, fundamental frequency, vocal energy, or intensity and energy in the voice's spectrum and these qualities are experienced by observers mainly as pitch, loudness and voice quality.

Speech and language therapists also recognize acoustic features of voice production (Fawcus 1986) in terms of pitch, intonation, intensity and quality (as well as the variables involved) in the development of voice disorders by attempting to describe the causes as functional or organic. Three conditions can affect phonation, according to Fawcus: the first is when the vocal folds show structural abnormalities; the second when the folds appear normal but demonstrate a disturbance of movement patterns; and the third when there is no apparent organic impairment of structure or function.

Variations in the normal 'healthy' voice will be observed during times of stress, anxiety, happiness, sadness, anger, denial and regression, and also in those who suffer profound hearing loss and in transsexualism. A voice disorder exists according to Aronson (1980) when quality, pitch, and loudness or flexibility differs from the voice of others of similar age, sex and cultural group.

The offender patient's vocal quality varies from within normal limits to no audible voice at all (aphonia) or, when apparently 'sounding' normal, that is without any obvious voice pathology, some patients will vocalize above or below their own normal pitch, others will vocalize using only partial voice, producing a husky, creaky, rough sound aided by considerable muscular tension of the neck and shoulders, and a few use inappropriate vocal volume either too loud or too soft, usually the latter. These vocal signs are significant and an indicator of personal distress or progress, most of which will resolve spontaneously during the course of psychotherapy. In some cases voice therapy may be needed to assist the production of a healthy voice.

LANGUAGE AND ITS ACQUISITION

Language is the most important tool of communication (Foss and Hakes 1978). It permits people to communicate tremendous ranges of attitudes and information, biases and truths. We don't really think much about language, we just use it. A native speaker of a language knows a great deal about his language that he is never taught, implying that learning the words of, for example, English script requires knowledge about the structure of words and that this is acquired through exposure.

According to Bolinger (1975), acquiring a language calls for three things: a pre-disposition; a pre-existing language system and a competence. The attainment of language is life-long and therefore learning never ceases (p.3). Bolinger emphasizes that language is never completely learned, that it is an enormously complex system and that the rate of learning a language diminishes rapidly so that well before adolescence it seems almost to have come to a stop (p.8). The learning curve starts at near infinity and ends by plunging rapidly towards zero.

The development of normal speech and language is also determined by appropriate sensory, motor and intellectual development and psychomotor maturation of the infant in an environment offering adequate communication. The quality of personal language that evolves during speech development is dependant not only upon the day-to-day experiences of life but upon the quantity, quality and style of language used in the domestic, social and educational environments and, overall, the child's use of language is thought to reflect that of his mother's verbal style (Gleason 1992). Obler (1992) informs us that language development of early childhood and even late childhood is different from that of adulthood since there is probably a core language all children learn, whereas the special language registers and skills of adulthood are relatively optional; only people who need them and find themselves exposed to them have a chance to acquire them. Much of adult language acquisition is not formally learned but is acquired in context; there are registers or styles of speech we need to acquire in our work and in our social relationships.

Mature language is efficient, and appropriate utterances are selected for psychosocial dynamics of the communication situation. Less mature language users are unable to select the appropriate code because they have a limited repertoire of the language form, and this is demonstrated by many offender patients both in their daily lives and in psychotherapy. It is important to emphasize, therefore, that in late adolescence and adulthood we can still acquire language skills. Linguists know that there exists the potential for long-term acquisition of language and there is speculation that there are actual changes in brain substrate organization for language throughout older adulthood, as throughout the life-span (Obler 1992).

The complexity and time span involved in the development of language leads us to believe that something more than the imitation of the language of others plays an influential role. Carey (1978) states that by the age of six years a child may have learned over 14,000 words, and if vocabulary growth begins in earnest at 18 months then this works out to an average of nine new words a day or almost one word per waking hour! By the time the child has reached adolescence he should have developed his own speech style and be able to moderate his speech depending upon his listener. It is thought that working class children are supposed to have only one code and that is the restricted code, as it has been noticed that these children lack the flexibility of vocabulary and grammar to demonstrate modifications. De Villiers and de Villiers (1978) describe how these children fail to recognize the listener's needs and they have not recognized that certain groups require different forms of address. This is thought to be caused either by delayed development or lack of social and educational opportunities. Disorders of adolescence which usually begin in early childhood are often well established chronic conditions by the time the teenager comes to treatment for psychosocial problems. It is now thought that language acquisition must be considered in terms of development of communicative competence.

'I am no good with words
I know what I want to say,
but somehow the words don't come out right.'

Poor communicators in early childhood are associated with behavioural problems which may persist. Severe limitation of language is seen to lead to behaviour problems in several ways; for example, sometimes patients use precocious language which they don't completely understand (echoing) thereby giving the impression that they are more able than they really are, and abnormalities in language development tend to have far reaching effects on many other areas of development (Gath 1987). High rates of persisting social, emotional and behaviour problems in children attending clinics or special schools for language handicap have been recognized and a whole range of psychiatric problems are found (Paul and Caparulo 1983), just as severe disorder of language can produce disturbances of attention, activity and motor skills. The frequent association between language and/or speech disorders in psychotic disorders suggests that children with linguistic impairment are at risk for psychiatric pathology (Cantwell and Baker 1985), that children with language and or speech impediments have been reported to present increased frequency of psychiatric disorder, and that the prevalence of speech and language impairment is higher among children with psychiatric disorders. Older aggressive boys present with poor verbal skills (Camp 1966) and communication disorders can contribute to problems of deviant parent/child interactions which could enhance the usual stresses of growing up and make the child vulnerable (Kotsopoulos and Boodoosingh 1987).

Speech and language therapy research leads us to believe that parental mistreatment may lead to children having difficulty processing language and thence to language disorder. The required skills, in particular verbal skills, are known to deteriorate under stress and children with learning disorders have difficulty in interpreting social situations. This is highly relevant with regard to mentally disordered offender patients. Law and Conway (1992) also report that developmental sequelae, of which children's speech and language difficulties are a part, are likely to be associated with the experience of abuse and neglect and Rodeheffer and Martin (1976) specifically refer to these children's difficulties in attending to instructions, their hyper-vigilance, their fear of failure, and the passive aggressive behaviour which may occur during testing. Knowledge of these difficulties is as relevant for assessments of speech and language as for other forms of developmental assessments. Abused children can also experience a sense of overwhelming loss; there is no one to whom it is safe for them to turn and therefore no one with whom to trust that special forbidden language of abuse

'you see it all and can tell no one.'

It is this 'not telling' which endures throughout childhood into adult life and eventually into therapy. Sharing 'the secret' becomes more difficult with time and the fear of retribution lives on maintaining negative cognitions and limited expressive language usage. Thus, the creativity of content of language and the flexibility, fluidity and spontaneity of utterance can be affected by developmental delay and other forms of speech pathology as well as mental illness.

THE EFFECTS OF MENTAL DISORDER ON COMMUNICATION AND SPEECH

Most forms of mental disorder exhibit changes in all aspects of communication and speech behaviour demonstrating incongruency between verbal and non-verbal behaviour as well as the quality and quantity of interpersonal interaction. The resulting effect on communication is possibly governed not only by social isolation and reduced motivation but by perceptual changes caused by the disorder, such as reduced visual and auditory awareness. France (1991) suggests that speech disturbance can be divided into three possible areas for consideration: first, the communication and speech pathology evident prior to the onset of the illness and possibly maintained and exacerbated by the illness; second, communication and language disruptions/disorder caused predominantly by the illness; and finally, additional problems resulting from drug and physical treatments, organic conditions such as brain damage, epilepsy and learning and hearing disorders. There is now a school of thought that those who eventually develop major mental illness such as schizophrenia may well have experienced developmental problems in the past and that there is a possibility that the emerging mental illness may be of longer duration than previously thought. Perhaps there are links that can be traced back to childhood connecting the language delay of childhood with a thought disorder of the later developing mental illness. Could this early influence on normal language development be in some way responsible for the later communication problems, experienced by many, once the mental illness is established?

Until recently it was assumed that the left hemisphere was dominant for language and the right hemisphere had little if anything to do with language, but recent studies of various language and communication functions which have considered right hemisphere damage have found that although basic language areas such as phonology, lexicon and syntax are not impaired in patients with right hemisphere damage, the ability to use language appropriately in broader pragmatic senses may well be affected (Obler 1992).

It is thought that there is more to language than phonology, syntax and lexical/semantics and there is a large body of evidence which demonstrates that right hemisphere disordered patients can present with impairments in non-componential, non-literal and more complex features of language which are context bound, such as understanding jokes, stories and metaphors. The aspects of language which evidence suggests are disturbed by right hemisphere damage are lexical/semantic processing, high level language processing and prosody (Bryan 1989). Studies have shown that the communication competence of these patients can be impaired at the level of discourse and that successful discourse requires a firm grasp of the context. Pragmatics is concerned with the context of language usage and encompasses the way in which knowledge about this situation, the participants, the topic at hand, previous parts of conversation and social conventions are used in language all of which can be assessed with Bryan's (1989) *The Right Hemisphere Language Battery*. This assessment also concerns how the speaker uses contextual as well as verbal and non-verbal aspects of the message to express a desired intervention and it would appear that there may be important links here between these disorders and ongoing research into personality disorders, and schizophrenia.

A schizophrenic may tend to be unaware of the fact that human relations are multi-polar phenomena (Reusch and Bateson 1987), since his cognitive processes appear to be disrupted. There is reason to doubt that the patient desires to communicate in the normal sense, hence the resulting semantic/pragmatic difficulties. When working in a group setting with schizophrenic patients and using video recordings of the group it is interesting to note how fascinated and how observant the patients are regarding the communication performances of others and how they are less observant of their own behaviour. They remark particularly on the immobile postures of others, their limited gestures, expressionless faces and boring/flat voices. These same patients later notice change and progress on the video and tend to be more observant regarding their own performance once they are used to working with video recording in therapy.

Barch and Berenbaum (1994) explored the relationships between information processing and language in order to further the understanding of language disturbances in psychiatric patients. The results of their study indicated that certain facets of information processing are associated with at least some of the language disturbances found in schizophrenia and they recommend further research.

LINGUISTIC COMPETENCE AND PSYCHOTHERAPY

Good communication skills are a precondition for successful participation in most forms of psychotherapy. The ability to engage in and benefit from psychotherapy also necessitates the ownership of sophisticated linguistic skills, from which, during therapy emerge the accompanying paralinguistic skills supporting the evidence of developing psychological well being and personal maturity. Communication problems experienced by mentally disordered offender patients are similar to other non-offenders suffering from mental illnesses, particularly if the onset of the illness was during the adolescent years and therefore before the acquisition of adult language and communication skills. During the assessment process we may learn that present communication problems reflect long traumatic histories of deprivation, separation, neglect and abuse, and when these histories are compounded with the communication problems accompanying major mental illness, it is not surprising that our patients are initially ill equipped to benefit from most forms of psychotherapy.

'I've never been one for talking
I've always bottled things up,
Other people have their worries
I shouldn't burden them with mine.'

'There was never anyone to listen.'

'People never believed me,
they listened but they didn't hear.'

'I couldn't talk about *these* things to anyone I *knew*.'

Linguistic imbalance in group psychotherapy is not only a handicap to individual patients but to the group as a whole. It is known that the development of language skills in a group is a slow process and that supplementary support and treatment to assist the development of linguistic competence is necessary in some cases. Patients themselves report that language deficiencies in individual therapy can exert pressures that initially inhibits development. A specialized vocabulary is needed to assist the descriptions of daily life (the here and now) to describe and rediscover the past and eventually to plan the future. The expression of grief and loss, past violence, abuse and neglect, and the ability to talk about the offence or offences and the time leading up to the offence demands a sophisticated vocabulary. Therapy offers the opportunity to encourage and rehearse some of the semantic/pragmatic difficulties which assist in the development of the psychotherapeutic dialogue. Long term effects of developmental language disorder can be partly redressed during psychotherapy; this is particularly relevant in the treatment of offender patients.

Speech and language therapy involvement in psychotherapy ranges from the use of cognitive and behavioural approaches, dramatherapy and psychodramatic techniques to supportive and psychodynamic psychotherapy. All these methods can be employed to stimulate communication competence and to improve vocal quality, expressive and receptive language development, with particular emphasis upon increasing the lexical store, and finally to enhance fluency of utterance.

Amongst the specialized battery of assessments and tests employed by speech and language therapists, to both diagnose the deficits and to promote the continuing development of language growth, are two additional therapeutic approaches. The first is personal construct psychotherapy which is based on George Kelly's theory that man continually attempts to predict and control his world and in order to do this he invents 'constructs' which are bi-polar, and it is through these constructs that he perceives events. It is presented as a completely formal stated theory: it accounts for all human behaviour, it makes philosophical assumptions explicit and it is concerned primarily with 'the person'. It is dependent upon language and therefore offers an extremely useful method of assessment of how the patient sees his world and his place in it. The second approach is that of neurolinguistic programming which is a model of human behaviour and communication which draws from the knowledge of psychodynamics and behavioural theories. It is concerned with the identification of both conscious and unconscious patterns in communication and behaviour and how they interact in the process of change (Dilts *et al.* 1980).

Li and Greenewich (1991) state that the task of the psychotherapist is to reach out for a common language to share with the patient, to express feelings, to form experiences and ultimately to reclaim a sense of self, and that this comes about through a shared language, and the single most important feature within the psychotherapeutic space is the freedom for communication of which talk is the most dominant feature. Psychopathology is defined by Reusch and Bateson (1987) in terms of disturbance of communication and they state that rehabilitation can only be carried out within the context of a social situation, and that therapeutically effective agents contained in psychotherapy are to be found in communication. Psychotherapy can then be used primarily as an attempt to improve the patient's communication.

Schank (1990) believes that we need to tell someone a story that describes our experience because the process of creating the story also creates the memory structure that will contain the gist of the story for the rest of our lives. Seeing similarities between these stories can lead us to recognize patterns of behaviour that will repeat themselves. Some people need to hear themselves played back to themselves so that the therapist becomes their memory, thus helping in some sense to provide some insight to their behaviour by simply employing a different indexing scheme from that of the patient. The stories we tell each other we also tell ourselves (a statement of ownership) and this in turn stimulates memory. In a group setting this can assist in the recalling of a story for another patient and is helped by the choice of echoed words and phrases from others. In a secure setting without a time limit and where open-ended psychotherapy can continue for years, the frustration for the patient of repeating 'the story' many times gives the therapist the opportunity to observe changing prosodic features. During the repetition of stories we may become aware of only few language changes, the style of the story may stay the same, but the subtle changes in prosodic features such as pitch, volume, stress and fluency of utterance highlight the patient's emotional contact between his 'story' and its ownership. We witness the emergence of remorse and developing empathy towards victims and others through changes in verbal and non-verbal expression, assisting the therapists to record progress.

Whilst sharing childhood memories in therapy we hear of the regression to childhood emphasized by recognition of defective early speech patterns, articulatory mispronunciations and occasionally, when under considerable stress, there will be a re-emergence of a dialect or accent which has hitherto been disguised or modified. Other forms of early speech pathology can also be unconsciously re-experienced by the patient and therefore detected by the therapists as genuineness; conversely, fluent speech styles can be used to destroy, camouflage or mislead.

Towards the end of psychotherapy a patient reported that she was now 'worth' something and was not now prepared to allow people to 'belittle' her or 'bring her down'.

'I want to be *me*
I've got my identity back.'

In the early days of therapy she was frightened of 'talking too much' and remembered how she was eventually able to talk using her drawings.

'I didn't know how to talk.'

By describing her drawings she was able to experiment with her own language, she found that it was 'safe' to use and a relief once she knew how she could trust both herself and her therapist. Her developing self-confidence, self-esteem and linguistic competence has not only

'given me insight into myself,
it helps me see what I am worth'

but has helped reduce behaviours of self-abuse and aggression towards others.

Systems Theory

Arnon Bentovim

INTRODUCTION

The term 'systemic approach' encompasses what is more commonly known as a family therapy approach. The development of the systemic notion aims to ensure that issues which involve the individual also extend their concern to the family and the social context in a single conceptual framework. Therapeutic work which flows from this approach includes the consideration of all involved with the problem. Systems thinking encompasses three different issues:

(1) A philosophy of observation to include the context as well as the object of concern.

(2) An approach to treating problems in families and those concerned with them.

(3) A number of methods of treatment.

Thus although problem behaviour, particularly offending, has to be considered as the responsibility of the individual who commits the criminal act, their offending behaviour as a problem needs to be understood in context. It is important to consider the offending individual and the intimate relationship which exists between that individual and other family members, their current and past history and their relationships within the wider social network of which a family and the individual is a part.

Identified problems, for example offending behaviour, need to be defined not only by the act but also by the way acts are socially constructed. A violent act is defined differently by the perpetrating individual, the victim, the family households of each, the extended family and institutions with whom household members have daily contact – whether this be educational, health, social services or the criminal justice context. The definitions of what is offending behaviour change over time: for example, the growth and recognition of phenomena such as child sexual abuse and the decriminalization of some consenting sexual behaviour (eg. homosexual acts), and the shift in ages of consent.

THE DEVELOPMENT OF SYSTEMIC APPROACHES

The concepts that underlie the collective title of general systems theory were originally developed by Von Bertalanffy (1962) in response to dissatisfaction with the reductionist tradition which saw events as cause and effect chains. Such thinking is embedded, for example, in psychodynamic models which see past events predicting future ways of relating. The alternative model was to study the pattern and form of the organization of biological systems, the family being seen as such a system (Jackson and Weakland 1961; Watzlawick, Beavin, and Jackson 1969). Observations of the family relied on the notion that a system was defined as an organized arrangement of elements consisting of a network of interdependent coordinated parts that function as a unit (Von Bertalanffy 1962). The particular family, therefore, develops characteristic patterns and core ways of being and relating. Such patterns are carried forward in life into subsequent social contexts by family members (Main, Kayman and Cassidy 1985). Clinicians attempted to analyze such patterns by seeing the whole family together, including the referred individual; they observed what went on between family members, and tried to understand how this related to presenting problems; they then attempted to convey their understanding in such a way that it could be used by the family to change what were perceived as unhelpful ways of relating.

An interest in treatment of the family as a group was stimulated by studies of communication patterns in families containing a schizophrenic member (Bateson, Jackson, Haley, and Weakland 1956; Lidz 1973). Several research groups began to examine the role of family factors in the genesis of schizophrenia and of various psychiatric disorders of childhood.

A focus on violence and offending behaviour in systemic approaches was introduced by Minuchin (1974) and his colleagues. They introduced the *structural* approach to family therapy. This work originated from the awareness that mental health problems and delinquent behaviour in children were sometimes more associated with major social stress, for example poverty, poor environment and immigration, than they necessarily were with the early history of family members. Families were helped to develop communication and social skills, and action techniques were introduced – such as the enactment of a conflict, or an emotional entanglement – in order to help the family find a new resolution to the problem presented. The therapist was directive and controlling: there was immediate supervision available to him through the use of the one-way screen, and immediate communication to the therapist to help him intensify his effect in promoting change within the family. Such approaches were introduced to help restructure a family whose rigid patterns were playing an important part in both triggering and maintaining destructive behavioural patterns (see Minuchin *et al.* 1975).

Other models of systemic thinking include *strategic* approaches (Watzlawick, Beavin and Jackson 1967, 1969; Watzlawick, Weakland and Fish 1974): this model assumes that complaints or symptoms arise as a result of failure to deal adequately with critical life transitions or stressful life events. The dysfunctional response and the solution which fails is the problem. So that, for example, inappropriate punishment for a perceived misdemeanour triggers off further aggressive responses which then become an escalating problem.

Therapeutic work thus focuses on the many solutions that have been tried (unsuccessfully) to resolve a difficulty: exceptions to the pattern of failure are sought no matter how small they are. This has led to a current school of 'solution focused' therapy which attempts to discover the exception to the normal problematic pattern (de Shazer *et al.* 1986).

The power and relevance of the symptom and its relationship to the way that systems patterns maintain the symptom, and the way the symptom in turn regulates the family and social system has been an important focus of systemic thinking. Hayley (1963, 1971, 1977) and Madanes (1991) have acknowledged the importance and power of the symptom and the part it plays in stabilizing family life. In this model, offending behaviour would thus be seen not only as a product of the complex set of relationships which impact upon and affect the development of the individual, but also, as a symptom – which may play a major role, and impact upon, individual and family life and social context – and have both a modifying and stabilizing role. Such an analysis has now extended to examination of offending behaviour in relation to such contemporary issues as feminist thinking about the gender structure in society, multi-ethnic perspectives, and the nature of the narrative structure of social discourse and relationships.

In recent years the split between psychodynamic and systemic ways of thinking have been bridged. Bentovim and Kinston (1991) have shown how traumatic and stressful events experienced by individuals in their family of origin, or in the current family, can have an organizing effect on current relationships, problem formation and problem maintenance. A powerful bridge between psychodynamic and systemic thinking is also provided by the Milan associates (Palazzoli, Boscolo, Cecchin and Prata 1978, 1980), who attempt to link an understanding of the unconscious processes which control family relationships over time with a systemic approach to changing the hidden rules in the family's patterns of communication. All behaviours are seen as working to preserve stability and coherence. The Milan group developed a highly organized and influential way of working; they use an observing team behind a one-way mirror, and have developed a variety of ways of practice which include careful formulation and generation of hypotheses to explain the problem and then, as it were, *in vivo* testing. The hypotheses are explored using a variety of questioning techniques which recognize, and attempt to challenge, the mutual influences and control which members of the family exert both on each other and on the therapists. A position of neutrality is adopted by the therapist, who asks, for example, questions of each member of the family: invariably he gets different answers – which can then be further explored to

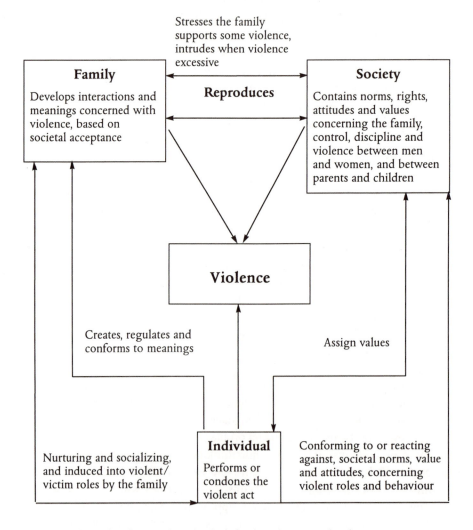

Figure 1 Relationships between the individual, family and society and violence

construct a total picture. The observing team helps the therapist in the room to explore the different ways in which a problem could be viewed by different family members and the way they are connected.

VIOLENCE AS A PARADIGM OF OFFENDING BEHAVIOUR

Figure 1 demonstrates a systemic approach which considers the relationships between the individual, the family, society and violence. This figure shows that all three agencies are concerned with the initiation and maintenance of violent interaction. Violence is placed in the centre to emphasize that it does not uniquely belong to any single setting, but can be seen as the property of each.

Society – which has a core of culture and a surface of behavioural conventions – contains a set of norms, rights, attitudes and values concerning what is deemed 'appropriate' violence, and what may be committed against whom and in what circumstances. Society legitimizes violence and approves the violence or 'discipline' of family members in its proper place. The family in turn becomes the setting of a violent act. Violent interactions and roles thus emerge as an integral aspect of this process and, in turn, create and regulate meanings within the family, and feedback to reinforce them. Individuals are nurtured, socialized and induced into violent or victim roles by the family: the individual then performs or condones the violent act and in turn creates, regulates and conforms to the family beliefs and meaning systems, and takes these into society.

Society stresses the importance of the family and supports a degree of expected violence/discipline: it will only intrude when violence is excessive, or when it defines violent or offending behaviours as unacceptable. Such definitions are influenced by complex, changing, and socially constructed processes. Privacy is a characteristic of the family as an institution: therefore, society cannot act unless there is sufficient communication to draw acts to the attention of those who can provide either social control, or therapeutic work to ameliorate such patterns. Society assigns values to individuals who in turn conform to – or react against – societal norms, values and attitudes concerning violent roles and behaviour. Until recently there has been an extraordinary lack of social consequence for aggression of all types. A 'blind eye' is turned, for example in domestic violence, and women may be blamed if they meet violence with violence, since such actions breach traditional societal norms and expectations. The woman who cannot escape from the violent home, and cannot protect her child, is often more the focus of condemnation than the man who perpetrates the violence. Only recently has there been a public debate, in terms of legal and moral responsibility, about the woman whose only perceived escape has been to kill the man who abuses her.

SYSTEMIC THINKING AND PATTERNS

People living in close proximity set up patterns of interaction with each other which have been shown to be made up of relatively stable 'items' which build up into sequences and patterns of behaviour (Kinston and Bentovim 1990). These 'items' involve family members in dyadic, triadic or whole family patterns of relating. They are often inter-generationally shaped, and – through inter-subjective responses – a set of complementary or symmetrical meanings comes to delineate the reality for individuals of their family contexts. A set of coherent myths and scripts (Byng-Hall 1986) emerge which can be general, for example 'ill luck has always dogged the Browns' or 'the Smiths have been an argumentative lot for generations' or 'John takes after his father, he's got the same eyes and he's a bad lot just like him'. Families thus replicate or recreate such scripts or meaning patterns, or they can attempt to reverse or overcome them, and mount a struggle to overcome their 'fate'.

A number of descriptive terms and 'domains' have been introduced to help to describe such family patterns (Bentovim and Kinston 1991). They include the *affective* life of the family; the *communication patterns* of the family; the *boundaries* which encompass the family as a whole and the way that they divide individuals from one another; the *alliances* between family members; the *adaptability* of the family and the *stability* of *organization and competence* for family tasks. A model is described which sees family contexts as functioning in a graded way from (1) an *optimal* level, (2) an *adequate* level, (3) a *dysfunctional* level, to (4) *breakdown* level.

It is also possible to describe larger institutions – such as hostels, or hospitals – where individuals (including ourselves) are in living or working relationships with each other using similar terms.

Optimal patterns of relationships in families or organizations occur where the nature and strength of relationships between family members is constructive and appropriate to their respective ages and roles. An *adequate family* or organization would be one where there are satisfactory relationships but with greater closeness or distance between some family members than others. A *dysfunctional family* or organization is one in which the patterns show serious discord or distance between members, and shifting or over-exclusive alignments. It is noted that children in such families repeatedly detour parental tensional conflicts. *Breakdown in a family* or an organization is shown by serious deficiencies. Family patterns show marked splits, scapegoating and severe triangulation where parents achieve closeness through attacking a third family member, or there is isolation of all family members.

Using such concepts it is possible (1) to delineate what is specific about the family/organization through the observation of concrete items of interaction; (2) to understand the meaning of the particular family's interaction by using the multi-generational family history to deepen understanding – which enables the therapist to make a more complete holistic formulation; (3) to provide a complete account of the family/organization in context; (4) to predict – on the basis of clinical and research knowledge – what the family/organization might become if therapeutic interventions were to be successful.

CHARACTERISTICS ASSOCIATED WITH OFFENDING BEHAVIOUR

The importance of looking at the systemic characteristics associated with offending behaviour lies in an examination of 'the pattern which connects' (Bateson 1973). The distinction between a model of 'cause and effect' needs to be expanded. If the factors associated with criminality are examined, it is noted significantly frequently that the individual has often become caught up in a series of relationships into which he or she has been inducted, and which will remain as future 'working models' of relationships.

Studies of juvenile delinquency repeatedly note the association with factors such as neglect, lack of parental supervision or failure to exert discipline. A further association is a lack of active parental responsiveness to children's antisocial acts, and a consequent failure of the individual to develop a self-regulating pattern towards a more socially responsible position. There may be deviant family values, such as drug and alcohol abuse, and the modelling of antisocial behaviour by parents. Such experiences can have a deep influence on subsequent behavioural responses and relationships both within future families and the wider society. A family climate of pronounced discord, conflict, abuse and family violence in turn induces a set of meanings and realities for a young person which will propel that person into a re-enactment and repetition of such patterns themselves.

There has been considerable recent interest in the development of protective factors which will interrupt such patterns. The following factors are noted to have a protective effect in ameliorating negative modelling and the stressful impact of 'negative living contexts'; educational opportunity; positive peer group influence; positive effort by teachers and the expectation of achievement; the intervention of community agencies; living in neighbourhoods of low delinquency; elements of family cohesiveness and consistency and development of at least some positive relationships with some family members.

PATTERNS OF TRAUMATIC STRESS AND OFFENDING BEHAVIOUR

Highly dysfunctional and breakdown level family/organizational patterns and beliefs are often related to major stress. Such stress may be defined as a 'disorganizing event' and can arise within the current family/systemic context, or may have origins in the past but still exert an effect on current functioning. If stressful events are of sufficient severity they can become traumatic and have long-standing 'traumatogenic' effects. It has been shown that such events can have an organizing effect on both individual and family relationships over lengthy periods and result in a 'trauma organised system' (Bentovim 1992b). The notion of 'problem-determined' or 'problem-organized' systems was introduced by Anderson, Goolishan and Windermans (1986). They based their thinking upon systemic/constructivist views concerning the way that communication about problems itself creates a system, that is, a problem-determined or problem-organized system. This is paralleled in the way in which highly traumatic events, interactions, and responses to violent offending acts come to 'organize' the reality and the perceptions of those participating – including the professionals. Through such processes the responsibility of the abuser is minimized, and the victim or some characteristic of the victim is seen as adequate 'cause' of the abuse. Responsibility is not placed where it belongs.

Helplessness is associated with the dynamic/systemic effect of powerlessness, with feelings of 'invasion' and psychic pain, and the absence of protection from the environment.

Individuals who are caught up within such systems feel a sense of grievance and a desire for revenge which are characteristic of those involved in offending behaviours. The systemic approach to therapeutic work attempts not only to develop an understanding of the offending individual in terms of the factors which have led to his offending, but also the context in which he or she is currently living and the influence of others in triggering and maintaining offending patterns. It will concern itself, too, with the effect of the individual and his offending behaviour on his family and social context. This requires a number of levels of assessment and analysis. An assessment of dangerousness not only requires an assessment of the individual, but also those in the living and social context who may have a significant role in the triggering and maintenance of such patterns.

Gurman, Krisken and Prusoff (1986) have identified the ingredients common to all models of systemic therapy, whether with individuals, families, groups, or within organizations. These include (1) helping to change the perception of the problem by all those in the systems; (2) modification of communication between individuals and within families and organizations; (3) the creation of alternative modes of problem solving; (4) modification of the degree of distress, or anger associated with symptomatic behaviour; and (5) a modification of the breakdown/dysfunctional modes of family functioning.

Because of the powerfully organizing effect of serious offending, particularly within the family, there has been a modification of thinking and technique. Instead of working with the family group from the outset, working with the family is now regarded as an aim to be achieved through individual, sub-system or group work.

Research on systemic approaches (Gurman *et al.* 1986) has demonstrated the effectiveness and power of systemic therapeutic interventions and their value, for instance, in the modification of offending behaviour, for example within family contexts (Bentovim *et al.* 1988).

Personality and Sexual Development, Psychopathology and Offending

Peter Fonagy & Mary Target

AN OVERVIEW OF PSYCHOANALYTIC THEORIES

Scope of the Chapter

There are no psychoanalytic theories of crime. Crime is a legal or sociological, not a psychoanalytic, construct. Psychoanalytic theory therefore considers criminality under the heading of character or personality disorder. Each psychoanalytic theory takes a different approach to explaining how individuals who are more likely to come to be considered as criminals may have developed that way. Thus criminality may be linked to different character pathologies within different psychoanalytic frameworks and all such frameworks contain somewhat distinct formulations of each character pathology. We will consider some major psychoanalytic theories of two forms of character disturbance most commonly linked to criminality: narcissistic personality disorder and borderline personality disorder. Reviewing all these ideas falls beyond the scope of this chapter. Here our focus will be on psychoanalytic theories of personality rooted in theories of psychosocial development.

Antisocial personality disorder is seen in most psychoanalytic traditions (e.g. ego-psychology) as a combination of extremes of particular personality types: individuals who are selfish, grandiose, lacking in empathy and identity (narcissistic), or are impulsive, violent, self-harming, socially maladapted, emotionally labile (borderline) personalities. This chapter provides a selective review of certain psychoanalytic theories, including classical and ego psychological models, and US object relational approaches to such personality disorders and the implications for the understanding of criminal behaviour are explored. Other psychoanalytic models are considered elsewhere in these volumes.

Freud's (1905c) psycho-sexual theory of development was revolutionary in presenting a predominantly developmental view of adult psychopathology, in that he begun to construct an understanding of adult disturbances in terms of infantile and early childhood experience. The details of the model were etched in by Karl Abraham (1927) who identified specific links between character formation, neurosis and psychosis on the one hand and instinctual development on the other. Contemporary followers of Freud proposed alternative foci for clinical study, but all were based on developmental formulations: Adler's (1916) focus was on the child's feelings of inferiority as the roots of the adult's striving for power and maturity; the Hungarian analyst Ferenczi (1913) outlined the vicissitudes of the child's development of a sense of reality and the simultaneous sacrifice of fantasized omnipotence; Rank's (1924) focus was at an even earlier stage, that of the birth trauma, which in his view underpinned all subsequent human conflicts, defences and strivings; even Karl Jung's (1916) model may be considered a developmental one, if in a somewhat negative sense, in that he proposed true maturity and mental health to lie in the giving up of the 'child-self'.

More recent psychoanalytic theories continue to follow a strictly developmental motif. Anna Freud (1936) provided a developmental model of ego defences and later (1966) a comprehensive model of psychopathology based on the dimensions of normal and abnormal personality development. Melanie Klein (1935, 1936), influenced by Ferenczi and Abraham, was a pioneer in linking interpersonal relationships to instinctual developmental factors to provide a radically different perspective, both on severe mental disorders and on child development. Meanwhile, in the US Heinz Hartmann (1939) with Kris and Lowenstein (Hartmann, Kris and Loewenstein 1946) provided an alternative, equally developmentally oriented framework, focusing on the evolution of mental structures necessary for adaptation, and elaborated on the common developmental conflicts between mental structures in early childhood. Margaret Mahler (1979) and her colleagues (Mahler, Pine and Bergman 1975) provided psychoanalysts in the North American tradition with a dynamic map of the first three years of life, and ample opportunities for tracing the developmental origins of disorders. Fairbairn (1952a) traced the development of object seeking from immature to mature dependence; Jacobson (1964) explored the development of representations of self and other. Kernberg (1975) drew on previous work by Klein, Hartmann and Jacobson to furnish a developmental model of borderline and narcissistic disturbances; Kohut (1971, 1977) constructed a model of narcissistic disturbances based on presumed deficits of early parenting.

Unfortunately, early theories have not been supplanted by later formulations and most psychoanalytic writers assume that a number of explanatory frameworks are necessary in order to comprehensively account for the relationship of development and psychopathology (see Sandler 1983). So-called neurotic psychopathology is presumed to originate in later childhood at a time when there is self–other differentiation and when the various agencies of the mind (id, ego, superego) have been firmly established. The structural frame of reference (Arlow and Brenner 1964; Sandler, Dare and Holder 1982) is most commonly used in developmental accounts of these disorders. Personality or character disorders, as well as most non-neurotic psychiatric disorders, are most commonly looked at in frameworks developed subsequent to structural theory (e.g. borderline personality disorder, narcissistic personality disorder, schizoid personality disorder). Here, a variety of theoretical frameworks are available, including the structural, most of which point to developmental pathology arising at a point in time when psychic structures are still in formation (see, for example Kohut 1971; Modell 1985).

PSYCHOANALYTIC MODELS OF DEVELOPMENT

Freud's Model of Development

Major Shifts in Freud's Thinking

Freud and Breuer (1895) initially believed that he had discovered the aetiology of neurosis in the actual event of childhood seduction. In this conception the interpersonal event of the early trauma was represented in a distorted form in the neurotic symptom. For example, a child of eight with hysterical blindness may have achieved relative internal safety by 'shutting his eyes' to the memory of having witnessed his mother's rape. This model posited no mental apparatus, it reflected the physical conversion of energy. For example, he wrote in 1894: 'Where physical sexual tension accumulates – anxiety neurosis.' (S. Freud 1894a, p.192).

The turning away from his seduction hypothesis in favour of his second model, emphasizing fantasy driven by a biological drive state, discredited psychoanalytic theory as a social theory of development. It led Freud (1905c) to attempt to explain all actions in terms of the failure of the child's mental apparatus to deal adequately with the pressures of a maturationally predetermined sequence of drive states. Adult psychopathologies, as well as dreaming, jokes and parapraxes, were seen as the revisiting of unresolved childhood conflicts over sexuality (Freud 1900, 1901, 1905b). For example, he saw anxiety as arising from the failure of repression of unacceptable sexual wishes (Freud 1905c, p.224).

The fundamental influence of the social environment again found a preeminent place in the emerging analytic theory with the third major shift in Freud's thinking (Freud 1920, 1923, 1926), This new structural theory was to survive long after Freud because of the compelling fit with clinical observational data in the dual instinct theory (Freud 1920). For example, the significance for psychopathology of the child's struggle with innate destructive and self-destructive forces was finally fully recognized. At this time, Freud (1926) also revised his view of anxiety from being a biologically determined epiphenomenal experience associated with inhibited drives, to a psychological state linked to the perception of internal (instinctual or moral) or external danger. The danger situation was specified as the fear of helplessness resulting from loss (loss of the mother, her esteem, loss of a body-part or loss of self-regard). This revision restored adaptation to the external world as an essential part of the psychoanalytic account, and recast the theory into more cognitive terms (Schafer 1983). Freud nevertheless retains the concept of a more primitive form of anxiety which arises in an involuntary automatic way 'whenever a danger situation analogous to birth' had established itself (Freud 1926, p.162). It is this automatic pervasive anxiety and the associated state of overwhelming helplessness which is warded off with the help of 'signal anxiety' which prompts the ego to limit the threat of a basic danger situation (see Yorke, Kennedy and Wiseberg 1981).

This final revision in Freud's thinking provided a developmental framework based around the tripartite structural schema of id, ego and superego (Freud 1923, 1933, 1940). The hypothesis that conflicts within the human mind are chiefly organized around three themes (wish versus moral injunction, wish versus reality and internal reality versus external reality) has had extraordinary explanatory power. In particular, the ego's capacity to create defences which organize characterological and symptomatic constructions as part of the developmental process, became the cornerstone of psychoanalytic theorization and clinical work in the US (Hartmann et al. 1946) and Britain (Freud 1936).

The limitations of Freud's developmental model are manifold, and the subsequent elaboration of psychoanalytic theorization is testament to the cultural context-dependent nature of psychological theory and the need of subsequent theorists to make their own contributions to the culture or context in which they live. Perhaps the most important post-Freudian contributions have been in the domains of the cultural and social context of development; the significance of early childhood experiences; the developmental significance of the real behaviour of the real parents; the role of dependency, attachment and safety in development alongside the role of instinctual drives; the synthesizing function of the self; the importance of the non-conflictual aspects of development. Many of these shortcomings were pointed out by Freud's contemporaries who frequently moved away from organized psychoanalysis under a cloud, at least so far as Freud was concerned. Their association with these themes may have delayed general consideration of them within mainstream psychoanalysis. For example, Jung's rejection of libido theory drew attention away from the undoubted advances he made in the understanding of narcissism and his development of a theory of the self throughout the life cycle (Jung 1912, 1916, 1923).

Freud's Views of Crime and Criminal Tendencies

Freud never concerned himself specifically with criminal behaviour. His views, however, continue to exert a significant influence on psychoanalytic thinking in this area. In 1908 he wrote:

> 'Our civilization is built upon the suppression of instincts… Each individual has surrendered some part of his possessions – some part of the sense of omnipotence or of the aggressive or vindictive inclinations in his personality… The man who, in consequence of his unyielding constitution, cannot fall in with this suppression of instinct, becomes a "criminal", an "outlaw" in the face of society – unless his social position or his exceptional capacities enable him to impose upon it as a great man, a "hero".' (1908a, p.187)

Thus, Freud's view of criminal tendencies contains many of the components which were to be emphasized by many post-Freudian psychoanalytic thinkers. He considers constitutional predisposition to be a critical factor in the development of criminality. He sees weakness of repression to be the primary cause along with a failure to renounce infantile omnipotence. He sees untamed aggression as central but remains sensitive to the proximity of criminality and personality disorders, such as a narcissistic personality (the 'hero') which is further stressed in his paper *On Narcissism* where he links sociopathy with excessive narcissism. He explains the common fascination with the 'criminal' as an almost envious stance taken by us with their 'blissful' state of mind which allows them to adopt libidinal positions which we have been forced to abandon.

Perhaps somewhat less valuable are Freud's attempts at classification of criminality. In his paper on character types encountered in the course of psychoanalytic work (S. Freud 1916c) he traces all crimes to either incest or parricide. His argument for this is less than compelling and has largely been abandoned by later writers. In the course of the same review, he distinguishes psychopathy (guiltless crime) from criminals whose actions arise out of a sense of guilt (conscious or unconscious). The latter group, he feels, commit their acts to relieve their vague sense of inner torment by deliberately creating situations where punishment will be inevitable – a manifestation of unconscious guilt. The psychopath he feels 'develops no moral institutions' (p.333) – later he termed these 'psychical structures' (S. Freud 1925b, p.275) – which would prevent them from entering the world of crime.

Classical psychoanalysis was already sensitive to the most critical aspects of understanding delinquency. Karl Abraham in 1925 suggested that 'impostrous' antisocial tendencies could be understood as long term consequences of 'psychological undernourishment' during childhood (p.304). Abraham felt that the lack of love which characterized the early childhood of such individuals undermined their capacity for object relationships, causing a regressive enhancement of their narcissism and a lifelong hatred of the other. The limitations in their capacity to form relationships critically undermined their ability to enter and resolve the challenges of the Oedipal stage, leaving them vulnerable in all future social relationships. The absence of successful Oedipal resolution explained their failure to make lasting bonds, their remaining self-centred, their excessive need for admiration, bragging, fraudulence, perverse chaotic sexuality, and chronic tendency to disappoint and betray others.

Freud was pessimistic about the usefulness of psychoanalysis as a treatment method for criminals. The superego was seen by him as an essential component of successful psychoanalytic treatment. This view has been largely borne out by later developments and most current psychoanalytic forensic clinicians would accept that the psychoanalytic treatment of such individuals requires significant modifications of technique which permit the evolution of psychic structures which are developmentally compromised in individuals with criminal tendencies. Freud's lack of experience with this group prevented him from making appropriate recommendations about the nature of these modifications and the development of the entire forensic field within psychoanalysis suffered as a consequence.

The Structural Approach

The Structural Approach to Development
HARTMAN'S EGO PSYCHOLOGY MODEL

Freud's model was refined and advanced in the ego psychology of Heinz Hartmann and his colleagues. Hartmann (1939) demonstrated how psychoanalysts frequently used the developmental point of view in an oversimplified and reductionist way. His concept of the 'change of function' (p.25) highlighted how behaviour originating at one point in development may serve an entirely different function later on. The internalization of parental injunction may, through the mechanism of reaction formation, lead the child to adopt a stance repudiating the anal wish to mess and soil through excessive cleanliness and orderliness. The same behaviour in the adult may serve quite different functions and is likely to be independent, to have achieved secondary autonomy (Hartmann 1950), from the original wish. The failure to recognize this has been termed the 'genetic fallacy' (Hartmann 1955, p.221). Similarly, the persistence of dependent behaviour in adulthood cannot be treated as if it were a simple repetition of the individual's early relationship with the mother.

Sandler and Dare (1970) point out that whereas the infant's first year of life may be considered as characterized by oral dependency, such longings are likely to occur at any phase at times of stress, when the child wishes to have what he fantasizes was true earlier. Adult behaviours are invariably seen as having multiple functions (Brenner 1959, 1979; Waelder 1930).

Hartmann's admonition continues to be relevant. The identification of what are presumed to be primitive modes of mental functioning in individuals with severe personality disorders (e.g. Kernberg 1975, 1984; Kohut 1977) is often regarded as evidence for the persistence or regressive recurrence of early pathogenic developmental experiences. Yet, even if splitting or identity diffusion were representative of early modes of thought (an issue which is in any case highly controversial, see Westen 1990), their reemergence in adult mental functioning may be linked to later or persistent trauma. The structural view of development, perhaps more than any other psychoanalytic developmental framework, attempts to take a holistic view of the developmental process, resisting the temptation to identify particular, especially early, critical periods (Tyson and Tyson 1990).

Following Anna Freud (1936), Hartmann, Kris and Lowenstein (1946) postulated an initial undifferentiated matrix which contains the individual's endowment and from which both the id and the ego originate. They also introduced the concept of an 'average expectable environment', which affirmed the importance of the parental contribution to development, and outlined a scheme for the phase specific maturation of autonomous, conflict-free ego functions, accommodating both environmental and maturational influences upon personality development. They described the self as gradually differentiating from the world during the first half of the first year, and the gradual evolution of the child's relationship to his or her own body and objects in the second half, as the influence of the reality principle is increasingly felt. In the second year, an ego–id differentiation phase emerges, marked by ambivalence, as the reality principle begins to assert its influence over the pleasure principle. The final phase is that of superego differentiation as a consequence of social influences, identification with parental values and the resolution of the oedipal conflict. Rapaport (1950), suggested a stage theory of the development of thinking which commences in hallucinatory wish fulfilment through the drive organization of memories, primitive modes of ideation and the conceptual organization of memories, until finally the capacity for abstract thought is attained.

Structural Model of Psychopathology
GENERAL FEATURES OF THE MODEL
Within the structural model, neurosis and psychosis of adult life are seen as arising when an individual's urge for drive gratification reverts from an age

appropriate mode of satisfaction to a formerly outgrown infantile mode. Such regressions are brought about by psychic conflict which the ego is incapable of resolving. The id's regression and the associated revival of infantile urges intensifies the clash with parts of the personality that have maintained a mature level of functioning and intense internal conflict is the outcome. The ego's failure to manage such conflict – the intensification of guilt and superego pressure, the intensification of drive demands as a consequence of the regression, and the greater inappropriateness of these demands in terms of age appropriate adaptation to the external world – leads to the formation of symptoms.

Symptoms are compromises, reflecting the ego's manifold attempts to restore inner equilibrium between the unacceptable drive representations and the opposing agencies of ego and superego. In other cases, it may be the regression of the ego owing to psychological and organic causes which is reflected in the pathology. In psychosis, the ego is seen as being threatened by complete dissolution. Essential ego functions may resume modes of functioning characteristic of early childhood and come to be dominated by irrational, magical thought and a failure to control impulses. Thus, whilst mental health is seen as the harmonious interaction between psychic agencies that function at age appropriate levels, mental ill health is seen as the result of the ego's attempt to reconcile developmentally contradictory impulses and aims. The pathogenic sequence is perceived as follows: (1) frustration; (2) regression; (3) internal incompatibility; (4) signal anxiety; (5) defence by regression; (6) return of the repressed; and (7) compromise formation and symptomatic disorders.

Symptomatic disorders are not the invariable developmental consequences of childhood fixations. Within the classical structural model, inhibition is seen as a powerful, albeit potentially quite crippling, way of reducing conflict between the psychic agencies. At extreme levels, inhibitions are seen as characteristic of personality disorders (Freud 1926). For example, an individual who avoids any kind of human contact which might stimulate drives and their associated affects, may be seen as schizoid in personality type. Sexual inadequacy (erectile dysfunction) may be seen as the inhibition of the expression of the sexual drive. Inhibitions may apply to the ego (see A. Freud 1936), whereby an ego function which has become psychically painful may be abandoned. Ego restrictions of this kind would be exemplified by someone whose conflicts over competitiveness would cause them to withdraw from sports activities and invest their energies elsewhere, for example in writing. Restriction of affect may occur with individuals who experience emotion as highly threatening.

STRUCTURAL MODEL OF BORDERLINE AND ANTISOCIAL PERSONALITY DISORDER
Individuals with borderline personality disorder were initially described in the psychoanalytic literature as patients who are unlikely to do well in classical psychoanalysis and frequently reacted adversely to it (Deutsch 1942; Stern

1938). The issue of modification of classical technique was also raised at an early stage (Schmideberg 1947). Knight (1953) was the first to propose a comprehensive developmental model of the disorder in terms of ego functions impaired by traumatic development. Among the ego functions he considered were: 'integration, concept formation, judgment, realistic planning, and defending against eruption into conscious thinking of id impulses and their fantasy elaborations' (p.6). Erikson (1956, 1959a), in his epigenetic sequence of identity formation described the syndrome of identity diffusion, which he saw as reflecting deficiencies in a sustained sense of self-sameness, temporal continuity of self-experience, and a feeling of affiliation with a social group of reference. Jacobson (1953, 1954, 1964) drew attention to how these individuals, at times, experience their mental functions and bodily organs not as belonging to them, but as objects which they wish to expel. They may also attach their mental and body self to external objects. She saw them as retaining an 'adolescent fluidity of moods' (1964, p.159).

Aichhorn (1935) was the first psychoanalyst seriously to concern himself with delinquent individuals and his techniques for addressing their problems were both imaginative and effective. His etiological formulations, however, were even more influential, perhaps because these were strongly endorsed by Freud himself (Freud 1925b). He proposed a dual deficit model. He posited a failure of progression from the pleasure principle to the reality principle in conjunction with a malformation of the superego in his developmental account of the disorder. This accounts for lack of impulse control in delinquent individuals, as longings for immediate gratification persist and remain unquestioned. Excessive strictness and overindulgence were both seen as causes of the child's failure to renounce the pleasure principle. His ideological notions stressed deprivation as not only impeding the renunciation of the pleasure principle but also disrupting the internalization of parental norms. This and the internalization of poor parental norms (in delinquent families) were put forward as explanations of superego dysfunction.

The two central components of Aichhorn's model (the dominance of the pleasure principle and an underdeveloped superego) were retained in most ego-psychological writings on antisocial personality (Friedlander 1945). The relative emphasis given to these two components and the type of early object relationships to which they may be traced differentiates later authors from this tradition. Models remain remarkably similar and etiological speculations seem more a function of the particular clinical population studied than genuine differences in the perception of the nature of the problem.

Aichhorn's revolutionary approach to treatment included a phase of 'seducing' the patient into the treatment process. Aichhorn believed that in order to renounce their narcissistic position and give up the pleasure principle in favour of the reality principle, delinquent individuals had to establish an idealizing relationship with their therapist. To establish a relationship which would compensate for the loss of narcissistic cathexis, the therapist had to be able indulge the patient and compromise traditional psychoanalytic technique.

Reich (1933) proposed a new structural conceptual framework for understanding personality types which he described as 'instinct ridden'. Following Freud, he proposed that in normal personality structure, the superego is able to elicit compliance from the ego, or at least to force the ego to make adaptations to these demands. By contrast, in instinct ridden personalities, Reich suggested that the ego kept the superego at a distance, causing it to be isolated and therefore unable to prevent the individual yielding to an impulse. Reich was clear that this did not mean that conscience (or superego) did not exist in such individuals; thus they might well manifest remorse or guilt in real, and at times overwhelming ways. Nevertheless, at moments of great instinctual temptations, the superego was isolated and therefore was unable to exert its inhibitory influence. A similar idea of partial or functional absence of superego restrictions is contained in Alexander's (1930) concept of the neurotic character.

Fenichel (1945) emphasized that the superego was not absent in these individuals, but pathological; not just isolated by the ego but also 'bribed' by satisfaction of some kind of ideal requirement or punishment. He felt that the pathological superego reflected the contradictions and ambivalences of the child in his relation to the primary objects. The early ambivalences of object relationships manifested in the tendencies of such people to fluctuate between rebellion and ingratiation, charm and seduction, followed by betrayal and revenge. Objectively, the early environment of antisocial individuals was seen by Fenichel as loveless, inconsistent and subject to frequent and radical change. Reciprocal object relations could not evolve under these circumstances; the Oedipus complex was not properly entered or resolved; its solutions were disorganized and weak. Hoffer (1949) explains this in terms of the child's idealization of the father, disavowing his true feelings, internalizing him as idealized, and identifying with his lies, deceptions, and even violence.

Further understanding of the nature and source of the structural deficits which may underpin criminality was provided by Phylis Greenacre (1945). The patients she describes are impulsive, affectively labile, have superficial relationships, manifest perversions, and show a characteristic incapacity to learn from past experience. Consequently, they are commonly highly self-destructive, abuse drugs and alcohol, and are trapped in various vicious cycles of provocativeness followed by punishment. Greenacre was the first explicitly to pinpoint the common failure of such individuals to distinguish signifier from signified, intentions from deeds, 'the substitution of the symbol of gesture or word for the accomplished act' (p.167).

Greenacre's formulation was in terms of assuming that such individuals had commonly experienced parenting from highly narcissistic figures who could not tolerate imperfections in their children, which they disguised or concealed in various ways. They were narcissistic extensions of the parents' fragile self structure, which would have been intolerably challenged by misbehaviour on the child's part. Being narcissistic extensions of the parent increased the child's frustration and aggression and intensified their need for a separate identity. The parents' determination to deny the reality of the child's vulnerabilities, led to a distorted sense of reality, making the child manipulative and opportunistic in wishing to create 'good' impressions. The externalization of their intense aggression, in combination with a lack of a solid paternal introject (usually because father was absent from the child's life for prolonged periods) leads to the creation in the mental world of such individuals persecutory external figures of ferocious strength and intensity, from which they spend their lives escaping, both in fantasy and in reality. Greenacre here describes something very close to the primitive and intense guilt, which is also pointed to by Kleinian writers, and is in contrast to classical phenomenological descriptions emphasizing the absence of guilt in antisocial individuals. Thus the apparent absence of guilt in antisocial personality is the ego's adaptation to an over-whelmingly intense and totally intolerable and destructive unconscious primitive guilt. Greenacre identifies a further important root for the intensity of these feelings. She suggests that the child internalizes the parents' shame and guilt concerning the child, who identifies with these feelings and attempts to rid himself of them by rebelling against them. Schmideberg (1949) also viewed the toughness of even the most hardened criminals as highly defensive, and acknowledged that the state of being free from guilt may be more apparent then real.

Friedlander (1945) should be credited with being the first to put forward a transactional model of antisocial personality. Along with other ego-psychologists, he suggests that the mother's inconsistent attitude to the child's instinctual life, augmented by violent emotional outbursts, undermines the renunciation of the pleasure principle and weakens the internalization of the superego. In an imaginative description of family interactional patterns, he points out that not only are attempts at the internalization of subsequent authority figures compromised by the failure to create a coherent structure in the child's mind around which parental demands may be organized, but also, under these circumstances subsequent punishments will not serve to 'strengthen the super-ego' (the person will not learn from punishment) because such aversive experiences fall outside the realm of morality and are experienced either as instinctual gratifications or as representing frustrations of gratifications, creating further hostility without the possibility of corrective emotional experience. This formulation raises important questions concerning the value of a penal system as the primary method for attempting to correct antisocial behaviour.

Kurt Eissler's (1949, 1950) contribution was primarily in providing a psychodynamic descriptive summary of the common features of antisocial personalities. He identified ten features which represent somewhat of a mixture of theoretical constructions and phenomenological descriptions: (1) predominantly narcissistic orientation (selfish motives); (2) paranoid view of world; (3) excessive sensitivity to displeasure; (4) an alloplastic tendency; (5) outward directed aggression; (6) weak and inconsistent system of values; (7) infant-like omnipotence alternating with feelings of helplessness; (8) an addiction to novelty (sensation seeking); (9) subtle body image disturbances; (10) concreteness of thinking and value systems and lack of capacity to benefit from experience.

Eissler's model of these abnormalities is also rooted in less then expectable early environments. Injury to omnipotent feelings in childhood which may take the form of a traumatic betrayal of the child, just at the time that he is ready to give up infantile omnipotence in favour of idealized relationships with adults, is regarded as the key to the mistrustful, evasive, defensively thrill seeking behaviour of such individuals. Most interesting in Eissler's formulation is his description of the delinquent's attitude to the new. In his view, the object relations experiences of such individuals lead them to be wary of novelty and, not surprisingly, they show a tendency to describe as new and exciting situations and experiences which they have encountered many times before. This adaptation to trauma by the creation of false novelty actually prevents them from genuinely encountering new circumstances and creates a substantial obstacle to treatment. In his treatment model, causing genuine surprise to such individuals in the course of therapy has an important place.

Johnson and Szurek (1952) moved away from the notion of generalized superego weakness and tackled the phenomenological problem presented by observing guilt in antisocial personalities by suggesting that superego lacunae (lack of superego in certain circumscribed areas) was the nature of the superego pathology. Such gaps in the superego were thought to occur because of the parents' unconscious wish to act out forbidden impulses; the child is unconsciously encouraged by the parents to act in amoral ways, but consciously discouraged from doing this. Their ideas in many respects resemble systemic formulations based on family therapy. They suggest that the child may be scapegoated, unconsciously chosen by the parents to act out their prohibited wishes and then punished severely for doing so, depending on the severity of the parents' superego structure. The child is thus presented with a potentially unresolvable dilemma: either he remains totally inhibited or he becomes particularly clever in actualizing the parents' unconscious fantasies. Maybe it is not surprising that antisocial individuals can at times appear very inactive, as if their intentionality were pervasively inhibited. The superficial charm and manipulative skills of antisocial personalities would be understood as deriving from the clever strategies required of them to satisfy unconscious parental demands whilst avoiding manifest injunctions on such behaviour.

Lampl-de-Groot (1949) suggested that the balance of the superego and the ego ideal explained why certain individuals became neurotically depressed, whilst others became antisocial. The former corresponds to a severe superego and strong ego ideal, whereas the latter is a consequence of a menacing superego and a weak ego ideal. Singer (1975) proposed a tripartite synthesis of the ego-psychology model identifying: (1) drive disturbances (stealing as acquiring an aggrandized penis to undo hidden feelings of being small, impotent, castrated and worthless); (2) disturbances of ego functions (heightened sensitivity to displeasure, disturbed reality testing, inability to delay action by fantasy); and (3) superego defects (the superego is corruptible (Alexander 1930), isolated (Greenacre 1945; Reich 1933), and riddled with lacunae (Johnson and Szurek 1952).

More Recent Psychoanalytic Contributions

Anna Freud's Model

That development is both cumulative and epigenetic (i.e. each developmental phase is constructed upon the previous one) is a fundamental tenet of all psychoanalytic developmental models. Anna Freud (1966) was one of the first coherently to adopt a developmental perspective on psychopathology, a precedent which is widely acknowledged by today's leading developmentalists (Cicchetti 1990; Emde 1988b; Sroufe 1990). She argued that psychological disorder could be most effectively studied in its process of developmental evolution and asserted that it was the profile or pattern amongst strands (lines) in development that best captured the nature of risks the individual child faced.

Anna Freud (1966) stresses that, for children, the degree of inner equilibrium compatible with normality is very hard to establish, as the forces that determine the child's development are external as well as internal, and to a marked degree outside the child's control. The child needs to integrate his constitutional potential, the influences emanating from the parental environment, and the expected vicissitudes associated with the gradual structuralization of personality. When one or other of these aspects of development depart from the expectable, disturbances of equilibrium are bound to occur and healthy development is jeopardized.

Anna Freud views such developmental disharmonies (deviations and asynchronies) as a background for psychopathology. Developmental pathology is, however, seen as separate and to some degree independent of the symptomatic pathology of Hartmann's structural model. For example, a simple insight-oriented treatment method is unlikely to be able to tackle the psychological difficulties faced by such a child (see A. Freud 1974, 1983; Kennedy and Yorke 1980). Treatment directed toward developmental assistance may, however, help to correct developmental discrepancies. Minor degrees of disharmony are ubiquitous (Yorke, Wiseberg and Freeman 1989, p.26). Gross disharmony, however, may in itself constitute pathology as well as being the focus of later neurotic development. In general terms, disharmony is seen as a 'fertile breeding ground' (A. Freud 1981, p.109) for later neurosis and more severe psychopathology, and the major constituent of non-neurotic developmental disturbances of the personality (personality disorders).

Anna Freud agrees with structural theorists in regarding severe personality disorders as reflecting structural deficits such as defects in reality testing, the dominance of primitive defences, limited capacities for anxiety tolerance, poor superego development. She explains these as developmental disturbances (deviations or disharmonies). For example, Yorke *et al.* (1989), suggest that the inadequate response by the mother to an infant's instinctual needs creates dangers and external conflict. Such disharmony of need and external environment will be most intensely felt when structuralization is not yet ready to sustain the pressures caused by the internal and external stresses thus created. Ego development will suffer because the internalizing and identificatory processes will be specifically threatened. Object constancy, for example, may not develop if the early relationship with the mother is disrupted by trauma. The failure to achieve structured compromise produces the labile character of borderline and other personality disturbances. Narcissistic character disorder is seen as rooted in early emotional deprivation which compromises the process by which objects (representations of people) are invested with instinctual energy. The individual attempts to identify with the frustrating and disappointing object, providing a focus for libidinal cathexis that heightens narcissism and cathexis of the self (ego-centrism).

Anna Freud, in her contribution to a Festschrift for August Aichhorn (1949), provided a developmental model of antisocial personality. She dates the critical experiences as taking place during the first year of the child's life when an absent, neglectful or ambivalent mother fails to provide steady libidinal satisfaction for the child. This prevents the natural progression of the child's interests moving away from his body needs and genuine interest in the object never develops so that the slightest disappointment is likely to lead to withdrawal from the object and a re-cathexis of the self and its body. Thus the primacy of body needs over object relationships is by-and-large retained. Destructiveness and criminality is a consequence of the failure of libidinal development to reach a stage where aggressive impulses are successfully bound. The child becomes destructive and later develops criminal tendencies.

Anna Freud distinguished the above form of deeply rooted criminal tendency from a less malignant form, where delinquent behaviours result from unconscious displacements of conflicts (pre-Oedipal and Oedipal) from the family setting to the outside world. This kind of behaviour is common in school-aged children and shows a far greater tendency to resolve spontaneously and respond to psychotherapeutic intervention. The child, for example, may act out primal-scene-related fantasies and get into difficulties at school for aggressive sexual behaviour, the root of which is not a flawed character structure but simply neurotic conflict. Other forms of neurotic delinquency may arise if a child's sexual behaviour (e.g. phallic masturbation) is frustrated by overly strict parental constraints on sexuality. The ego's adaptive activities may then be overwhelmed by sexual content. The recognition of this duality of delinquent behaviour is consistent with longitudinal, prospective studies of delinquency and is more sophisticated then many other psychoanalytic notions which tend towards homogenizing delinquent behaviour. However, the distinction suggested by Anna Freud has never been operationalized and is therefore of unknown relevance to the long term outcome of this problem.

The British Independent Group's Contributions to Understanding Personality Disorder

The key contribution by Fairbairn (1944) was the proposition that early trauma of great severity is stored in memories which are 'frozen' or dissociated from a person's central ego or functional self. This conception steps beyond the classical psychoanalytic notion of repression in developmental accounts of psychopathology. The classical model of pathogenesis (conflict → repression → reactivation of conflict → neurotic compromise) is still seen to apply to conflicts which reach the Oedipal (3–4 year) level. The Independent model applies to disorders of the self, thought to arise out of traumatic events before that age. Although their clinical formulations apply particularly to narcissistic and borderline personality disorders, the notion of multiple self representations is of profound importance in all domains of psychoanalysis. For example, the Independent approach to dream interpretation differs from the classical position, in seeing dreams as communication patterns between different parts of the self (see Bollas 1987; Rycroft 1966; Rycroft, 1979b).

Schizoid personality (Fairbairn 1940, 1952a) arises out of the infantile experience that love is destructive for the mother and therefore has to be inhibited along with all intimacy. In schizoid states the ego is so split that the individual may be mystified about himself and is transiently disturbed about reality (finding the familiar in the unfamiliar and *vice versa*). These individuals resist perceiving others as whole persons and substitute bodily for emotional contacts. They hide their love and to protect themselves from others' love, they will erect defences designed to distance others, seeming indifferent, rude or even hateful. Loving is dangerous and intimate relationships can only be maintained by retaining a part of the self which remains uninvolved. Often, since the enjoyment of love relationships is forbidden to them, they may give themselves over to the pleasure of hating and destruction. Fairbairn (1952a) differentiates depressive disorder from schizoid conditions in that it derives from later in infancy and is rooted in the infant's feeling that his aggression was destructive towards the object and has to be defended against (e.g. turned against the self).

Winnicott (1956, 1963) uses his formulation of the *false self* to elaborate a theory of antisocial behaviour, particularly in children (Winnicott 1956). He sees antisocial behaviour as starting in the environment's failure to adjust to the child, but its continuation to be ensured by an essentially 'reparative' function; it is an expression of hope, an attempt by the child to restore his situation to a pre-traumatic one. The outrageousness of the antisocial act is a cry of help, 'failing to find it, it seeks it elsewhere, when hopeful'. With development, the original symbolic meaning of the anti-social act is lost and it is replaced by secondary gain (economic gain replaces the symbolic possession of love from stolen goods).

In the case of destructive behaviour, 'the child is seeking that amount of environmental stability which will stand the strain resulting from impulsive behaviour' (p.310). This represents a search for lost environmental provision, an attitude of humanity, without which the individual feels no freedom to act or get excited. Therapeutically, Winnicott's insight is critical. The natural response to outrageous behaviour is outrage, and an expression of hope for a humane response is met with further deprivation and thus hope quickly withers away. The appropriate treatment is not psychoanalysis but an attempt on the part of the therapist to meet and match 'the moment of hope' (p.309) of the patient.

Kernberg's Integration of the Object Relations and Structural Schools

Kernberg, an analyst with a Kleinian training, writing and practising in the environment of ego psychology, achieved a remarkable level of integration between these two, quite possibly epistemologically inconsistent (see Greenberg and Mitchell 1983) developmental frameworks (see Kernberg 1975, 1976b, 1980, 1984, 1987). In Kernberg's theory of development, affects serve as the primary motivational system (Kernberg 1983). He suggests that combinations of a self representation, an object representation and an affect state linking them are the essential units of psychic structure. He sees affects as coming to be organized into libidinal and aggressive drives, always *vis à vis* interactions with a human object. To put this differently, he treats drives as hypothetical constructs manifested in mental representations and affects; these representations are of the self and object linked by some dominant affect state. The object is not just a vehicle for drive gratification, and the major psychic structures (id, ego, superego) are seen as internalizations of object representations and self–object relationships under the influence of various emotional states. The characteristics of internalization depend upon the affects active at the time. A superego may be harsh because of a prevailing affect of anger and criticism.

Kernberg (1976b) describes the concept of self-image as a component of the process of internalization. It is one of three components (the others being object representations and dispositions to affective states). There are also three processes of internalization: introjection, identification and ego identity, which correspond roughly to developmental processes involving the acquisition of experiences and behaviours which reflect an individual's self-image as well as his object representation.

His model of early development is based on reconstructions from the treatment of severely disturbed adults which are strongly influenced by Kleinian theory. It is less concerned with the child's real experience and focuses on the force of introjects and fantasies. Kernberg (1976b, 1980, 1984) is also strongly influenced by the work of Jacobson (1964) and proposes a three stage developmental theory associated with a theory of character pathology based on developmental failure.

Kernberg differs from other proponents of object relations theory such as Klein, Fairbairn, or Mahler, in that he focuses less on any particular time at which the currently dominant pathogenic conflicts and structural organization of the personality may have originated, and more on the current state of the patient's ideation. He accepts that subsequent development makes any one-to-one link between current state and the past risky. He sidesteps the distinction between Oedipal or pre-Oedipal problems which characterizes much of structural psychoanalytic writing. He believes that all levels of disturbance are more complex in severe personality disturbance but exist across the entire spectrum of psychopathology.

Here, the tolerance of ambivalence characteristic of higher level neurotic object relationships is replaced by a defensive disintegration of the representation of self and objects into libidinally and aggressively invested part object relations. Instead of the more realistic and readily comprehensible relationship patterns of neurotic personalities, he finds highly unrealistic, sharply idealized or (through aggression) highly persecutory self and object representations. These cannot be traced back to actual or fantasized relationships in the past, as he believes they do not correspond to any real relationship.

What Kernberg sees as activated in these patients are, for example, highly idealized part object relations formed under the impact of diffuse, overwhelming emotional states of an ecstatic nature, or equally overwhelming but terrifying and painful emotional states which signal the activation of aggressive or persecutory relations between self and the object. As the object relations are very poorly integrated, the reversals of the enactment of self and other representations may be very rapid. This can make relationships with such individuals confusing and even chaotic. For example, love and hate may exist in a dissociated way side by side; several object relations may be condensed into single images, and so forth. He identifies the central problem of borderline patients as the activation of primitive, overwhelming part-object relations which continuously alternate.

In contrast, the problem in the case of psychosis is the blurring of boundaries between self and object representation. Here, the protective quality of the defensive object relation fails because the confusion between self and object blurs the origin of the intolerable impulse. This is therefore reactivated without the protection of the defensive relationship pattern into which it was cast. Such patients will be frequently overwhelmed in any kind of intimate relationship.

For Kernberg (1967, 1977), the root cause of borderline states is the intensity of destructive and aggressive impulses, and the relative weakness of ego structures available to handle them. The good introjects are repeatedly threatened with destruction by the predominance of negative, hostile images and impulses which are necessary to achieve stability. Kernberg sees the borderline individual as using developmentally early defences in an attempt to separate contradictory images of self and others. This is necessary to protect positive images from being overwhelmed by negative and hostile ones. The wish to protect the object from destruction with only the most rudimentary psychic mechanisms at its disposal leads to the defensive fragmentation of self and object representations. Manifestations of the borderline condition therefore represent a continuation of an unresolved infantile conflict state. The defences of borderline individuals centre on the splitting (defensive separation) of contradictory self and object representations in order to forestall the terror associated with ambivalence. Splitting causes others to be perceived as either 'all good' or 'all bad' with the result that attitudes to them may rapidly shift between extremes. Primitive idealization, also a consequence of splitting, protects the individual from the 'all bad' objects through creating an omnipotent object in fantasy which is the container of grandiose identifications. Projective identification is seen by Kernberg as a by-product of the absence of self–object differentiation; the individual using this defence is left with a sense of empathy with the object of projection as well as a need to control him/her. The use of primitive denial ensures that the individual can totally disregard his experience of 'good' feelings toward the object when 'bad' feelings dominate his consciousness. Splitting also results in a 'diffuse sense of identity' which is characterized by a confused internal representation of the 'real' object, and an unintegrated primitive superego which sets unattainable ideals and internalized persecutory images. Since representations of the self are organized in a parallel fashion with those of others, splitting also leads to

'extreme and repetitive oscillation between contradictory self concepts...the patient, lacking in a stable sense of self or other, continually experiences the self in shifting positions with potentially sharp discontinuities – as victim or victimiser, as dominant or submissive, and so on.' (Kernberg, Selzer, Koenigsberg, Carr, and Appelbaum 1989, p.28).

Kernberg (1987) illustrates how the self-destructiveness, self-mutilating behaviour and suicidal gestures tend to coincide with intense attacks of rage towards the object. They can serve to re-establish control over the environment by evoking guilt feelings, or express unconscious guilt over the success of a deepening relationship. In some patients self-destructiveness occurs because their self-image becomes 'infiltrated' with aggression, so that they experience increased self-esteem and a confirmation of their grandiosity in self-mutilation or masochistic sexual perversions. The caring professions can respond only with despair to these patients' obvious sense of triumph in their victory over pain and death. Their efforts seem futile to the patient, who at an unconscious level experiences a sense of being in control over death. Self-mutilation, such as cutting, may also protect from the identity diffusion (derealization) which is a constant threat to the fragmented internal world of the borderline individual.

Kernberg (1970) groups together borderline and schizoid personality disorders, viewing both these as lower level character organizations (see also Kernberg 1967). The overlap is to some extent substantiated by empirical investigations demonstrating co-morbidity between the two conditions (Plakum, Burkhardt and Muller 1985) as well as overlaps in pathological psychic mechanisms (Grinker, Werble and Drye 1968; Gunderson 1985).

Kernberg (1975, 1976a, 1984, 1989) believes that patients with antisocial personality disorder usually have underlying borderline personality organizations. Because superego integration is minimal at this level and sadistic forerunners are easily projected outwards, there is deficient guilt, lack of goals, inauthenticity and erratic potential for sublimation. The function of the ego to synthesize libidinal and aggressive derivatives is impaired, leading to pregenital aggression, erratic work record and lack of goals and direction in life. The ego is not clearly differentiated from the ego ideal, and from the superego, leading to a chaotic mixture of shameful and exalted images of the self, deficient guilt, magical thinking and repetitive and contradictory behaviours. Primitive defences and poor object constancy leads to paranoid attitudes, unstable self-concept, superficial concern with others, and a lack of genuine empathy.

Antisocial behaviour occurs in most severe personality disorders because of the common underlying personality organization but is best treated as a sub-category of narcissistic personality (Kernberg 1970, 1971). The narcissistic features are invariably strong (self-centredness, grandiosity, and lack of concern for others). Superego pathology is more evident in these individuals and is behaviourally manifest in an absence of loyalty, guilt, anticipatory anxiety, and an incapacity to learn from prior experience. Kernberg (1989) takes the DSM-III-R approach to the diagnosis of antisocial personality disorder to task for concentrating on behavioural indicators at the expense of internal object relations, thus potentially blurring important distinctions between different character constellations. He distinguishes four groups of individuals: (1) those suffering from 'pathological self-love' who are thus self-centred, exhibitionistic, overambitious, and suffer from severe bouts of inferiority alternating with grandiosity; (2) those whose internal object relations are pathological and who thus manifest greed, envy, defences against envy, entitlement, appropriation of others' ideas and property, lack of concern for others and the predominance of exploitative relations with others; (3) those whose basic ego state is characterized by chronic emptiness, stimulus hunger, and a diffuse sense of the meaninglessness of life; (4) severe superego pathology, manifesting in a deficit of depressive position type sadness, and absence of guilt feelings and he also mentions the important component of an absence of self reflection in these individuals.

Kernberg saw narcissistic pathology as rooted in experiences of a rejecting primary caregiver who was cold but who was the only available source of comfort. The child inevitably falls back on the grandiose self. The child's rage reaction to protect the grandiose self is projected onto the parents who are then perceived as even less likely to meet his needs, and the child is increasingly restricted to the grandiose self for soothing and comfort. The term 'grandiose self' is one also used by Kohut (1968), but in a different way from Kernberg. For Kernberg, this aspect of the self contains the admired aspects of the child, the compensatory fantasies about the self as all-powerful, and a fantasized image of a loving and understanding caregiver. The needy parts of the individual remain dissociated from experience. The grandiose self differentiates narcissistic personality from borderline disorder. Whereas both manifest a predominance of splitting over repression (unlike obsessional or hysterical personalities which he sees as being organized around repression, (Kernberg 1984), narcissistic personalities have a cohesive, albeit highly pathological self.

Kernberg (1989) makes a helpful distinction between individuals with passive and active superego pathology; whereas the former is more likely to commit crimes of lying, swindling, forgery or prostitution, the latter is more likely to commit violent crimes, assault, robbery, and murder. Individuals with narcissistic pathology are more likely to present with passive antisocial behaviours, show some guilt and demonstrate sublimatory capacities. Malignantly narcissistic individuals are closer to the active type of Kernberg's antisocial personality schema, in so far as they are likely to manifest ego-syntonic aggression or sadism, or triumphant kinds of self-mutilation or suicidal attempts, and a strong paranoid orientation. Both should, in Kernberg's view, be carefully distinguished from reactions to abnormal environments, which may be neurotic or even normal adjustments (dyssocial reactions) and may emerge in studies of sub-groups where criminal behaviour is highly prevalent, and socially accepted.

The Attachment Theory Model of Bowlby

The infant comes into the world predisposed to participate in social interactions. The British psychoanalyst, John Bowlby (1969, 1973, 1980) was the first to give central place to the child's biological proclivity to form attachments, to initiate, maintain and terminate interactions with the caregiver and use him/her as a 'secure base' for exploration and self-enhancement. Bowlby's (1958, 1969) critical contribution was his focus on the infant's need for unbroken (secure) early attachment to the mother. The child who does not have such provision is likely to show signs of *partial deprivation* – excessive need for love or for revenge, gross guilt and depression – or *complete deprivation* – listlessness, quiet unresponsiveness and retardation of development. Later there are signs of superficiality, want of real feeling, lack of concentration, deceit and compulsive thieving (Bowlby 1951). Later Bowlby (1973) placed these reactions into a framework of reactions to separation: protest → despair → detachment.

Bowlby's attachment theory is unlike most other psychoanalytic developmental formulations in that it is, for the most part, prospective (Bowlby 1969). Laboratory investigations such as those of Brazelton and colleagues provided important support for Bowlby in demonstrating the innate social disposition of the infant, and the adverse consequences if expectations of social responsiveness from the caretaker are not met (see Brazelton 1973, 1982; Brazelton and Als 1979; Brazelton, Tronick, Adamson, Als and Wise 1975; Tronick, Als, Adamson, Wise and Brazelton 1978). He is also most bold in claiming that the infantile roots of pathology lie in *actual* realistically-based fears.

Bowlby (1973) takes a Balint–Fairbairn (as opposed to a Kleinian) approach to frustration and aggression. He maintains that anger may have survival value in alerting the parent who has withdrawn attention. However, when loss has become permanent and the parent is irrecoverable, the anger has no function yet may persist and even intensify in the absence of appropriate feedback mechanisms.

Bowlby (1969, 1973) suggests that disruption in the functioning of the attachment system will interfere with the child's developing capacities for regulating his behaviour, emotions and arousal. He argues that since children have many of their first experiences of emotional states (intense anger and anxiety, as well as love and happiness) in the context of their early attachment relationships, the quality of these relationships will determine their capacity for self-regulation at times of high stress. Insecurely attached children should therefore be more vulnerable to emotional and behavioural disregulation, and have fewer opportunities to elaborate the capacity to regulate emotional experiences, than secure ones (see also Ainsworth, Blehar, Waters and Wall 1978). Further, Bowlby (1973, 1980) maintains that secure attachment will generate internal working models of relationships characterized by an expectation of emotional as well as physical support, leading to positive self-concept and confidence in the availability and responsiveness of the other. Insensitive parenting will give rise to insecure models of relationships, characterized by lack of trust in the other and a self-representation as unworthy and undeserving of love and affection (see also Bretherton 1985; Cummings and Cicchetti 1990; Main, Kaplan and Cassidy 1985).

Broadly speaking, Bowlby's prediction that insecure attachments are associated with various later difficulties has been borne out by empirical research. Insecurely attached children appear to be more likely to experience fluctuating and unpredictable affective states, including intensely negative emotions such as excessive sadness and anger (Berlin 1993; Cassidy 1993). Insecure attachments are associated with maladaptive functioning in other contexts (Crittenden 1988; Field 1989), with problems of emotional disregulation (Kobak and Sceery 1988; Sroufe 1983), heightened sensitivity to stress (Lewis, Feiring, McGuffog and Jaskir 1984; Sroufe and Fleeson 1986; Sroufe and Rutter 1984), pervasive anxiety and distress (Grossmann *et al.* 1985) problems in interpersonal relationships (Erickson, Sroufe and Egeland 1985; Pastor 1981; Sroufe 1983), internalizing (Campbell 1987; Erickson *et al.* 1985) and externalizing (Armsden and Greenberg 1987; Lewis *et al.* 1984) disorders.

The issue of the continuity of psychological attributes across developmental stages has come to dominate debate within developmental psychology (Emde 1988a; Kagan 1984; Rutter 1987). Attachment research demonstrated that there are marked continuities in children's security of attachment, maintained probably by the stable quality of the parent–child relationship (Grossmann *et al.* 1985; Main *et al.* 1985; Sroufe 1985). There is no assumption of linear continuity (e.g. an overly dependent preschooler emerging from a very clinging infant, or an aggressive child emerging from an infant with many tantrums). Rather, Bowlby's theory assumes complex developmental relationships: for example an affectively dependent infant becoming a self-reliant schoolboy, a prediction which has been confirmed by research (Sroufe 1983).

In 1969, Bowlby identified three psychological states associated with the disruption of early attachment in the first three years of life. Following on from the acute distress of the protest state, the despair state is characterized by preoccupation, withdrawal and hopelessness. Most pertinent, from our viewpoint, is Bowlby's third state, which is thought to follow prolonged separation, that of detachment. Detachment represents an apparent recovery from protest and despair, but there is no resumption of normal attachment behaviour following the refinding of the object. The infant is apathetic, and may totally inhibit bonding. There is an intensification of interest in physical objects, and a self-absorption which is only thinly disguised by superficial sociability.

In 1946, Bowlby (1946) linked affectionless psychopathy to the absence of a maternal object and to a biological predisposition. The term 'affectionless' is perhaps unfortunate in the light of the common clinical experience that emotional detachment from others in the past and present does not stop psychopathic characters from repeatedly and aggressively engaging with others (Meloy 1992). In primary psychopathy (Hare and Cox 1987; Meloy 1988b), the violence is predatory; it is planned, purposeful and apparently emotionless. By contrast, affective violence is not predatory; rather it is a reaction to a perceived threat and is accompanied by heightened emotional (autonomic) arousal (Meloy 1988a). The attachment system may be involved in both predatory and affective acts of violence; while in the former case the individual seeks the object and the purpose of such proximity seeking is primarily destructive, in the latter case proximity triggers an intense defensive reaction of a violent kind.

Although a significant proportion of individuals with criminal records meet diagnostic criteria for borderline or narcissistic personality disorder, it would be foolhardy to claim any kind of isomorphism between borderline personality disorder (BPD), as defined phenomenologically, and criminal acts. From an attachment theory perspective, we may, however, identify commonalities at the level of psychic mechanism between individuals in the two groups. Recently, Meloy (1992) made a systematic attempt to link the object relations theory approach to BPD to a wide variety of violent criminal behaviour. For example, he explored cases of ego-dystonic, sudden violent acts which appear to be impulsive rage reactions without a prodromal period. These acts would be exemplified by Intermittent Explosive Disorder whose typical victim is a spouse, lover, boyfriend or girlfriend (American Psychiatric Association 1987; Felthous et al. 1991) or more chronic obsessive preoccupations with the future victim where depression, helplessness, and a conscious sense of tension build up over a period of months and years to be 'released' by a violent act. A small scale controlled study showed sudden murderers to be apparently ambivalently attached to dominant mothers and to experience their fathers as rejecting, negative and hostile (Weiss, Lamberti and Blackman 1960). The fragmentation of the self-structure through splitting and projective identification makes such individuals vulnerable to injuries to the perception of the self (criticisms, insults, belittling rejection), which are common precipitants of the violent act (Blackman, Weiss and Lamberti 1963). Ruotolo (1968) came to the same conclusion in a clinical investigation of five sudden murderers. Some authors stress the symbolic meaning of either the violent act or the victim (Revitch and Schlesinger 1978, 1981; Wertham 1966). The violent act is directed against a split-off part of the self with which the individual is projectively identified. Rather than pursuing Meloy's excellent analysis, I would like to explore the applicability of our own attachment theory formulations of BPD to certain types of criminal behaviour.

Gacono and Meloy (1992) used the Rorschach to investigate sixty DSM-III-R Antisocial Personality Disorder prisoners of both psychopathic and nonpsychopathic type. Antisocial personality disorder was associated with pathological narcissism and omnipotence. Narcissism was allied with lack of affectional relatedness (indicated in the Rorschach by low mean and frequency of texture responses); with a relatively high number of 'hard', non-human or part-human objects; a failure to represent whole people. Evaluative comments were predominantly negative, idealization was rare and predominantly directed towards non-human objects. These tendencies were stronger in psychopathic than in non-psychopathic individuals.

Gacono, Meloy and Berg (1992) extended these findings to an outpatient sample of narcissistic and borderline personality disorder individuals. Compared to these groups, psychopaths showed minimal capacity for either attachment or anxiety. Non-psychopathic antisocial personality disorder individuals tended to be more anxious and easily provoked into feeling threatened than psychopathic individuals with the same diagnosis.

In a further study, Weber, Meloy and Gacono (1992) studied adolescents with conduct disorders, with dysthymic inpatients as a comparison group. Conduct-disordered adolescents manifest emotional detachment and devaluation observed in the prison population of psychopaths, but to a lesser degree. Conduct disordered adolescents showed very weak desire for relationships compared to depressed adolescents, and were indifferent to people as whole, real, and meaningful individuals. In line with Deutsch and Erickson's (1989) findings that undersocialized conduct-disordered adolescents had disrupted early life and attachment experiences, the study found socialized delinquents could be less severely affected on these measures. These findings may be interpreted as psychometric evidence for disturbance of attachment relationships in at least some conduct-disordered adolescents.

Bruhn and Davidow (1983) demonstrated that the earliest childhood memories reported by delinquents could be distinguished from a matched non-delinquent sample of youngsters. One of the strongest distinguishing features was the way other people were represented in the early memory. Delinquents recalled them in terms of whether they helped or hindered their activities but not as three-dimensional characters. The non-delinquents were much more likely to embellish their portraits of others by recalling personality traits and other distinguishing characteristics.

Davidow and Bruhn (1990) replicated this study with 71 delinquents matched with 71 non-delinquents under control on age, SES, and family constellation. Particularly striking was the amount of description of the other.

The majority of delinquents gave minimal or moderate descriptions, whereas non-delinquents tended to give extensive portraits of the other. In a similar vein, parents were recalled as not available to help, offering minimal assistance or as causing injury. Davidow and Bruhn note a qualitative difference in the description of the other person: in the delinquent individual the description tends to be self-referred as well as negative (e.g. 'he was mean to me'). In the control group, the other person is described as a separate human being (e.g. 'my father was jumpy and nervous').

Interestingly, considerable epidemiological research related to attachment theory formulations of criminal behaviour has been carried out in the context of large-scale studies inspired by social control theory. Social control theory (Durkheim 1951; Hirschi 1969; Kornhauser 1978) proposes that crime and deviance will result when an individual's bond to society is weak or broken. In Hirschi's (1969) formulation, there are four elements to the social bond: attachment, commitment, involvement, and belief. Attachment refers to affective ties with parents, schools and friends. Changes across the course of life that strengthen the individual's bond to institutions of social control will reduce criminality, whereas transitions which weaken the bond will be associated with increases in deviance.

Although in these large-scale studies measures of attachment tend to be superficial, the results are in line with the assumption that criminality involves disturbance of attachment processes. For example, marriage is likely to reduce criminality if the individual is strongly (securely) attached to his/her spouse. In Sampson and Laub's (1990) re-analysis of the Glueck's data of 800 individuals in both delinquent and non-delinquent childhood groups those who had weak ties to work and family were far more likely to engage in crime and deviance. Adolescent delinquents and matched controls were both more likely to show adult antisocial behaviour if their attachment to their spouse, occupational commitment, or job stability were weak. Over three-quarters of the delinquent group with adult criminal records had weak attachments to their spouse. Attachments made a highly significant independent contribution to the prediction of criminal activity, even when a history of prior convictions had been controlled for, and amongst married men this was stronger than either job stability or occupational commitment.

Shoham et al. (1987) were able to distinguish impulsive or planned violence in a population of prisoners on the basis of attachment to the family. Individuals who appeared to be attached to their family were more likely to be impulsively violent. Lack of punishment in childhood was strongly associated with planned violence.

Marcos, Bahr and Johnson (1986) reported a questionnaire study of over 2600 adolescents and found that self-reported drug use was most highly correlated with drug-using friends, although parental attachment and religious attachment also contributed to explanations and life time drug use. Judith Brook and others (Brook, Whiteman, Brook and Gordon 1981, 1984; Brook, Whiteman and Gordon 1983; Brook, Whiteman, Gordon and Brook, 1984; Brook, Whiteman, Gordon and Brook 1985; Norem-Hebeisen, Johnson, Anderson and Johnson 1984) in a series of studies offered convincing evidence indicating that aspects of mutual attachment may insulate young people from drug use. Brook, Whiteman and Finch (1993) looked at drug use over a ten year period in 400 children in order to identify the reason why attachment may provide a protective function. In this longitudinal study she was able to show that earlier child aggression appeared directly to influence drug use, lead to adolescent unconventionality, and difficulty in *later* attachment relationships, which in turn lead the young person to drug abuse. The study offered clearer results indicating that earlier aggression decreases the likelihood of later attachment for women. Weak parent–child attachment (measured by question-naire) at 13–18 years was seen to lead to unconventionality (rebelliousness, lack of responsibility, intolerance of deviance), which in its turn led to drug use. Aggression (assessed on the basis of maternal reports, included anger, non-compliance, temper tantrums, aggression with siblings), was a powerful predictor of low attachment, and to a lesser extent of unconventionality and drug use. This suggests that parent–child attachment has an important recip-rocal role. Aggression, as we have seen, may be the outcome of inadequate early attachment relationships but may also cause a weakening of the parent–child bond, and in this way contributes in an important way to the development of deviance.

Only a handful of studies have succeeded in linking traditional work on attachment with these large-scale epidemiological findings concerning the ecology of crime. For example, Shaw and Vondra (1993) demonstrated that risk factors normally considered to be related to delinquency and criminality (e.g. parental criminality, over-crowding, quality of relationship with a signifi-cant other), were more commonly observed together in families of insecure infants. These challenging findings suggest that infant security and risk factors considered relevant to the child's choice of a deviant developmental trajectory may be inter-related. At the present state of knowledge it is not possible to determine which may be of primary significance.

Even were there more such studies, the logic of the link between large-scale epidemiological investigation and the single-case orientation of clinical work is not entirely clear from an epistemological viewpoint. Very often, the bare facts of epidemiological associations are precisely that. For example, the influence of marital relationships on criminality will be hard to understand until measures of marital quality are better able to tap the meaning of the relationship to the individual, rather than just overt signs of difficulty such as marital conflict. From a clinical point of view, we know that an individual may have an extremely strong attachment to a fraught, sado-masochistic relationship. Measures such as the Adult Attachment Interview will need to be developed for all important current relationships if the impact of adult attachment relationships on criminality are to be appropriately assessed.

Stern's Approach to Infant Development and a Possible Alternative
Formulation of Criminality

Stern's (1985) book represents a milestone in psychoanalytic theorization concerning development. He challenges many of the ideas of previous approaches to developmental schemas. His work is distinguished by being normative rather than pathomorphic and prospective rather than retrospective. His focus is the reorganization of subjective perspectives on self and other as these occur with the emergence of new maturational capacities.

His model uses four different senses of self, each with an associated domain of relatedness: (1) 'The sense of emergent self' involves the process of the self coming into being and forming connections (from birth to two months of age); (2) 'the sense of core self' (from between two and six months of age) and 'the domain of core relatedness' is based on a single organizing subjective perspective and a coherent *physical self*; (3) the 'sense of *subjective self*' and the 'domain of intersubjective relatedness' (between seven and fifteen months) emerges with the discovery of subjective mental states beyond physical events; (4) the sense of 'verbal self' which forms after 15 months.

The capacities underlying the sense of subjective self include a number of clinically extremely relevant mental functions, which have only been elaborated by developmental researchers over the past 10 years. Its earliest manifestation may be an understanding of the mental state of attention which is evident in normal infants from about nine months of age in the monitoring of the gaze of the mother (Butterworth 1991; Scaife and Bruner 1975), and through gestures such as protodeclarative pointing (Bates *et al.* 1979). That infants apprehend the intentions and motives of others is evident in gaze monitoring, as they appear not only to check where someone is looking, but also how the person is *evaluating* what they see, as is clear in the phenomena of social referencing (Sorce, Emde, Campos and Klinnert 1985). Such emotional communication can be conveyed through the face or the voice by a parent or familiar caretaker, and it can regulate behaviour towards an object, a location or a person (Boccia and Campos 1989; Camras and Sachs 1991). In protodeclarative pointing, children appear to use the pointing gesture as a comment on a topic of interest, concern or fun (Baron-Cohen 1991; Tomasello 1988). Phillips, Baron-Cohen and Rutter (1992) found that normal 9–18-month-old toddlers respond to an ambiguous action of an adult by instantly looking at the adult's eye, but do so on only a minority of occasions when the adult's action is not ambiguous. Thus infants from this stage appear to sense the congruence or lack of congruence between their own state and that of another person.

The sense of verbal self and the domain of verbal relatedness represents a move to a stage where oneself and other people can be represented as storehouses of knowledge and experience. This experience may be shared, which involves the ability to objectify the self, to reflect upon mental contents and to use language to communicate. Baron-Cohen (1993), identifies six different classes of mental states of which the developing child comes to have an appreciation at different moments.

(1) Understanding beliefs, particularly understanding that a belief may be false was considered by Dennett (1978) as a litmus test of the child's capacity to develop an understanding that people have minds and mental states, and that mental states relate to behaviour. Wimmer and Perner (1983) designed a famous false belief test in which the child's (true) belief and the child's awareness of someone else's different (false) belief were contrasted. They showed that around three to four years of age, normal children pass such a test.

(2) Desire is often regarded as the other key mental state of folk psychology (Dennett 1978). Together, belief and desire explain most behaviour. For normal children, desire is understood earlier than belief. Wellman (1993) shows that desire is understood by most normal two-year-olds. The oppositional behaviour of two-year-olds may be interpreted not as a desire to establish separateness (see Mahler *et al.* 1975), but as evidence of their growing awareness of the frustrating difference between their own and their parents' desires (Wellman 1990).

(3) Understanding knowledge appears to be easier than understanding belief for normal children (Wellman 1990). This may be because knowledge is true belief, and misrepresentation (which involves false belief), is not involved.

(4) Understanding pretence is regarded by some psychoanalytic workers as the earliest, and perhaps most important, developmental achievement on the way to symbolization (Fónagy and Fonagy, in press). Understanding that something can be something while at the same time knowing that identity to be inappropriate (e.g. that a chair is a tank), is a crucial characteristic of mental functioning at the level of meta-representations (Leslie 1987). This can be argued to be one of the roots of language, as well as of artistic capacity (Fonagy and Fonagy, in preparation). The moment at which true pretence arises is a controversial issue, some developmentalists finding evidence for pretence in the second year (Leslie 1987),

whilst others see genuine pretence as evident only in three- and four-year-olds (Lillard 1993).

(5) Understanding perception appears easier than appreciation of the other mental states previously considered. Whereas belief, knowledge, desire and pretence are all *opaque*, that is, inferred rather than observed perception applied to the physical world. Flavell, Everett, Croft and Flavell (1981) report that understanding of perception is well within the ability of normal two-year-olds, who can readily judge if someone saw something or not. Until three to four years of age they cannot master the more complex task of how something will appear to someone from a different perspective.

(6) The development of an understanding of emotion is perhaps the most relevant form of understanding of mental states for clinical psychoanalysis. Harris (1994) reviewed empirical work on the child's understanding of emotion. Early in the first year of life, infants begin to respond selectively and appropriately to the emotional expression of the caretaker. Infants of ten weeks manifest affective states appropriately, but not by mimicking of the mother's expression (Fernald 1992; Haviland and Lelwica 1987). Infants also expect the caretaker 'to be emotionally responsive to their own expressive signals' (Murray and Trevarthen 1985) and have no similar expectations of mobile but non-human stimuli (Ellsworth, Muir and Hains 1993). The child also understands the intentional nature of emotional states – the fact that they convey an appraisal of objects or persons in the child's environment (Boccia and Campos 1989).

Infants of depressed mothers 'expect' less emotional responsiveness and therefore gaze less at their mother (see, for example, Cohn *et al.* 1986). Infants generalize this expectation toward the stranger (Field *et al.* 1988). There is evidence that the effect is cumulative and it shapes the behaviour of strangers interacting with the infant who behave less positively towards him or her (Cohn, Campbell, Matias and Hopkins 1990; Field *et al.* 1988).

Infants also understand anger in the caregiver and respond to it by crying, looking angry or just watching their mother in an expressionless fashion (Haviland and Lelwica 1987). Toddlers understand affect between others such as covert tension between the parents or overt conflict (Cummings, Zahn-Waxler and Radke-Yarrow 1981, 1984). Laboratory observations indicate that a simulated quarrel is most likely to be associated with a freezing response with subsequent aggression, and to sensitize children to further similar experiences (Cummings, Iannotti and Zahn-Waxler 1985). Children appear to understand quarrels differently; whilst for some it serves as a licence to engage in hostile behaviour, for others it is a stimulus that arouses solicitous concern. Children assimilate such exchanges into larger causal schemata encoding general assumptions about how quarrels arise, who is to blame and how one may avoid and ameliorate the experience (Harris 1994).

Two- to three-year-olds appropriately distinguish among and can name various emotional states, and appear to understand the equivalence between their own states and those of other people (Bretherton, Fritz, Zahn-Waxler and Ridgeway 1986; Brown and Dunn 1991; Dunn, Bretherton and Munn 1987). Wellman, Harris, Banerjee and Sinclair (in preparation), report that children up to four years of age almost invariably explain emotion in terms of an intentional target, a person or a physical object at which the emotion is aimed.

Stern's starting point is the 'emergent moment' which is the subjective integration of all aspects of lived experience that takes its input from emotions, behaviours, sensations and all other aspects of the internal and external world. The emergent moment is seen as deriving from schematic representations of various types: event representations or scripts, semantic representations or conceptual schemas, perceptual schemas, and sensory-motor representations. He adds to these two further, clinically highly relevant, modes of representation: 'feeling shapes' and 'proto-narrative envelopes'. These schemata form a network which he terms 'the schema-of-a-way-of-being-with' (see also Horowitz 1991; Kernberg 1976a).

The 'schema-of-a-way-of-being-with' is conceptualized by Stern from the assumed subjective point of view of the infant who is in interaction with the caregiver. The infant's experiences across a number of domains are organized around a motive and a goal, and in this sense echoes Freud's (1905c) original formulation of drives and object relationships in the Three Essays. The goals which organize these moments are not only biological, they include object relatedness, affect states, and states of self-esteem and safety, as well as physical need gratification, be it hunger, thirst, sexuality or aggression. The representation will contain a proto-plot with an agent, an action, an instrumentality and a context which are all necessary elements for the comprehension of human behaviour (see Bruner 1990).

Although Stern (1994, 1985) implies many links to pathological states he does not propose a comprehensive model of psychopathology. A number of workers, equally committed to integrating findings from developmental research with clinical goals, have proposed models, loosely based on Stern's developmental approach (Fonagy, Edgcumbe, Moran, Kennedy and Target 1993; Fonagy and Moran 1991). Work with case records at the Anna Freud Centre (Fonagy and Target 1994; Fonagy and Target, in press; Target and Fonagy 1994a, 1994b), in conjunction with research on the determinants of early relationships (Fonagy, Steele and Steele 1991a; Fonagy, Steele, Moran, Steele and Higgitt, 1991b; Steele, Steele and Fonagy, in preparation; in press) has led to an extension of certain psychoanalytic assumptions concerning the nature of psychic change in child analysis (Fonagy and Moran 1991). In these papers we delineated two models of the psychoanalytic treatment of mental disturbance. The first (the synthetic model) describes the mechanism by which the patient is helped to recover threatening ideas and feelings which have been repudiated or distorted in the course of development as a result of conflict and defence. The second model (the mental process model) draws attention to the therapeutic effects of engaging previously inhibited mental processes within the psychoanalytic encounter. This engagement tends to occur primarily through patient and analyst focusing on the thoughts and feelings of each person, and how the child understands these. The two models entail distinctions between two types of pathology, requiring two types of analytic work, with different predicted rates of change.

The notion of unutilized mental processes offers a conceptual bridge between psychoanalytic work with children and advances in cognitive science; it also stresses the therapeutic value of a mentalizing or reflective capacity, which independently emerged as important in the parent–child attachment relationship. Furthermore, it offers a theoretical explanation of a long-established clinical finding, that children with marked developmental or personality disturbances require longer treatment, with modifications of classical psychodynamic technique (e.g. A. Freud 1966). This theoretical basis leads us to predict that there will be clear differences in technique, levels of change, and rates of change depending on the depth of personality disturbance in a child.

This approach may be exemplified with some ideas about the role of inhibition of mental functioning in borderline personality disorder (Fonagy 1991; Fonagy *et al.* 1993). The theoretical ideas outlined above, concerning a connection between disturbed attachment, inhibition of mental processes and personality pathology, are being examined in a study of BPD. The hypothesis is that an early and sustained history of trauma and abuse in these individuals would be associated with inhibition of their capacity to envisage mental states (reflective self-function). This has been supported by both a cross-sectional and a longitudinal investigation. Patients who met Gunderson's criteria for BPD were rated as having lower reflective self-function than control groups of patients with non-psychotic psychiatric disorders of equal severity. The inpatient psychotherapeutic treatment of BPD patients was associated with an improvement in reflective self-function in all cases who showed substantial symptom reductions in response to the treatment. These findings offer preliminary support for the hypotheses that (1) part of the disturbance of BPD patients may be understood in terms of a deficit of mentalizing functions, and (2) that these functions are inaccessible to such patients, but may be recovered in the course of psychotherapeutic treatment.

There is considerable evidence which supports the possibility of conflict-induced deficits in the functioning of mental processes which normally evolve through constitutionally determined developmental pathways (or, to use Waddington's (1966) term are 'canalised'). Adlam-Hill and Harris (1988), for example, compared nine-year-old boys attending ordinary schools with boys of the same age attending schools for the emotionally disturbed. Members of the latter group frequently failed to distinguish real from apparent emotion, implying that the disturbed family environment which characterized most of these children in some way impeded the normal development of the capacity to understand how and in what situation feelings could be hidden. They were particularly unlikely to see any need for concealing feelings if the other person's feelings were at stake. Mary Main (1993), from an attachment theory perspective, found evidence that ambivalently attached children, who are most likely to have had experiences of emotional entanglement with their primary caregiver, are also most likely to deny the inherent privacy of mental state. Main argues that such children continue to assume that their caregivers have access to their innermost selves, and that they themselves can read the thoughts of an attachment figure. From a broader psychoanalytic perspective, we would claim that the child defensively inhibits his capacity to accept the mental separateness of the mother because to do so would entail the pain of experiencing her incomprehension of his feelings, beliefs and desires (Fonagy *et al.*, in press).

Evidence is also accumulating that suggests that these fundamental cognitive processes underlying the understanding of mental states are far more vulnerable to the vicissitudes of environmental experiences than previously thought. There is evidence to suggest that the development of the capacities underlying the false belief task may be enhanced by the proximity of a sibling (see Jenkins and Astington 1993; Perner, Ruffman and Leekam, in press). Close interaction with a sibling who is of a similar age enhances the child's understanding of mental states. Preliminary data from our own prospective study, as well as data reported by Main (1993), is consistent with the view that a secure attachment to a caregiver enhances the child's capacity to explore the mind of that person and facilitates the evolution of emotional self-awareness and a theory of mind.

Following the philosopher, Davidson (1983), and psychoanalytic exponents of his work (see Cavell 1988a, 1988b, 1991), we believe that getting to know our own minds is a process of familiarizing ourselves with the mind of another. The child perceives and eventually comes to recognize himself in his caregiver's perception of him. We believe that the development of the self entails the internalization not of the object, good or bad, as classical object relations theory posits, but rather, that it is the caregiver's image of the intentional infant which comes to be internalized and comes to constitute the core of the child's mentalizing self. Incoherent perception of the child's mental state therefore places the child's self-development at risk. Accurate perception of the child as a psychological being is particularly critical when the caregiver's own history of deprivation places her at risk of recapitulating her own adverse early relationship experiences with her child (Fonagy *et al.* 1993).

An inhibition of the capacity to envision the state of mind of the other may be assumed to disable the normal aversive emotional reaction which we experience when we observe distress in others, particularly when the distress was caused by ourselves. The development of moral behaviour may crucially depend on this negative emotional state, without which the distinction between conventional and moral behaviour (Turiel 1983) may never be established.

Blair (1992) examined the attributions made by criminals diagnosed as showing antisocial personality disorder (APD) and other criminals without a diagnosis. He compared their responses to a number of stories which could normally be expected to evoke guilt, happiness, sadness, or embarrassment in the protagonists. The happiness story concerned an individual winning the pools, the sadness story a person coming last in a competition, the embarrassment stories involved three forms of audience condition (no audience, passive audience or negative audience) with the embarrassing acts being, for instance, dropping a tray of food. The guilt stories were also divided into three groups: person harm (a man punches another man), object harm (a man smashes up public property), and unintentional harm (to either property or person). Differences emerged both in the intentional and unintentional person harm stories: in both cases, APD individuals made fewer guilt attributions and more indifferent attributions than other criminals. Both groups made fewer guilt and more indifferent attributions than normal controls. Attributions of happiness and sadness emotions were not different between the groups.

This study, despite its small sample, offers support for the contention that certain criminals lack the capacity to envision the state of mind of victims' distress. On the basis of the investigations of BPD we are inclined to assume that these difficulties arise because of failures of the primary attachment relationships. We have some preliminary evidence that is consistent with this point of view.

There are a number of research teams working with prison populations using the Adult Attachment Interview (AAI). We have almost completed a small study of prison hospital patients with a matched group of psychiatric controls. There were 22 male patients in the prison sample, mean age 27.6 years. Eleven had been sentenced by the end of the study; the remainder were on remand. A further five patients were convicted subsequently. Their crimes ranged from attempted burglary, theft, damage to property, taking and driving away, handling stolen goods, obtaining property and services by deception, gross indecency, possession and intent to supply heroin, importation of drugs, grievous bodily harm, malicious wounding, multiple armed robbery, kidnapping, rape, murder. They were interviewed using Structured Clinical Interview for DSM-III-R (SCID I and II) structured interviews to obtain DSM-III-R diagnoses. They all had at least one Axis-I disorder (80% three or more diagnoses) and 91 per cent had at least one Axis-II diagnosis (American Psychiatric Association 1987). Fifty per cent had a DSM diagnosis of borderline personality disorder. The average GAF score for the group was 47. These patients were individually matched with patients from a sample of non-psychotic inpatients.

Although we have not completed the analyses of our data, a number of striking correspondences have emerged between a subgroup of these 22 criminals and the borderline patients in our psychiatric sample. In this subgroup, entangled classifications were also the most common; extreme deprivations in childhood were commonly and convincingly reported, and these mostly involved severe physical abuse at the hands of borderline or psychotic parents. The interviews were marked by incoherence and a notable lack of an 'intentional stance' towards both attachment objects and the self.

The offenders could be divided into two groups on the basis of the patterns of AAI ratings: those in Group 1 were predominantly classified as Dismissing, Entangled–Preoccupied or Autonomous, had Reflective Self Function (RSF) ratings higher than the median and were unlikely to be classified Unresolved/Disorganized or Cannot Classify. Group 2 subjects matched the borderline diagnoses in terms of AAI, although not all of them met DSM diagnostic criteria. They tended to be classified Entangled–Preoccupied or Cannot Classify, none were designated Autonomous, and all but two scored above five on the lack of resolution of trauma scales, they scored below the median on coherence of mind and reflective self function, and had histories of abuse. This group could also be differentiated in terms of the crimes they committed. The index offenses of prisoners in Group 1 were predominantly crimes against property, whereas those of prisoners in Group 2 were largely serious, violent assaults including rapes and a murder associated with pathological jealousy.

This is only a pilot investigation, but the results are promising to the extent that they link the AAI narratives to index crimes. Naturally, a likely alternative account to the one proposed here is that it was these crimes which caused the disorganization of the attachment system, and which permeated the interviews of Group 2. The less serious offenses may have made less impact on the representation of relationships.

We propose that crimes are often committed by individuals with inadequate mentalizing capacities, as part of their pathological attempt at adaptation to a social environment where mentalization is essential. We assume that these individuals did not have access to meaningful attachment relationships which would have provided them with the intersubjective basis for developing a metacognitive capacity capable of organizing and coordinating their internal working models of relationships. The disavowal of the capacity to represent mental states (momentary or permanent) may be a key component of crime against the person. Thus, violence against another may not be possible unless the mental state of the other is insufficiently clearly represented for this to block the violent act. Violence is a solution to psychological conflict because of the inadequacy of the mental representation of the mental world in the minds of these individuals. Their metacognitive capacity is limited, and they experience ideas and feelings in physical, often bodily, terms.

This, of course, opens a whole avenue to adaptation. Unpalatable ideas may be felt to be removed by destroying the physical object which embodies that idea. We have proposed (Fonagy, Target and Moran 1993) that aggression is a defence to safeguard the self from thoughts and fantasies which it does not have the representational capacity to protect itself against through mental manipulation. Similarly, aggression in disruptive children is an adaptation to the activation of discordant internal working models by a caregiver, through disruption of the relationship. In more severe disorders, this defence might come to be integrated within the working model of relationships, thus aggression may become a part of self-assertion. The violent act is, we suggest, aimed at destroying symbolic representation (Fonagy and Target, in press b). The assault on the perpetrator's fragile sense of self has to be removed. As one murderer put it: 'Either he or I must die, something has to give' (Meloy 1992, p.58).

Psychotic and Borderline Processes

Patrick Gallwey

INTRODUCTION

The overlapping of badness and madness creates a domain of popular and deep anxiety. The really bad, serial killers and the like, provoke fascination and are usually perceived as mad, yet the fear of unleashed savagery compels retribution and punishment. It is unlikely, if the violence has been extreme and especially if there is more than one victim, that a plea of diminished responsibility to murder due to an abnormality of mind will be achieved by the killer. This is true even when, as in the case of the serial killer Sutcliffe, there is clear evidence of psychosis. Madness has been a defence against crime from the middle ages but the universal belief in the untamed ferocity of human nature finds affirmation and celebration in such rare individual atrocities. The tradition that humans are instinctively antisocial and, without dire threats of punishment, likely to run wild, inspires the punitive element in most religions and is the central philosophical plank of criminal jurisprudence. It seems to have inspired Freud to write his three essays on sexuality (1905c) and to continue the idea in the concept of the id (1923) and is taken for granted by many educated people. It has been seriously challenged by some social anthropologists (Montagu 1979) and an alternative to instinctual hedonism has been put forward by the object relation theorists of the British School of psychoanalysis following Fairbairn (1944) and in a more complex way by Klein (Klein 1957). Freud's belief in unstructured pleasure seeking drives, looking for gratification with any object as a utensil and only socialized with difficulty by repression, is still held unquestioningly by many analysts. Klein (1946), whose ideas opened up the psychoanalytic study of psychosis, was less pessimistic than Freud in so far as she believed that the infant was quite naturally capable of forming a loving relationship with the mother from the beginning. However, as we shall examine later she believed this primary bonding was reliant upon omnipotent phantasy and threatened by innate destructiveness. She linked this destructiveness to Freud's belief in inborn passivity, which he named the death instinct (S. Freud 1920), a theoretical move that is too much for many analysts, but her thinking over the question of inborn envy is in line with Freud's gloomy view of human instinct (Klein 1957).

It is also broadly the case that most psychoanalytic theories of early mental life view it as dominated by omnipotent phantasy, with an infant who is either totally out of touch with reality or only grasping a very modified and grandiose form of it. Psychosis tends to be seen as a regression to these primitive omnipotent states of mind. Thus, in the main, psychoanalysis views human nature in its unmodified early aspect as mad, bad and selfish; the psychological equivalent of original sin. This is not a very encouraging start, I'm afraid, for anyone turning to psychoanalysis for guidance as to where goodness can be discovered in those who are both psychotic and maladjusted.

Something of a paradox is experienced by those working with patients who have endured very great abuse, neglect and childhood suffering, as have many criminals: what impresses most is how well they have managed and not so much how evil they have become. It is quite extraordinary how brave is the childhood spirit that can survive the extremes of abuse with some hope and sanity intact and keep going in spite of crippling damage during crucial periods of development. Criminals become known for the suffering they cause but what has led them to become the way they are or to any awareness of the goodness they have managed to retain is usually lost in the outrage that they understandably create. In fact, to mention such realities is to risk the charge of being 'soft on crime' and to provoke a bluster of enthusiasm for even harsher punishments, as if to add more suffering to the appalling equation will somehow put things right. There appears to be a universal need to confine criminals to a domain of punishment from which we exclude ourselves. In spite of reliable research that demonstrates how crime is the outcome of early prolonged disruption to the basic necessities of nurturing (West 1982), offenders continue as popular moral scapegoats, particularly so for politicians on the look out for votes: so that recently members of the government have recommended more punishment and less understanding and have, apparently seriously, suggested that the fear of hell should once more be instilled in children as an antidote to maladjustment!

Bad behaviour is, of course, a major cause of widespread misery and it is understandable why many people have a fantasy that it can be completely banished. That this is also an apparently informed idea is more serious because, as a consequence, the very social harmfulness of crime is never properly tackled. Empirical research into the causes of crime is ignored and many psychoanalysts and those who follow still view criminal behaviour as a simple expression of instinctual aggression. In spite of the work of Bowlby (1973) and Winnicott (1984), and partly because of the problems of undertaking long term detailed psychoanalytic research with criminals, psychoanalytic writing on the psycho-pathology of bad behaviour tends to stick to simple adaptions of standard theory.

Although crime is a relatively neglected area of psychoanalytic theory making, this is not true of psychosis and borderline states, the theory and practice of which have been extensively developed, particularly in the UK, the USA and in South America. However, I want in this chapter to approach the subject of psychotic and borderline states, and crime, from a somewhat different perspective. I hope this perspective does justice to the fact that, in their different ways, psychosis and criminal behaviour represent a grievous failure in the quite amazing capacity for social interdependency and altruism in human nature that is taken for granted by the mentally well. In order to do this I shall advance a theory of normal development which I hope adds a fresh dimension to current theories of psychosis and of crime. First I shall give a short and incomplete account of the way psychoanalysts have viewed the question of madness.

THE PSYCHOANALYTIC APPROACH TO THE PSYCHOSES

Perhaps the first serious psychoanalytic contribution to psychosis was made by Freud in his paper 'Mourning and Melancholia' (1917). In a previous paper (1911b) he had postulated that a case of paranoid psychosis was a reaction formation to unconscious homosexual wishes – the case of Schreber. Unlike the paper 'Mourning and Melancholia' which derived from direct observations of patients in depressive psychosis, this paper was purely speculative and he had never met the patient he wrote so much about. He had already, in his work on narcissism (1914a), included psychosis as one of the ways in which withdrawal of the object relating instincts into the self could be manifested. However, it was not until 'Mourning and Melancholia' that he put forward a theory based on direct clinical observation to explain the manifestations of a psychotic condition. Freud believed that the melancholic was demonstrating a pathological identification between the self and the dependent object. How-ever, he then went on to make a move which is very characteristic of psychoanalytic thinking, to formulate this as the return to an earlier stage of normal development, rather than seeing it as pathology *per se*, so that the illness becomes essentially a maturational regression. The pathological identification that Freud believed explained melancholic states became a variant of a universal mechanism in which the relinquishment, under the impact of reality, of being the central object of the parent's love, was achieved through an omnipotent phantasy of incorporating the abandoned object cathexis into the ego and setting up the object there as part of the structure of the self. Freud believed that every abandoned object cathexis was managed in this way, and that object relationships with the parents in particular, especially the father, resulted in the incorporation of the object into the ego, thereby creating a super-ego, representing the internal seat of conscience and morality (Freud 1923). Although it is perfectly reasonable to construct a link between the excessive self-reproach of the melancholic with the less self-torturing conscience of a normal individual, Freud's thinking results in an omnipotent phantasy coming into play as part and parcel of normal human development. Depressive illness and everyday moral self-regulation becomes part of a continuum. Psychopathology lies simply in the extent and quality of depressive activity.

The development of a psychoanalytic approach to psychotic states took an enormous move forward as a result of the theories of Melanie Klein. Like Freud, she relied on introjective identification (an omnipotent phantasy involving the oral incorporation of the object into the self) as a normal developmental process, most importantly and most fundamentally when the good and loving aspects of the mother's breast are taken in to form the foundation of the primitive ego. She formed her ideas on ego development whilst she was working clinically with disturbed children using her special play technique (Klein 1932b). She noticed that, after her child patients made aggressive attacks during play, there would be a marked increase in paranoid anxiety in relation to the object that had been the target of the aggression. Detailed observation of the play of these disturbed children and imaginative construction of the phantasies that could be presumed to be represented in the play, led her to conclude that, in order to protect the ego from the anxiety created by aggression, the aggressive aspect of the self would be split and projected into the object that was felt to be responsible for the violent feelings. This created an object that contained the projected part of the self, now experienced as part of the identity of the object and therefore disowned and disassociated. The self was divested completely and omnipotently of the aggressive aspect of the self, so what remained was an idealized self in unconscious introjective identification with an ideal object. This good internal object was continually re-experienced in the giving and non-frustrating aspects of the external nurturing breast. The frustrating aspects of the mother would be perceived as one and the same as the intrapsychic bad, persecutory object (Klein 1957).

Klein, like Freud, assumed these highly omnipotent mechanisms to be part and parcel of normal development. The original introjective identification of the good breast, seen as fundamental to the coherence of the ego, places omnipotence not only at the heart of normality, but as a *sine qua non* for the development of sanity. Although this is not finally achieved until the other omnipotent mechanisms of splitting and projective identification are finally relinquished – in the depressive position – nevertheless, the introjected good object remains as the sheet anchor of ego coherence and growth. Should the depressive position not be traversed then the ego will remain flawed by the splitting and there is a persistent paranoia. The seeds of psychosis have then been sown.

The identification of the self with an ideal object has been described by Rosenfeld (1971) as libidinal narcissism since the confusion between the self and the object obliterates the real difference between the self and the other, a proper perception of which is essential to dependent object relating. Klein saw this consequence of her theories upon the nature of the ego: in discussing the oceanic feeling she expressed the view that full contact with the world of goodness and beauty is essentially narcissistic and based upon the fundamental union of the self with the good breast which is the source of all such experience.

Like Freud's, Klein's theories maintain a continuum between mental illness and normal states of mind. Whereas the continuum for Freud is between depressive illness and normal human conscience, for Klein it is between paranoid and schizoid states and the universal tendency in human nature towards persecutory anxiety and a paranoid outlook on life, embodied in self-righteous xenophobia, supported by stereotypical mythologies of good-ness and evil. She was also able to explain some features of normal mourning and combined these with the paranoid element characteristic of many depres-sive states of mind including, of course, depressive illness (Klein 1935).

Klein's theories have been very influential in the UK, not only on those who follow her theories closely but also on those analysts who have worked more independently, such as Winnicott and Balint (Rayner 1991). There have been two main consequences: (1) the psychotic elements in apparently neurotic states of mind became analyzable and (2) a number of analysts in this country, notably Bion, Rosenfeld and Segal, have used these theories in the clinical approach to the treatment of psychosis.

It would be impossible, in the space available, to summarize the richness of much of this work, but I will select one or two key features of the work of Bion, Rosenfeld and Segal. I wish to highlight their points of departure from Klein which I feel are valuable in advancing our understanding of the enormous shift that occurs when individuals move from non-psychotic to psychotic states of mind, or live out on others the equivalent of destructive phantasies.

Both Bion and Segal have made contributions in relation to the develop-ment of psychotic thinking. Segal (1957), in an important paper, examines the concrete thinking to be found in psychosis. She suggests that in normal development, 'symbols' arise because of the gradual ability of the infant to recognize the difference between the self and the object and to form a bridge between the two. This perception of separateness requires the management of separation anxiety: if this proves intolerable, it will be obliterated by projective identification, producing a phantasy of 'oneness'. If this occurs, then instead of the creation of symbols which represent the thing symbolized, the symbol becomes a thing in itself – what Segal calls a symbolic equation. This gives rise to the concrete thinking characteristic of many psychotic states of mind.

Bion, on the other hand, in his extensive writing on the development of thinking and disorders of thought in psychotic states, asserts a quite different emphasis. He suggests that the development of normal thinking is reliant upon the same mechanism – of projective identification – and that it is a universal primitive form of communication between the infant and the mother. He postulates that, in a process he called reverie, the mother accepts the projective identifications of the infant – such as the fear that a part of itself is dying, and through a process he calls alpha function, alters that fear so that the infant can re-introject the now manageable part of itself (Bion 1961b, 1962). He suggests that this activity is a form of thinking carried out on behalf of the infant by the mother who is able to act as a container for unmanageable fears that the infant cannot process. Here Bion is extending to projective identification the healthy role that Klein saw in introjective identification, namely an omnipotent phantasy acting as a process to establish healthy mental functioning. Bion's theories on the development of normal thinking are, of course, in direct opposition to Segal's. Whereas Segal uses projective identification to explain the failure in the development of normal thought, Bion uses it as a mechanism for its formation. This disparity never seems to have been fully reconciled among Kleinians. Segal (1991) recognized the problem and suggested a mental space in which symbols could begin within Bion's concept of the mother as a container. She is plainly uneasy, however, at the issue of the confusion of identities which is a defining characteristic of projective identification, and fails eventually really to resolve the contradiction in their ideas.

In my view Segal's original understanding of the negative role of this process on symbol formation was much more helpful than Bion's because it keeps splitting and projective identification as a mechanism essentially leading to pathology, whereas in Bion's work, the mechanism is used to account for normal as well as abnormal states of mind.

Rosenfeld (1987), who worked extensively with actively psychotic patients, gave accounts of both projective identification and introjective identification producing narcissistic states in which the difference between the self and objects in the world were destroyed by the obliteration of separateness and individual differences. He became more and more of the view that it was important, in the analysis of borderline states and psychotic individuals, to try and help the patient recognize the dependent part of themselves, which often emerges in the analytic material as a child part of the patient. The dependent self is the sane part of the self, which could be attacked by other aspects of the self that are unable to manage the impact of reality and so seek a grandiose refuge in omnipotent phantasy. In a key paper (Rosenfeld 1971) he describes the malignant narcissism of certain borderline states and how essential it is to alert the patient to the fight going on within themselves, between different aspects of their personality, as well as to the attacks upon the dependent object. In these gravely ill patients he attempted to help the patient rescue the dependent part of themselves, which was often trapped in fearful omnipotent confusion. He also, in his later work, expressed the view that early dislocations in nurturing, in which the dependent self had been unable to thrive, were recreated in the illness and within the transference. In treating such ill patients, these early impasses to development needed to be understood by a close examination of the counter-transference. He believed that many obstacles in the treatment of disturbed patients, particularly senses of frustration and hopelessness in the analyst, were potentially very fruitful areas of study since they derive from the early dislocations in development, so that if they can be understood then the patient can be helped to get better (Rosenfeld 1987). In this part of his work there is less emphasis on envy, as the central variant causing grave pathology, than exists in the work of Klein and Bion.

Envy is an important concept because it introduces the innate element into the genesis of psychopathology. It can result in greed or refusal to take in good experiences, with unconscious violent attacks upon the source of them. Since it is essentially anti-life and anti-reality, it has great explanatory value for borderline, perverse and psychotic states of mind and has proved enormously important in the analysis of destructive forces within the individual's person-ality. In Rosenfeld's work, however, one finds another dimension entering his thinking and he persuaded those he supervised not to rely on the consolation of envy in their patients as a way of explaining the lack of progress in the analysis but to examine their own emotions and difficulties in perception which could be standing in the way of releasing the patient from some perennial impasse within their inner world. It seems to me that the emphasis by Rosenfeld on identifying the normal dependent part of the self as the sane element within the personality offers another way of understanding the basis for mental health in terms of a primitive part of the self which is not dominated by omnipotence. The development of psycho-pathology can then be understood as any inter-ference with this essential healthy dependent function and not as a simple persistence of the primitive or a regression to omnipotent levels of develop-ment.

Fairbairn (1951), who was also concerned with the impact of schizoid mechanisms in the development of mental disorder, held a different view from Freud and Klein, insofar as he saw instinct as essentially adaptive. He pointed out there could not be an instinct that did not have a goal and the goal was always some form of attachment to an object. This has always seemed to me a very sensible view because it is difficult to understand how human beings could have developed in the extraordinarily successful way they have if this were not the case. The idea that madness and badness are the essence of human nature and require curbing and modifying by benign parents in a controlling and civilizing society, makes the question of how civilizing restraint on the supposedly uncivilized passions could have come about in the first place. I find it more satisfactory to adopt a model of mental health which does not rely on omnipotent phantasy and which does justice to the importance of human interdependency on the one hand and the features of adaptability and inventiveness on the other.

AN APPROACH TO THE PSYCHOSES VIA A THEORY OF MENTAL HEALTH

The model that I use is a modification of some of the ideas of Fairbairn, Kohut, Bion, Segal and Rosenfeld and having at its root Freud's inspired revelations. It seems to me very sensible to see instinctual patterns of behaviour, and their counterpart in mental life, as essentially object seeking, as Fairbairn (1951) maintained. However, he does not go into much detail about how the self as an object in its own right comes into being. Kohut (1971) has attempted this in his views on narcissism which, although sometimes difficult to follow, nevertheless highlight the importance of a relationship between the mother and the child which, if lacking in some essential ingredient of exclusivity, can result in a persistent unconscious and partly conscious hunger for such a state of affairs. This leads, of course, to a very unrealistic set of expectations of the world and much destructive reaction formation. Kohut's ideas have been taken as an alternative to the more destructive theory of narcissism stressed by the Kleinians, post-Kleinians and by Kernberg. It seems to me, however, that they begin an account of early mental development which does justice to the realities of infantile behaviour and need, in the way that Bowlby (1969) puts forward in his views on attachment, but within a frame of reference that can be integrated with established analytical models of the mind. In my model of mental health I have tried to incorporate Bowlby's observation of children and Rosenfeld's description of the dependent part of the self as a foundation of sanity from which thinking and other mental development can grow, from an instinctual starting point that is based on the observation of children and infants as developed by Bowlby.

Bion (1962) describes the concept of an object, such as the good breast, coming about as a result of the successful realization of the instinctual preconceptions of such an object. For him the realization of preconceptions form basic prototypic objects whose functions, when introjected, enable the mobile linking together of simple elements of experience in a way that leads eventually to the capacity to think. However, his theories rest very much on the successful conceptualization of the object and the introjection of some of its aspects, such as the primitive nipple and penis, to form a basis for the self's ability to link with the object externally and to link primitive thoughts together internally, again relying on the omnipotent mechanism of introjective and projective identification as the basis for these healthy achievements. If one applies the same formula, however, to a preconception not only of the object but of the self in a dependent relationship with the object, which is after all the biological reality, then one can suppose that, where nurturing is successful in so far as primary bonding is encouraged to occur, then the self will realize not only pre-conceptions of the nurturing objects but also those aspects of its self which have responded to the good nurturing. The capacity for the progressive development of ego function including primitive thinking will then depend on the realization of the innate potential within the self and not on an omnipotent phantasy of acquisition of the object or its functions.

Using this model of development, the self is progressively realized, hand in hand with progressive realization of different aspects and functions of the object. This will result eventually in a dual concept of a complete self in a dependent and interdependent relationship with complete objects, in which the omnipotent mechanisms of splitting with projective and introjective identification have played no direct part. *Primary identification* is a good way of describing this development of healthy and entirely realistic achievement. The omnipotent mechanisms of splitting with projective or introjective identification may have played a part in protecting the early identifications that have been realized from destabilization in the face of excessive stress, but in my view, since they are essentially secondary phantasies (see below) they will not be available until at least some degree of primary conceptualization of self and object have been achieved.

The very first 'elementary concepts' are in all probability the building bricks of whole object identifications but already in their early form will have the separate duality described above. I use the term 'e-concept' to distinguish them from the whole object concepts which form eventually the primary identifications of self and dependent object (e-concepts can be inferred from the nature of pathological part objects that cannot be integrated, found in the analysis of many psychotic patients). The early dual primary concepts will, of course, include the reality of separateness and create the necessary conditions for the development of symbols to bridge the gap between the self and the dependent objects – a gap which has both functional and spacio-temporal realities. It is these realities which are the source of early and later healthy conflict in terms of frustration of need, fears of loss, of being left behind and dying and, intertwined with all this, problems of aggression, jealousy and envy. Anxiety is essentially a response to a threat, real or perceived, to the safety of the self and or the dependent objects. This is true in whatever stage of development the threat occurs.

I take the view that there are pre-conceptions needing realization to form primary concepts, appropriate to all stages of instinctual development, although the later in life they occur the more difficult they will be to distinguish from learned configurations. The early linking instincts take the form of *prospecting functions, holding on functions* and *substantive functions*, all of which are innately present in mutually realizable forms both in the infant and in the nurturing parents; particular, of course, the mother in her feeding capacity.

Prospective functions on the infant's side are connected with searching for the object of need and on the nurturing mother's side by alertness to these needs. Prospective functions, when successful, give a sense of optimism and trust in existence, a sense of potency, a sense of being in a safe space and a belief that home can be located. The ability to conceptualize the absent object is a consequence of having first been able to find it. This promotes the toleration of separation and the early enjoyment of independence. The eventual development of the logical constant of negation is laid down when abstract thinking becomes possible.

Sight, hearing and smell are all utilized in prospective functions and when their realization is faulty then the conceptualizations that are eventually made, rather than being benign and containing a loving valiancy, will be marked by fear, anger, suspicion and despair. Trust, optimism and potency will be absent. The inability to conceptualize the absent object will at its worst result in a basic confusion of identity or, if separateness is achieved, then the ability to tolerate absence will be very reduced. A pessimistic voyeurism replaces hopeful searching and the fear of evil eyes, of spying and being spied upon dominates a world in which the location of safety is never clear.

Holding on is the next function and depends upon the mutual holding functions of the infant and the parents. The instinctual behaviour of infants in grasping with the hands and mouth and the complementary need in mothers to hold and be held by their infant results in a sense of boundary – the psychic skin as described by Bick (1968). Good experiences in this domain will result in a sense of being well contained by the object and being well contained in one's own skin. Shape, size, a sense of proportion and the affirmation of difference are conceptualized. The conditions for the logical connectives of conjunction and disjunction are laid down as well as the capacity for attention, concentration and the belief in the existence of choice. Bion's (1962) description of the contact barrier, allowing some thoughts to be held in mind while others are kept as a penumbra of associations, would also derive from successful holding on. Clearly, when holding on is faulty, these positive qualities are lost. A fear of contact and an inability to contain emotions together with an excessive fear of falling to pieces will occur. Dysmorphobias, inability to tolerate boundaries, claustrophobic entrapment and confusion with a cold mechanical cruel object are the most serious outcomes.

Substantive linking is the final stage in a progressive series of linking activity in which a sense of substance of the object and a sense of fullness within the self, is achieved through the exchange of warmth, food and love. Belief in the achievement of reward, of happiness, of creative outcome and the specificity of cause and effect are achieved and will make possible the logical connectives of material implication and material equivalence when the capacity for abstract thought is acquired. The eventual capacity for deductive reasoning is inspired by the completion of the total process. Clearly, its faulty realization will result in problems connected with emptiness, a sense of poverty, a lack of depth in emotion or a sense of being full of hate and fear. More serious defects are confusion with an empty object or an inability to have a sense of meaning other than being in a black hole. Added to the previous failures a desperate autism is heralded. The capacity to think will be profoundly affected and show itself through difficulties in learning to talk, to read or to write. The popular label of dyslexia includes many whose difficulties are due to failure in primary linking. Such thought disorders spring from the failed or faulty achievement of primary separateness and are therefore more intractable than similar ones that are the outcome of the obliteration of separateness due to secondary narcissistic confusion between self and object as the result of projective or introjective identifications.

However, when the development progresses reasonably well, then at a very early state in neonatal life, an inchoate concept of the self will be achieved in a safe dependent relationship with a nurturing object and this irreducible dual concept (the primary identifications) will form the basis of all ego functioning and later development. It seems to me to be equivalent to the central ego of Fairbairn and it represents the sort of early integration that Klein mentions in her later work. In my model, once this essentially dual object has been successfully conceptualized, from what can be described as primary phantasies (the instinctual preconceptions), then the way is open for the development of secondary phantasies which will give rise to imagination and thinking and the provision of mental buffers against stress.

SECONDARY PHANTASY

Secondary phantasies are the outcome of separateness to which the self is heir, once the primary identifications of self and other have been achieved. The difference between the self and the dependent object – the psychological and physical gap – will be a primitive perception. It has two aspects: a spacio-temporal one in which absence impinges, and a functional one of differences in need. Secondary phantasy forms the psychological bridge that keeps the self in touch with the object internally both during its absence and during the vicissitudes of attachment.

Secondary phantasies will begin as simple memories and anticipations. Their emotional content will be a reflection of the way the primary identifications were acquired, complicated by the emotional experience of the spacio-temporal and functional gaps. This in turn will determine the extent to which the realities of experience will be altered by secondary phantasies to maintain comfort and ultimately avoid the anxiety of threat to the ego.

Shortage of space prevents a full discussion of the role of secondary phantasy, as I envisage it, but certainly Freud's understanding of dreams as wish fulfilment and the preservers of sleep, which have become known as ego defences (A. Freud 1936) describe something of what I have in mind. However ego defences have traditionally been somewhat over defined into rather rigid categories. The imagined alterations in the realities of dependency both remembered, perceived and foreseen that I discern in my patients, whose purpose is to reduce stress and maintain psychic equilibrium, are only classifiable by *the degree of omnipotent detachment from the primary dependent object*. I have called this the psychosynthetic activity of secondary phantasy. I believe this can be achieved, even from the beginning, without such a fundamental alteration as will obliterate the link with the dependent object.

Loss of this link can come about as a result of flights into grandiosity so that the self wanders too far from the dependent link or by splitting and projective identification in which the functional link is broken. These more omnipotent defences are reserved for extreme states of stress, when less profound alterations of reality, which do not involve the complete loss of contact with the dependent object, have failed to achieve the sense of safety that the ego requires. The maintenance of the link between the self and the dependent objects is reflected in secondary phantasy as an acknowledgment of the truths of interdependency and combined with the constraints of reality on attempts to realize psychosynthetic phantasies in the world, and provides the human relevance to invention, discovery and the development of social institutions. This contact with interdependent truths is the essence of all creative activity and I have called it the psychopoetic function of secondary phantasy. Psychosynthesis and psychopoesis, although appearing to work in different directions are really different components of the same mental function so that at any one time the configuration of experience will have a truth factor that reflects the extent to which the truth can be tolerated without undue threat to the ego. The pull away from reality or towards it is reflected in a highly changeable and active internal world of phantasy, affecting and being affected by the interaction with the external world. If the primary identifications have been adequately realized, then the potential for logical reasoning will have been laid down. There is, after all, only one set of absolute truths and that is in the irreducible realities contained in the primary concepts. However, provided the preconception of the way the primary identifications have been realized has itself become a concept, then abstract reasoning can occur with the concept of absolute truth values being included as part of psychosynthetic activity. This results ultimately in the development of logical reasoning and mathematics. Experimental science follows on as the attempt to realize absolute truth values in the external world and as a result is only indirectly relevant to human happiness and need, contributing as much danger to mankind as comfort and safety. The real world of interdependent existence is essentially artistic and will, in health, tolerate and exploit the lack of formal truth value in most statements, will gain meaning from degrees of ambiguity, extra meaning from metaphor and thrive on the emotional subtleties of non-verbal communication. The mistake of academic psychology and much sociology is not to have recognized the artificial domain of their chosen methodology.

To lose relevance in an attempt to hang on to certainty is too high a price to pay and although psychiatry has wandered down that path, the real needs of patients have kept most clinicians alive to the elusiveness of human reality. By and large they use scientific method as an aid to patient care and not as a way of seeking personal existential reassurance. The contrary argument that they have attempted to define such a reality is well developed by Foucault (1988). He makes important points, for the attempt to impose strict truth value on interpersonal thinking is the characteristic of theocracies and political tyrannies and usually results in appalling state criminality and cruelty through the imposition of conformity to institutional 'goodness', which is precisely the argument of the antipsychiatry movement.

However let us not digress further. When things have gone well enough, the fortunate individual will be heir to strong primary identifications and a mobile repertoire of secondary phantasy, will be able to buffer stress while coming to terms with its meaning and through psychopoetic adjustment to an acceptable truth take, via thinking, adaptive or adventurous action. Provided the link with the primary concepts is maintained, such a process, however socially eccentric it may be, will have relevance to the interdependent needs of the group in which it occurs and integrate the individual socially at the same time. This is the hallmark of sanity and positive social participation.

Failure to realize the dual primary concept of self and object necessary for the definition of separateness, or primary identifications that are so faulty that secondary phantasy fails, occasionally or habitually, to maintain the dependent link between the self and the dependent objects, will result in insanity or behaviour unmodified by secondary phantasy. We will look at each of these possibilities and the different outcomes in turn.

AUTISTIC ENTRAPMENT

If there is a profound failure in the realization of the primary preconceptions then the inchoate self will remain trapped inside an unidentified object and no proper realization of the self or dependent object can come about. Within this autistic domain there will be confusion, great terror and much rage, with an increasing despair and helplessness. This state of affairs is functionally equivalent to the sorts of confusion arising from profound projective or introjective identification of the self with the dependent object that occurs in later severe narcissism. However, in this primitive confusional state the situation is not reversible unless the realization of the vital preconceptions is brought about in sufficient time for the deficit to be overcome. If this is too long delayed then, even if later realizations succeed in providing sufficient concepts of self and object to equip a functioning ego, there will remain an autistic area that will be a source of very great vulnerability and disturbance. If the failure in realization is sufficiently prolonged, a frank autistic state occurs with a child trapped inside an ill-defined object unable to construct secondary phantasies and therefore unable to play, explore the world, develop or properly communicate.

However, when the failures are less prolonged and extensive, then autistic elements derived from faulty e-concepts (the equivalent of Bion's beta elements) which cannot be integrated into the ego, remain as highly anxiety provoking impenetrable defects in ego structure. These will be experienced as fearful black objects or as an ubiquitous nameless dread. Since they contain no concept of separateness, there is no spacio-temporal or functional gap to bridge, hence symbol formation is absent or rudimentary. Autistic elements cannot therefore be incorporated into secondary phantasy and are not dreamable or thinkable. They give rise to night terrors rather than nightmares. If they do appear in dreams or in fantasy then they are often experienced as black infestations or a fierce feeling of nameless dread. Sometimes some degree of separateness has been achieved and they emerge then as bits of the self confused with bits of the object, or perhaps as terrifying faces with horrific eyes. Such objects can also come about as a result of fragmentary splitting and projective identification (see Bion 1962 on bizarre objects). If at all possible the two need to be distinguished from each other, since the latter derive from the fragmentation of achieved primary objects, whereas the former result from primary failure and are therefore more anterior and more malignant.

Autistic elements will always pose a threat to the ego, but the degree of potential destabilization will depend upon the quantity and content of the autistic distress and the effectiveness of the ego defences against the anxiety. Space prevents a very full discussion of the various possibilities and in any case the connection between the clinical conditions that are explained by this model and the presumptions of causation are very far from established. However three broad categories can be postulated.

(1) An ego which is able to seal off autistic lacunae, which in themselves do not contain an extra threat from violent experiences, and in such a way that there is no very great immediate persistent anxiety. This encapsulation will be achieved by splitting and is presumably possible because the subsequent achievement of the dual primary identifications is sufficiently good to enable such efficient omnipotent psycho-synthesis to be mobilized. When this is less good, then bouts of neurotic anxiety, obsessional thinking or disorders of mood are a pronounced feature and indicate a hard pressed psychosynthesis due to a leaking of the autistic elements.

The resultant personality structure will be incomplete, so artificial, over controlled, false personality characteristics are likely. The potential for psychotic illness is always present and occurs when the encapsulation fails. This may come about as the result of significant stressful life events, particularly those that interfere with the realization of more adult preconceptions such as genital sexual conceptualization or child rearing. These later preconceptions may themselves produce internal changes that awaken the unrelinguished drives of the autistic domain. Perhaps the cause of schizophrenia is the release of overwhelming autistic anxiety which progressively undermines an ego that is already fundamentally flawed within each element of its total structure by the original failure in primary identification. Such a pathological situation could well arise from an innate deficit in linking functions of the self, operating psychologically at all crucial stages of primary developmental opportunity and having specific counterparts in neuro-physiological abnormalities. Once the sealed off early deficiency becomes released, the functioning ego can only be rescued from catatonic annihilation by elaborate grandiose psychosynthetic defences of splitting and projection, giving the first rank symptoms of schizophrenia.

When the primary autism is not so invasive then the illness is likely to be more transient as in many schizo-affective conditions, or self-limiting as in severe disorders of mood.

(2) The same encapsulated arrangement of the primary autism but with a contents that carries the sequelae of violent life-threatening experiences. The failure in primary linking is always life-threatening since, in order to survive as a going proposition, the self needs to realize its own identity within the concept of the dual dependent identifications. Hence the malignant anxiety of autistic entrapment. This failure usually comes about through passive deficiency in the response of the mother or in failures in the drive for attachment in the infant.

Where there is an aggressive or violent component to this failure on the part of the environment then the sense of catastrophic and violent threat carried within the autistic experience will be that much the greater. Then, when the encapsulation fails, there is no possibility of psycho-synthesis protecting the ego, so that not even psychotic phantasies, however grandiose, can come to the rescue. Violence and anxiety are lived out in catastrophic behaviour that may be unrestrained or homicidal.

Sometimes, when the encapsulation is not so complete, so that there is a small degree of leaking of autistic anxiety, the self will have some psychosynthetic way of handling this. Since the contents of the primary narcissism are not capable of symbol formation in their own right, this management will involve splitting and projective identification of the unintegratable elements or their organization, often through sexual deviant behaviour, into a collusive relationship. When the destructive and violent elements are too strong, then only extreme varieties of collusion or frank criminal abusive behaviour results. A more complete account of these varieties of borderline psychopathology can be found elsewhere (Gallwey 1985). In that contribution I used Bion's formulation of beta-elements which arise in his theory from splitting and projective identification and the arguments therefore need to be reformulated within the terms of the model of psychopathology that I have come to prefer and have set out here.

(3) Where there is an autistic deficit of varying proportions and content which has not been sealed off by an ego capable of efficient psycho-synthetic activity. In this state of affairs the individual will demonstrate a life long disturbance with the characteristic history of night terrors, early behavioural problems, hyperkinesis, repetitive destructive play, unsatisfactory early interpersonal relating and the likelihood of self-medication with psycho-active drugs in the face of persistent and ubiquitous anxiety. If the parental environment has been more passively or subtly disordered than is the case in many delinquent histories, then the individual may be less behaviourally disturbed but more isolated and enclosed, with severe difficulties in communication and achievement. Individuals who have failed to encapsulate their autistic elements are likely to meet diagnostic requirements of borderline or other similar varieties of personality disorder within the standard psychiatric nosologies.

We will now discuss briefly the other situation, namely a significant but lesser degree of interference in the realization of the primary preconception of self and dependent object which I term dysmorphia.

DYSMORPHIA

Since no nurturing can be ideal and since there is a good deal of variation in the extent of innate passivity, there will always be some unevenness in the path to the achievement of the primary identifications leading to individual personality variations and vulnerabilities, broadly compatible with mental health. However, past a certain point these types of deficit will give rise to significant problems which at their worst will not be sharply distinct from those produced by autistic entrapment. The important difference is that these deficits will not have prevented the realization of the primary preconceptions of self and dependent object, so that separateness has been achieved, with a functional and spacio-temporal gap in which secondary phantasy can begin to develop. The specific nature of the disruption to the primary identifications, which I have termed dysmorphia, is reflected therefore in the nature and content of the secondary phantasies. If the dysmorphia is severe enough it will produce active psychopathology or significant vulnerability that affects mental health and social adjustment. The ways in which this occurs are complex but, as has been indicated, the steps in linking between the self and the dependent object of prospecting, holding on and substantive contact, variously contribute to the final distortion in the primary identifications with the emotional distress that accompanies this.

The term dysmorphia is intended to cover both the structural and emotional distortions. It results in disturbances in identity and body image, basic reduction in existential confidence, feelings of impotence and inadequacy, diminished capacity to tolerate separation and general vulnerability to stress both from life events and in accomplishing later developmental realizations. Secondary phantasy is affected and will reflect the specific nature of the problems over linking as described above. Psychosynthesis will predominate over psychopoesis because of the degree of anxiety with which the ego has to cope. There will be a greater pressure towards grandiosity with severe stretching of the link with the dependent object as well as a tendency toward the more omnipotent defences of splitting with projective and introjective identification.

When the nurturing environment continues to be neglectful or abusive, secondary phantasy formation will be extremely impoverished. Problems in connection with learning and an inability not only to manage stress but to engage with the external world in a creatively imaginative way, will result in the development of a personality disordered way of life. As I have discussed elsewhere (Gallwey 1991) much compulsive delinquency is due to an impoverishment of psychosynthetic capacity, including the more omnipotent psychotic defences, resulting in the individual manipulating the external world in order to bring about the sort of rearrangement in reality that would otherwise have been achieved through the operation of psychosynthesis. Criminal acts, criminal sub-cultures and prison society reflect this mixture of entrenched, often ruthless, manipulation of others, that is tainted with grandiose wish fulfilment and the realization of nightmare.

Some other criminal activity, together with a great deal of non-criminal maladjustment, is due to the attempt to realize secondary phantasies, not as psychopoetic thinking resulting in inventive exploration of the world, but in the service of secondary phantasies which carry cruel and revengeful feelings which have lost the dependent link with a nurturing object. Such phantasies are usually grandiose or represent an attempt to realise a narcissistic rearrangement of the dependent realities based on splitting and projective identification (Rosenfeld 1971). I disagree with Rosenfeld in relation to those who present as libidinal narcissists, who in my experience have a malignant narcissistic aspect somewhere in a split off realm, often projectively identified in an object by whom they seem to be cruelly victimized. They often suffer from depressive illness and if this split suddenly closes, the eruption of violence can be homicidal. The persistence of severe splitting with projective or introjective identification results in manifestations of psychosis, borderline states or destructive behaviour close to that which has been described above in the discussion on primary autism.

In fact, from an immediate point of view the origins of the clinical states and the nature of the core psychopathology may be impossible to elucidate. The presence of an encapsulated autistic area is suggested when persistent severe anxiety, increase in psychotic symptomatology or destructive acting out accompanies an apparently successful psychotherapeutic working alliance.

This takes us to the therapeutic consequences of this model of psychosis and mental health.

THE PSYCHOTHERAPEUTIC STRATEGIES

It is always unsatisfactory to advance modifications of psychoanalytic theory without bringing substantial clinical examples and this chapter suffers from that shortcoming. Indeed, the same is even more the case when describing therapeutic issues. However, the demands of space are such that only a bare outline of the treatment implications of the model set out above can be undertaken.

I shall confine myself to two main issues. The first is the question of therapeutic goals and the second some very general implications for technique that arise from the model of psychopathology that has been advanced.

From what I have said regarding the profound nature of the various psychopathologies in borderline conditions, in psychotic states and their associated maladjustments, it will be realized that to rectify the defects is in most cases an unrealistic goal. Before attempting psychotherapy, an assessment of the vulnerability of the ego to being overwhelmed by destructive anxiety and the very great unfulfilled needs that lie within areas of severe ego dysmorphia or autistic confusion must be carefully made.

Anyone who presents in a borderline or psychotic state and is reliant on drugs or alcohol, has a history of significant behavioural problems, or who has been abused or severely neglected in childhood must have a very full period of appraisal before psychotherapy is attempted. A separate assessment should be undertaken by the prospective therapist, who should never rely completely on the opinion of the referring agency, whoever they may be. The therapist will have to carry the direct pressures and anxiety of the therapeutic relationship, so it is vital to sit down with the patient and try to get some idea of what one is in for. Careful history taking is all important not only in relation to childhood and presenting problems but also the extent and severity of failures to cope, especially attempts at suicide, other episodes of self-harm, criminal or violent behaviour, reliance on intoxicants, the quality of supportive relationships, as well as the course, severity and chronicity of any mental illness.

Many patients in forensic psychiatry will be extensively traumatized and the risk of making their situation much worse by over expectation or a failure to provide adequate support for the frailty of their egos is a very real one.

Many will have massive dependency problems and a great burden of anxiety, with which they may have managed to cope in one way or another. It is very unwise to involve such individuals in a treatment in which the dependent transference or the core pathology is gathered, unless one is ready to try to carry on when the inevitably demanding angry acting out behaviour arrives. Otherwise it will be impossible to see the treatment through to a reasonable conclusion. Many tragedies involving both therapists and patients have come about because the therapist, having come under pressure from severe disturbance in the patient or aggressive demanding behaviour, capitulates quite suddenly, leaving their patient in a much worse state than they were before the ill-conceived psychotherapy was begun. Many patients who have disorders of the type described in this chapter may require, during crucial phases, a managing psychiatrist or supportive mental health team. This should ideally be set up before the work begins if the depth of the disorder can be foreseen. Many such ill patients will of course already be in an institution, so that integration of the treatment with the multi-disciplinary team can occur. Even when such precautions are undertaken, the anxiety and pressures of working with this group of patients is very considerable, so that adequate supervision and a level of training that gives some chance of effective work is imperative.

What then can be put forward as psychologically beneficial for this group within the framework of the sort of psychotherapy that is available at the present time?

First and foremost comes the importance of a down-to-earth appreciation of the extent of the patient's problems, measured against the extent of the therapist's ignorance of what it's all about. It is much better to stick to conveying those realities with an attitude of real concern for what the patient is up against, than to use the situation as a vehicle for one's own set of theoretical preconvictions or need to enjoy making inventive formulations. The patient, who will be in real need of understanding, will have either to accept them as a kind of religious duty or face the added anxiety of being blamed for undue resistance when things get worse. Disturbed and ill patients benefit from someone sharing their sense of being in the grip of a force that threatens their identity, safety or capacity to think. They fear madness and fear they will never get better or recover their lost personality strengths. To have the opportunity to share these kind of anxieties with a psychotherapist and not to have to put on a brave face or find refuge in denial may be more enhancing of recovery than attempting more detailed explorative work. The acceptance of the role of neuroleptic drugs goes hand in hand with this approach as does the need to understand the staff group reactions to one's patient, which may be a formidable task in non-therapeutic environments such as prisons.

However, there is always the chance of a more detailed understanding of severe pathology and if this can be achieved, it can be of lasting benefit.

In the model of primary linking, the functions of prospecting, holding on and substantive experience will be conveyed in the transference through the various expressions of secondary phantasy, both in psychosynthetic and psychopoetic response to the dependent relationship with the therapist. This supplies a real opportunity to lessen the deficit in the primary identifications, particularly if the disordered linking problems can be picked up, when their sensitive interpretation may rectify quite specifically the dysmorphia that has been their consequence. Obviously, a patient's sense of a lively prospecting therapist who enables them to feel psychologically held in a substantive way will depend upon the sensitivity and skill of the therapist and on the frequency of the sessions. Achievement of inroads into autistic entrapment is hard and requires interpretations that demonstrate an understanding of the fear of becoming lost and trapped in confusion. When the patient decompensates into an autistic state, the fact that they will have lost the capacity to link thoughts together or to conceptualize an individual object as a constant entity will make ordinary interpretive work impossible. Under these circumstances contact can sometimes be made by simply interpreting the nature of the problem and why that has arisen; by saying, for instance, how the patient feels that objects and people seem to change all the time and how they feel trapped and muddled with what should be outside them.

With less autistic patients the study of difficulties in following what the patient is trying to say may reveal subtle disorders of thought. Particular attention to the nature of muddles in the construction of logical statements can then be related to specific problems in the linking functions. For instance, those who have failed to achieve satisfactory holding on may be at times very hard to follow even when they are apparently describing everyday occurrences.

Instead of seeing this as resistance or asking for clarification it is worthwhile trying to see what it is that is missing, what logical connective, say an 'if' or 'but', would help to make sense of what they are trying to formulate. This can then be related to feeling unheld or even dropped. I have found this analysis of problems in comprehension a sensitive route to making contact with specific misfortunes in primary linking and a valuable way of freeing obstacles to progress. The advantage of working in this rather detailed way with those who have been emotionally deprived is that, when affinity of thought is achieved, the patient experiences a duality of linking within the terms of the analytic functions that will to some extent reproduce the kind of physico-emotional experience that they missed out on at an earlier stage. This greatly reduces their clamour for more direct reassurance and greatly enhances the therapeutic alliance.

The length of the treatment is another important factor and the time constraints need to be made clear from the outset. Again one is reminded of the importance of having some idea of what is a reasonably realistic goal and integrating a psychotherapeutic approach with general psychiatric care (Jackson 1991). As he describes, psychoanalytic understanding of the psychotic world of ill patients is a powerful aid to their treatment and management. Such understanding should, of course, include other approaches such as well-conceived cognitive strategies, which may be more appropriate with disturbed patients than attempting transference-based or other interpretive approaches. A specific approach to the omnipotence of psychotic experience (Chadwick *et al.* 1994) is the kind of well thought out cognitive therapy that needs to be developed. Group treatment in these cases may be very valuable (Cox 1976) and provides a very good opportunity to make contact with disguised pathology through the study of the group's difficulties in communicating with each other along the lines mentioned above.

In setting out these thoughts and modifications to theory I do want to stress that they represent the conclusions reached in direct clinical work with patients both as a psychoanalyst and clinical psychiatrist. The model derives from the work of the major psychoanalytic theorists and represents an attempt to integrate and reconcile a variety of different theoretical positions which, because of the problems of refutation unique to psychoanalysis, tend toward the dogmatic.

It will be recognized that the model makes redundant the concept of the id and diminishes the depressive position as a distinct developmental requirement by substituting a more continual 'depressive' pull towards reality in the psychopoetic function of secondary phantasy. All instincts become ego instincts and, although essentially self-preservative, are also social in so far as the preservation of the self is inextricably connected with innate interdependent capacity. Death instinct is maintained not as an instinct *per se* but as a specific innate deficiency in the range of primary linking functions which serve the instinctual preconceptions of a primary object relationship. Primary phantasy as the mental counterpart of instinct (Isaac 1952) forms the central thesis of this model. The metapsychology of super-ego formation is taken out of omnipotent phantasy so that conscience becomes the resultant of fortunate experiences of acquiring basic identifications within the framework of a good dependency.

I hope the model has some meaning and usefulness for those working in this perplexing and poorly understood field of human misery.

Theories of Aggression and Violence

Felicity de Zulueta

INTRODUCTION

The terms aggression and violence are often used interchangeably. However, whereas aggression is understood by ethologists and biologists as a normal form of social behaviour we share with other animals, its manifestations should not to be confused with violence, which is essentially human and relates more to the meaning we give to a destructive form of interpersonal or even personal behaviour. For example, a man kills another: this can be interpreted as a 'bestial' act of violence and 'the inevitable manifestation of our instinctual drives' or, as a 'legitimate act of courage in the defence of the nation', or as 'necessary for the preservation of law and order'.

These different interpretations depend upon how individuals perceive themselves and the world they live in: they are related not only to people's personal experience but also to the social and cultural matrix to which they belong.

Whatever form violence takes, the fact that humans resort to such behaviour suggests that there is a thinking subject doing something to another who, from the observer's point of view, would be defined as 'human', be it an infant in the case of abuse, a woman in the case of rape, a man in the case of murder.

But how do those who commit acts of violence perceive their victims? What is going on in the minds of those who torture and kill? What is the victim in the eyes of his or her tormentor at that moment? And what drives the attacker to this cruel behaviour?

Some of the answers to these important questions lie in the close study of the effects of loss, abuse and psychological trauma on the attachment relationships of both children and adults. What emerges most clearly from this research is that the individual can only exist in relation to the 'other': this finding is crucial to our understanding of human violence. One could go further and say that is the denial of our intrinsic biological and psychological need for the 'other' that may partly explain the length of time that it has taken to begin to understand the origins of human violence.

Indeed, the more we explore the subject of human destructiveness, the more we realize that what is at stake is not so much a scientific enquiry regarding its origins but more a philosophical and religious debate about human nature. This is an old debate in the West, dating back to the fourth century AD. At that time, some early Christians, such as Julian of Eclanum, believed that if humans die or suffer it is because they belong to nature and are mortal beings. However, Augustine rejected this view: how could the plight of sick or deformed children be explained if it were not due to the fact that 'sin' was transmitted from parents to children. By blaming mankind (and sexuality in particular), Augustine gave a meaning to human suffering and evil at a time when plagues and wars were ravaging Europe. His belief won the day: Julian of Eclanum and his followers were excommunicated and the myth of 'original sin' is still with us, manifest in the current belief that mankind is intrinsically violent and driven by what Freud (1920) called the 'death instinct'. The latter not only reflects a traditional view in the continuous debate regarding human nature but also humanity's desperate struggle to give a meaning to pain, violence and death. This need to feel guilty in the face of disaster is a way of making sense of the incomprehensible and of regaining some sense of control when faced with total helplessness: victims of trauma, incest or abuse all tend to cling to the belief that they are in some way to blame for what happened to them (de Zulueta 1993, pp.11–12). Fairbairn described this need to feel guilty as the 'moral defence' (1952b, pp.65–68). The abused child would rather see himself as 'bad' in order to make the parents 'good'. At the level of his internal object relations, he will cling to his 'bad rejecting objects' with resulting destructive behaviour.

> 'What Freud describes under the category of the "death instinct" would thus appear to represent for the most part masochistic relationships with internalised bad objects. A sadistic relationship with an internalised bad object would also present the appearance of a "death instinct".' (Fairbairn 1952b, p.79)

For Fairbairn there is no need to postulate a 'death instinct' to describe sadistic or masochistic behaviour: it can be explained in terms of the individual's object relatedness.

However, what needs to be taken into account in this debate is that there is, underlying the belief in the human species' innate destructiveness, the assumption that individual gratification is what drives mankind: such a view presupposes that the individual's need for the other is essentially materialistic.

This fits with our Western cultural premise concerning the central importance of the individual in relation to society. This assumption, shared by Freud
(and many of his followers including Klein (1930) and Kernberg (1976a)),
ethologists (Lorenz 1966) and sociobiologists (Wilson 1978), is that we
operate as individuals with innate drives, including aggressive drives, that need
to be discharged: the 'other' is essentially an outlet for the individual's
gratification. Not only does this simplistic approach fail to address recent
findings regarding the aetiology of human destructiveness but it precludes
further thinking regarding the importance of the relationship which exists
between the perpetrator and his or her victim and the sociocultural context in
which this relationship is being acted out.

As we have seen with Fairbairn, there are also psychoanalysts who hold the
opposite view, based upon the assumption that we are essentially 'object
seeking'; that is, relationship seeking (Fairbairn 1952b; Kohut 1977; Suttie
1935). This view implies that outside relations are what lead to frustration,
self-destruction and violence because we are essentially social animals (Zulueta
1993, pp.64–77). This approach could be seen to represent the opposite view
of human nature, the view that human beings are essentially loving, like Jean
Jacques Rousseau's 'noble savage'.

These beliefs reflect two profoundly incompatible visions of life and of the
fundamental nature of human experience (Greenberg and Mitchell 1983,
p.406). Neither opinion can really help us understand the origins of human
violence unless it is backed by scientific research evidence. This will remain
the focus of the rest of this chapter.

Paradoxically, it is because of current interest in the study and treatment of
victims of human violence such as war, concentration camps, child abuse and
rape, that we are beginning to realize just how much human beings depend
upon their attachments to one another. Trauma has, in fact, been defined as
'the sudden cessation of human interaction' (Lindemann 1944).

These findings come as no surprise to those involved in the study of
attachment behaviour in early childhood and it is to their findings that we need
to turn first in order to understand the aetiology of human destructiveness.

THE IMPORTANCE OF ATTACHMENT BEHAVIOUR IN THE UNDERSTANDING OF HUMAN VIOLENCE

We are indebted to the British psychoanalyst, John Bowlby (1988, p.81) and
to his American colleagues for having made us aware of a hitherto unrecog-
nized and yet crucial reciprocal relationship which appears to exist between
our need for the 'other' and our destructive behaviour.

What is now clear is that human beings, like all mammals, are born with
an innate predisposition to form intense attachments to their primary caregivers

(not necessarily their mothers), and then to their secondary caregivers. The vast literature in the field of attachment has been reviewed elsewhere (Zulueta 1993, p.43–77), and I will attempt to present here some of the most relevant findings in terms of our interest in forensic psychotherapy. The separation studies (with the sequential response of protest, despair and denial) carried out on primate infants and their mothers reveal that:

(1) Attachment behaviour has a psychobiological substrate.

(2) It is a form of behaviour partly mediated by opiates – so much so that one researcher describes social bonding as an 'opiate addiction' (Panksepp, Siviy and Normansell 1985, p.25). Indeed the distress symptoms produced by separation are similar to those seen in narcotic withdrawal states and they involve aggressive behaviour. This implies that emotions are at the root of social bonding: pleasure is the outcome of attachment mediated by endogenous opiates. Separation produces distress and aggression. These findings lead us to postulate that the mechanisms underlying love and hate may be reciprocally related.

Developmentally, the process of attachment is achieved through a complex process of psychobiological attunement between the infant and caregiver (Stern 1985, p.140–42). This allows the infant's early physiological and hormonal systems to be regulated by her primary caregiver, functions that the infant gradually acquires as she develops. Hofer (1984) maintains that it is the presence of internalized 'biologic' regulators within the interaction that determine the infant's response after separation.

For example, if bonnet macaque monkeys are obliged to forage for food rather than receiving it *ad libitum*, the mother–infant relationship becomes more tense with increased maternal rejection and increased infant independence. When separated from their mothers, these infants show the normal 'protest' behaviour of the acute phase but become markedly depressed in the second week of separation. This does not occur in their usual environment (Rosenblum and Sunderland 1982).

This study, amongst others, shows how the nature of the mother–infant relationship prior to separation can have important effects on how the infant behaves after separation. Hofer suggests that this response is linked to the presence of the internal 'biologic' regulators which, if disrupted through deprivation or trauma, can produce an altered response to separation or loss. He also thinks that such regulators are important throughout life.

Harlow's research on maternally deprived rhesus monkeys produced, amongst other abnormalities, grossly inappropriate aggressive behaviour (Harlow and Mears 1979). For some researchers, this is attributed to the reciprocal manifestation of a damaged attachment system.

These physiological changes are accompanied by parallel psychological and behavioural developments arising from the interaction between mother and infant which lead to the development of the self and the internalization of 'working models' or 'object-relations'. Hofer (1984) suggests that the 'biologic' regulators are precursors of these mental representations or 'psychologic' regulators: the latter may well allow us to endure temporary separations without full scale bereavement responses (p.192).

The complex process of psychobiological attunement between the infant and her caregiver is to be replayed throughout the individual's subsequent relationships and is at the heart of her attachment to others. This implies that any disruption of this essential developmental process leads to serious long term effects both at a physiological and psychological level. Thus the trauma of loss, deprivation or abuse (whether physical, emotional or sexual) can all have longstanding effects on the individual's capacity to form satisfactory relationships, her sense of self and, in particular, her potential for violent behaviour. Satisfactory attachments, which are essential for our emotional well-being, are dependent on our capacity to become attuned to the 'other'. Ainsworth, Blehar, Waters and Wall (1978) in the USA have shown that the 'securely' attached one-year-old infant (as determined by the Social Isolation Test) of a 'good enough mother' has the self-confidence and the capacity to form satisfactory relationships: the 'other' for such an individual is perceived and treated as another human being whose needs can be empathized with and attended to.

On the other hand, the insecurely attached infant, who has been emotionally deprived or abused, has little self-confidence and tends to relate to others with hostility. Such an infant shows an unexpected response to their mother on her return in the Strange Situation Test: she avoids interacting with her caregiver whilst remaining in fairly close proximity to her. Although the child appears to be emotionally detached, her heartbeat indicates that she is highly aroused.

This 'avoidant' (or Group-A) behaviour appears to arise when an infant is placed in an intolerable conflicting situation by her caregiver. Usually, threats of any sort arouse in the infant a tendency to withdraw from the frightening object and make close contact with her caregiver. However, what if mother is both threatening and forbids contact, as the mothers of these infants tend to do? The infant can displace her attention elsewhere and thereby 'cut herself off' from feeling both angry and fearful in relation to her mother, on whom she totally depends: she has learnt to dissociate in order to preserve her love object and her 'secure base'. This form of defence is very common in all victims of psychological trauma.

Such an 'avoidant' response is found in 20–25 per cent of one-year-old infants in the USA, whilst 63 per cent are securely attached (Group-B). The remaining 12 per cent are also insecurely attached: they display anxious behaviour in relation to their mother as a result of her inconsistent behaviour and behave in an ambivalent manner upon her return in the Strange Situation Test (Group-C).

The study of attachment relations is beginning to provide important evidence as to the links between the infant's attachment patterns, the formation of internal working models (or object relations) and the development of the self.

One such study is of particular interest: nineteen pairs of children aged four to five years old were observed at play.

In those pairs where one or both partners were Group-A children, there was victimization: in five of these pairs one partner continuously victimized the other, both verbally and physically. In these couples the abuser had an 'avoidant' attachment response in the Strange Situation Test and the victim was also insecurely attached (Group-A and Group-C). Securely attached children were neither abusers nor victims (Troy and Sroufe 1987).

These findings are important for our understanding of human violence and its links with Group-A attachment responses. They also help us to understand how object relations are internalized: the fact that a Group-A child can be either victim or victimiser suggests that it is the relationship, the self in relation to the 'other', which is internalized. What researchers have also noted in particular is the high stability in the infant's reunion behaviour with mother. This stability is explained by the fact that, once established, patterns of attachment tend to be self perpetuating. This allows the individual to preserve a sense of continuity in terms of his or her sense of self. For this to be achieved, perceptual and cognitive distortions have to play an important part in the maintenance of the Self: we tend to perceive the world as we need to see it.

An example of this kind of cognitive distortion is provided by Frodi's (1985) study on the effects of infant crying on caregivers (p.363). The baby's cry is always aversive, producing a similar effect to that of being repeatedly insulted or being given an electric shock. The effects are even more marked if the subjects watching the video were told that the baby was either 'premature' or 'difficult' when, in fact, the child was normal. A smiling baby elicits a positive reaction for most people. However, for abusive mothers both smiling and crying appears to be aversive.

The same observation has been made with abused children who, faced with a crying peer, will respond negatively and may even hit the other child (Main and George 1985). This response could be attributed to the fact that 'avoidant' children may find the crying unbearable because it could remind them of their own pain and, possibly, of the way their caregivers dealt with it, too.

Conclusion

What these studies on attachment behaviour appear to show is that deprivation in all its different manifestations results in attunement failure and that the resulting *avoidant* child grows up with little self-confidence and perceives the 'other' much as she perceives herself to be, as a dehumanized being, or, as 'part object'.

Such insecurity has important implications in terms of self for it results in a desperate need to have some sense of control over the 'other' who thus becomes an object of exploitation or abuse and is perceived as a dehumanized other. Indeed, the loss of an important relationship to the self – otherwise described as self object failure – in an insecure personality is tantamount to an attack on the self, with all that this entails in terms of destructive narcissistic rage and the associated cognitive and physiological manifestations mentioned above. One last finding that is of particular relevance for psychotherapists working with those who abuse and victimize is that it is not so much the experience of rejection and trauma that determines how secure people feel as adults, but the capacity they have to gain access to the information about their childhood and how coherently they can organize such information. This could be seen as an important function of the therapeutic experience, which should aim at providing a 'good enough' attachment relationship to help the patient rediscover that which was helplessly endured and then defensively 'split off' in order to survive.

THE IMPORTANCE OF PSYCHOLOGICAL TRAUMA IN THE UNDERSTANDING OF HUMAN VIOLENCE

If psychological trauma is defined as 'the sudden uncontrollable disruption of affiliative bonds' (Lindemann 1944), it is no coincidence that there is considerable overlap between attachment disorders and psychological trauma: those are the result of a disruption to the attachment system. Both lead to disruption of the attachment system with all that this implies in terms of psychological defences, biological manifestations and violence.

Freud (1896a) was one of the first to suggest the possibility that what was then called hysteria was the outcome of child sexual abuse in childhood. His findings and theories were rejected by the psychiatric establishment, and later by Freud himself.

Nearly one hundred years later many psychiatrists are still doubtful about the role of sexual abuse or chronic psychological trauma in the aetiology of psychiatric disorders. However, there are studies which do show strong links between sexual abuse, borderline personality disorders and eating disorders (Brown and Anderson 1991; Herman, Perry and Van der Kolk 1989; Mullen *et al.* 1993), as well as between sexual abuse and perversions (Welldon 1988).

The long term effects of psychological trauma or post traumatic stress disorder (PTSD) are no longer denied. This syndrome recognizes the wounding of the human psyche during states of terrifying helplessness. It took a devastating war and the defeat of a world power for the importance of psychological trauma to be recognized again. PTSD essentially recognizes a biphasic response to traumatic events involving, on the one hand, the reliving of these events in some form or another and, on the other hand, a sense of numbness and reduced responsiveness to the outside world.

Dissociation and Re-Enactment

Traumatized people find themselves reliving their traumatic experience mainly through intrusive thoughts in the form of visual flashbacks, nightmares, or recurrent memories, or through the actual re-enactment of the event. In the latter, the subject may play the role of victim or victimizer. It is this particular consequence of psychological trauma that is a major cause of violence, one that is all too often neglected but which can be at the root of what appears as cold or unprovoked violence occurring many years after the original trauma. In such individuals, damage to the attachment system and to the self results in intense rage that is often split off from consciousness.

> *Vignette*
> 'In 1968, a Vietnam veteran lit a cigarette which led to the murder of his buddy by the Vietcong. On the anniversary of this death, for the next eighteen years, he carried out an 'armed robbery' by putting a finger in his pocket and carrying out a 'holdup' in order to elicit police gunfire. His unconscious re-enactment only came to an end when he discovered its meaning.' (Van der Kolk, 1989, p.391)

What is most striking in the study of psychological trauma is to discover how the psychobiological effects of trauma often remain hidden by the human psyche's vast repertoire of defences. Painful memories are lost to consciousness as the individual literally dissociates himself from feelings or thoughts that are too disturbing to acknowledge. This is how abused children and trauma victims cope with the unspeakable pain of their past. It is only when these dissociated feelings are triggered back into consciousness by an internal or external stimulus that the dissociated rage and its accompanying perceptions are brought back into action (although not necessarily into consciousness), often to recreate the very pain to which the victim was subjected, either in himself or in the 'other', as we see happening with parents who abuse their children as they were abused or with 'battered wives' who recreate their childhood abuse with their male partners.

Repetition Compulsion

As a result of the failure to integrate the traumatic experience into declarative memory, trauma can become organized at a sensory or somatic level which is difficult to change (Van der Kolk 1994). As a result, the traumatized individual is likely to be exposed repeatedly to states of high arousal which cannot be handled because of an associated inability to modulate such experiences, both biologically and psychologically. Indeed, victims of chronic trauma cannot use symbols and fantasy to cope with their feelings and therefore tend to act rather than think. This state of mind is what has been termed alexythimia.

Links between social bonding and opiate addiction have also been confirmed in men suffering from PTSD.

Vignette
'A group of eight Vietnam veterans suffering from PTSD were exposed to a fifteen minute clip of a Vietnam war film: seven of the men showed a 30% reduction in perception of pain and were found to have released the equivalent of 8 mg of morphine.' (Pitman, Van der Kolk, Scott and Greenberg 1990)

As Van der Kolk (1994) points out, one of the functions of the mother–infant attachment relation is to modulate physiological arousal in the infant. When subject to deprivation, these infants appear to develop less opioid receptors and therefore need higher levels of endogenous opiate secretion to feel soothed. They may then resort to all kinds of addictive behaviour including compulsive re-exposure.

In childhood victims of sexual abuse who suffer from prolonged and repeated trauma, otherwise known as complex PTSD (Herman 1992, p.119), this tendency to re-enact the abuse is further reinforced by another defence, which is that of perversion (Welldon 1988). These victims sexualize their attachment relations just as their abusing parents did. The resulting ritualized form of behaviour defends the individual against overwhelming feelings of pain and loss of control.

Vignette
A young woman who has been both physically and sexually abused in childhood cannot bear the feelings which emerge at the end of her therapy: terrified of her own rage and dependency, she fends off these feelings by becoming an omnipotent seducer whose central aim is both fusion with and control of her object-therapist in the service of her threatened self.

One of the main findings in PTSD sufferers and child abuse victims is the sense of guilt which these people feel and which also compounds the need to repeat the trauma. Identifying with the aggressor gives the child victim a sense of control and power that is desperately needed. But, such an identification with the abusing parent also implies a belief that the child is 'wicked' and needs to be punished. As Fairbairn (1952b) points out, the abused child will cling to this belief in his own badness because in becoming 'bad' such a child also makes his objects of attachment 'good' and this gives him a part to play in his downfall, hence the term 'moral defence' (pp.65–67).

For the developing child this leads to splitting of the caregiver into idealized good and bad rejecting part objects and a clinging to the paranoid schizoid position seen very clearly in borderline personality disorders.

Thus, both child and adult victims of psychological trauma hold onto this need to feel bad and therefore in some way responsible rather than totally helpless. This moral defence could be seen to have found its cultural equivalent in the myth of original sin. As Freud was to admit, the death instinct may well serve the same function. he wrote: 'It may well be that this belief in the internal necessity of dying is only another of those illusions which we have created to bear the burden of existence' (1920, p.39).

IMPLICATIONS FOR FORENSIC PSYCHOTHERAPY

The Therapist's Need to Deny the Reality of the Trauma and the Dangers of Re-Enactment

Working with the victims of psychological trauma makes people realize that we all need to hang on to a belief that we are both invulnerable and have some control over our lives. The meaning we give to the world about us is terribly important. The helplessness experienced by those who have been traumatized, whether perpetrators or victims or both, can really threaten these 'secret psychoses' or normal delusional beliefs of everyday existence.

This threat, in addition to the pain, rage and violence these patients communicate, either directly or through massive projective identification, makes it even more likely that those involved with the treatment of traumatized individuals will seek to deny the reality of their patients' experience. This therapeutic denial is made more likely if the therapist relies on a psychoanalytic theory and/or personal psychoanalysis that does not acknowledge the reality of trauma and the dangers of re-enactment. In such cases, repetition of the denied abuse in the therapeutic setting becomes quite likely, particularly with victims of child sexual abuse. It was Foulkes (1964) who pointed out that the psychoanalytic encounter can so easily be used by therapists as a way of dealing with their own needs and trauma: 'the psychoanalyst really defends himself by psychoanalysing others' (p.151). This can lead to therapists developing their own unconscious identifications with their patients, making them even more vulnerable to the effects of projective identification and re-enactment.

Thus, both therapists and patients can get caught up in either the unconscious re-enactment of their patients' perverse defences, with all the excitement this engenders, or in a re-enactment of the psychological trauma itself. The result is a perversion of the therapist's professional's relationship, much as takes place between abusive caregivers and their children.

Importance of Supervision

These observations make it absolutely essential for all involved in the psychotherapeutic treatment of forensic patients to have some form of supervision, a space to think about what is happening, or not happening, in the therapeutic relationship, a place to be supported, confronted and held, through what can be an overwhelming experience for both the therapist and the patient.

Also, if violence is to be understood as the reciprocal manifestation of attachment gone wrong, the treatment of those who resort to socially destructive behaviour requires a capacity to give as well as the humility to know when therapy itself may simply not suffice to give a patient a 'good enough attachment experience' to let go of the need to be 'bad'. It may well be in some patients' interests to remain 'bad'.

CONCLUSION

The crucial importance of attachment as a major motivational system in our species and of its reciprocal links with violence is only just beginning to be recognized (de Zulueta 1993, pp.41–75). What is now being suggested, as a result of studies on attachment and psychological trauma, is that there are at least two dimensions involved in the manifestation of human violence. The first stems from the neurophysiological underpinnings of the attachment system and their profound disruption as a result of trauma and abuse.

The second arises from the self in the form of narcissistic rage derived from a matrix of internalized early attachment relationships bolstered by powerful psychological defence mechanisms such as denial, dissociation, splitting, projection and projective identification, all commonly used when dealing with trauma and abuse.

In other words, if love and hate are reciprocally related, affiliative and destructive behaviour are the different manifestations of the same underlying attachment system and its psychological representations at the level of the self. These conclusions are not easy to hold onto when working in the field of forensic psychotherapy. When treating patients whom society has labelled as 'evil' and whose perverse and cruel activities cannot fail to engender feelings of horror and fear in all of us, it is hard to believe that we all share the same ceaseless need for the 'other'. But, as Bowlby (1988) reminds us: 'human infants are pre-programmed to develop in a socially co-operative way: whether they do or not turns to high degree on how they are treated' (p.9). In other words the forensic patient does to his objects what was once done unto him.

The Origins of Rage and Aggression

Neville Symington

INTRODUCTION

It is a mistake to think that psychoanalysis has one theory. Psychoanalysis is a clinical methodology that encompasses a wide range of theories. Nowhere is this more evident than when psychoanalysts start to discuss the cause of aggression. At its most simple there are two theories. The first states that aggression arises when a human being's basic needs are frustrated. This theory is based upon the homeostatic theory of motivation, which states that the organism has a built-in tendency to equilibrium, to homeostasis; when inner tension arises the organism is programmed to reduce that tension through incorporating food, water or finding an object that will satisfy a sexual need. Aggression arises when one of these needs is frustrated. Aggression is therefore a reaction to frustration. The other theory states that aggression is a basic instinct in man. Those who hold the latter theory say that man is a savage creature by nature, but those who follow the former state that man is essentially benign and only becomes savage when frustrated of his basic biological needs. I believe that both theories are wrong. The homeostatic theory is wrong because it fails to account adequately for certain areas of human experience such as a person's love of beauty, the individual who dies for his country, and, emotional and mental satisfactions in favour of which an individual will be prepared to sacrifice pleasures associated with the homeostatic theory. Although there must be few analysts today who hold the homeostatic theory, there are many who hold what is in fact one of its consequences: that aggression arises through frustration of a basic biological need. Some would extend this to include frustration of emotional needs. The theory that man is innately aggressive does not give sufficient account of the transformations of instinct which have progressively taken place in the evolution of mankind. I want therefore to put forward another theory and to do this I will start from a piece of experience and its interpretation.

Vignette

In the early 1970s I worked as a psychotherapist at HM Prison Grendon, near Aylesbury, England. Grendon is a psychiatric prison, and group therapy is the treatment of choice (Parker 1970). I was also associated at this time with an organization whose goal was the social rehabilitation of prisoners. It was the philosophy of this organization that rehabilitation started from the day that a man first went to prison. For this purpose then I went one day to interview a man who had just been remanded in custody at Wandsworth Prison. This young man had entered the house next door to where he lived, where he found the ten-year-old girl, Isabella. He pulled her by the hair around the top landing and then dragged her screaming down the stairs. When he got her to the ground floor he raped her and then killed her by bashing her head against a wall.

I was shown into the interview room by the prison officer and I sat on a wooden upright chair with the prisoner opposite me and a bare wooden table between us. He spoke in an affectionate manner towards me; he was nervous and looked very young. He looked bewildered, as if he had been catapulted into this world from another planet. After explaining to him the purpose of my visit and asking him for the date of his trial, and he giving me some details about his legal representation, I set about asking him about his crime. He had known Isabella quite well, I gathered. The problem arose when it came to the day of the crime. He remembered that he had gone on his bicycle down to the greengrocer. He had come back and he had seen Isabella in the garden and he had gone to play with her and then there had been an accident. I pressed him to tell me exactly what had happened. 'We were playing along the stairs', he told me, 'and then Isabella screamed.'

'What made her scream?'

'She was hurt.'

'Can you remember what happened?'

'It wouldn't have happened if her mother had been there. She should have come back. Young children should not be left on their own. You never know what might happen to them.'

He then wandered off as if in a dream. He started to talk about Isabella's mother, Josephine:

'We used to be together, you see.'

'You mean you were having an affair?'

He smiled with embarrassment and apparent guilt. I pressed him to talk but he remained silent. I tried to talk of other things. At one moment he murmured,

'Isabella saw us.'

'Is that what made you attack her?'

'Hair. Oh heavens – stairs.' He then murmured:

'Accident – Oh no!'

He was now only semi-talking to me. I had the impression that some visual images were flashing across the 'memory screen' and he was giving his reaction to them. At this point in the conversation a very strange thing happened to me: I fell asleep, or at least I would have done so had I not struggled with all my might against it. It was in the morning. I was sitting on a hard wooden upright chair. He commented:

'What, sleepy?' and he smiled again with embarrassment.

It was as if an anaesthetic slug had been fired into me. I struggled on with the interview but all my energy was directed towards keeping awake. The interview came to an end. I returned for a second interview about a week later. Again when we talked of his crime he went into his 'memory screen' mode and I was overcome with sleepiness.

A week after the second interview he went on trial at the Old Bailey, was found guilty and received a very long prison sentence. A few days later a prison officer opened up his cell in the morning and found that he had hanged himself.

I will give you my reconstruction of these events. The facts were that he had committed the crime of which he was accused. When I was interviewing him I don't think that he was consciously suppressing knowledge or lying to me. I think a part of his mind had blanked out his crime and just the odd flashes came back to him but not what he had done himself. My conjecture is that subsequent to the trial a memory of what he had done came back to him and that is was as a consequence that he hanged himself.

DISCUSSION

In a psychoanalytic treatment the analyst represents a part of the patient's mind which I have termed the *embryo mind*. Speaking generally, we know the mind's enormous potential. The human race has been blessed with Plato, Michaelangelo, Shakespeare, Mozart, Kant, Marx, Einstein and hosts of others too numerous to name. We all know the heights of which the mind is capable. It is my experience as a psychoanalyst that many minds have a latent potential capable of considerable creative emotional work. This is the emotional correlate of what Vygotsky named the *proximal zone*. He meant by this that part of the mind which is capable of further cognitive development. The *embryo mind* is the *proximal zone* but applied to the emotional sphere of the mind. It is the *embryo mind* that the analyst represents. The phenomenon of the analyst as external representative of this inner capacity of mind is called the *transference*. My mind was knocked for six when I was interviewing this violent prisoner. On the basis of my *countertransference* I am led to infer that his *embryo mind* was being violently smothered by a part of the mind which is known in psychoanalytic discourse as the *archaic superego*. I have found a model of the mind where different parts are, in relation to other parts of the mind, indispensable for understanding the emotional phenomena I encounter in clinical work. So my own personal experience of being slugged by an anaesthetic dart in itself leads to the inference that his *embryo mind* is being violently attacked. This inference receives confirming evidence in view of the fact that the memory of what he has done to Isabella has been almost entirely obliterated. This paralleled the fact that my mind was not entirely knocked out – a small part remained struggling.

There are three main aspects of this constellation of physical and mental action:

(1) A savage tyrant part of the mind – the *archaic superego* – is attacking the part of the mind with all the creative potential – the *embryo mind* – with the result that events of great importance are wiped out.

(2) The young man attacks with great brutality a ten-year-old girl.

(3) In interview with the young man an analyst's mind is nearly knocked unconscious.

Number Two is an infamous public event; Number Three is a personal private event passing between two people; Number One, however, is an entirely private inner drama. Now I want to trace things in the following manner.

The hypothesis is that the murderer blotted out the memory of what he had done because he felt so appallingly guilty. As you can imagine it was a crime which was reported in the media and sent ripples of shocked outrage through the public community. The world at large experienced the horror which the criminal himself could not experience. It is a phenomenon often observed in clinical psychoanalysis that what is not experienced by the agent himself is projected outwards and experienced in the wider community. The only person who had no conscious horror of the event was the man who perpetrated it. My hypothesis is that to allow himself to know what he had done caused an insupportable guilt. It was guilt, therefore, that led him to blot out the memory of what he had done. The anaesthetizing of my mind was the external correlate of this blotting out of the memory of his crime and the source of this attack on my mind was the very same guilt. My further hypothesis is that the emotional origin of that savage attack upon Isabella was also guilt.

Guilt is a feeling consequent upon an action. Guilt only makes sense if it was within the field of possibility for me not to do the action which produces the guilt. What I am saying, then, is that in the murderer there was a prior guilt that led to the killing of Isabella; that there was enormous guilt about the slaughter going on in his own mind. When he killed Isabella he had entirely surrendered himself into the power of that part of his mind which Melanie Klein (1975) first named the *archaic superego*.

The guilt about the inner situation is so great that it impels him to dramatize it in the outer world. When the inner drama is catapulted into the outer world an actual killing occurs and the man is caught and sentenced to prison. Punishment is society's revenge against the perpetrator of the crime but it is also the medicine of healing. This is, paradoxically I believe, the driving motive behind the crime. This is illustrated most clearly in Dostoievsky's (1870) *Crime and Punishment*. The novel opens with Raskolnikov brutally axing the old woman to death. The main portion of the book describes Raskolnikov's doubt: 'Shall I or shan't I confess?' He finally does confess and is sent off to hard labour in Siberia. The reader understands, however, that through the relationship with Sonia the punishment is the first step towards recovering a sane mind. With my murderer at the moment at which recovery might have started he killed himself.

CONCLUSION

Guilt may be the instigator of violent outbursts of the sort I have tried to describe. In such outbursts aggression – which is a natural endowment of human beings – is used destructively rather than constructively. I have sketched the activity in the mind, using an example, that produces this guilt. To go into how these activities in the mind originated would take us into another area of inquiry. What I am stating is that it is guilt, a guilt which is not conscious, which accounts for these sudden outbursts of violent rage. This process was first described in the psychoanalytic literature by Freud (1916a).

To return to where I started, these violent outbursts of murderous rage neither occur because a biological need has become frustrated nor because aggression is innate in man. The problem is in whose service the aggression is being employed. It is when it is employed against the potential capacities of the mind that guilt arises. A person does not feel guilt unless there was an alternative activity open to him. The origin of some violence lies in guilt. This means that an inner unconscious decision has been made. That the origin of violence is to be found in the ego rather than in an instinctual urge means that it is a personal construction in which it is possible to find meaning. There is, therefore, some hope because the possibility of constructing things differently is always there. The more we understand guilt and the way it comes about in the mind the more chance we have of arriving at measures which are prophylactic against the eruption of violence in our society. It is to this I believe that we should address ourselves.

Murderous Guilt

Nikolaas Treurniet

INTRODUCTION

Scientific research into the psychoanalytic process is difficult to conduct with any degree of methodological soundness. After all, the basic observations are not public, nor, usually, are the ways in which observations are arranged, deduced and summarized – in order either to develop or test hypotheses. The clinical retrospection by which post factum causes are deduced from consequences produces circular thinking (Wallerstein 1991). Conversely, the psychoanalytic process is often disturbed in an unacceptable manner when basic observations are made public in a methodologically responsible way, although this is viewed rather differently from the way it used to be (Weiss and Sampson 1986). These restrictions severely limit research. Ever since countertransference has become a respected concept, justifiable doubt has arisen about the analyst's ability to give an 'objective' report on what happens in an analysis. As in the law there is good reason for applying *unus testis nullus testis* – one witness is no witness; more than one person is necessary to make argumentation credible: a *tertium comparationis*, an objective correlative. Through our knowledge of child development we do know how important the triangular relationship is for the development of the sense of reality. So the more witnesses there are, the better. In every analysis the danger of a *folie à deux* is very much present. Hence the vital importance of supervision, consultations with colleagues, clinical study-groups and so forth. In the Netherlands, Verhage (1994), in particular, has rigorously formulated and applied this principle to clinical practice. This chapter will describe one particular aspect of such an application: the exploration of unconscious determinants of a crime. (See also category (4) in the next section.)

FRAMEWORK OF THE RESEARCH

The analysis – forty-five minutes five times a week – took place in a residential setting, the Van Mesdag Clinic in Groningen for delinquent patients placed in government custody. At the time the analysand, a man, was twenty-seven years old. His crime was murder. The analyst wrote a report after each session on the day itself, but never during the session. The reports, covering twenty sessions each (known as one period), were sent to four different commentators who, independently of one another, sent in their written comments divided into specific categories, to a central registration point, to which no one but the leader of the project, Verhage, had access – not even the analyst himself. Once every six months, that is, after each five or six periods, the commentaries were sent to all members of the project group. The analyst produced a synopsis of these, setting out the agreements as well as the differences, after which this material was discussed for one whole day. This discussion was recorded on tape, typed out and then sent to all the participants. The analyst was supervised at a frequency of once a month. The supervisor did not write commentaries himself, but did attend the six-monthly discussion and contributed to it. The categories by which the commentators judged the material were as follows:

(1) *Transference neurosis:* How do you perceive the patient in the real situation? What is most important in the process of transference neurosis? Which actual factors, as opposed to the analytic technique (e.g. the residential setting or other artefacts or external influences), have influenced the process and so altered the material?

(2) *Structure:* Which change in the defence mechanisms, other ego functions and/or object relations do you find important during this period? Likewise for drive organisation and superego/ego-ideal formation.

(3) *Technique:* Which interventions by the analyst have brought about changes in the material and/or influenced the process?

(4) *Crime:* Has anything during this period helped in your opinion, to 'explain' the patient's crime or at least to make it more explicable?

(5) *In the realm of speculation:* What interpretation or behaviour on the part of the analyst would you have omitted or vice versa: What kind of influence would this or could this have had on the analytical process and what are your arguments for this?

Each of these categories was subdivided into factual commentary on the one hand and speculations, hypotheses and predictions on the other.

The team of commentators consisted of two women and two men. Both women were very experienced analysts from Amsterdam (Jeanne Lampl-de Groot and Bets Frijling-Schreuder). Both men were from Groningen, one of them being a very experienced analyst indeed, with considerable experience in forensic psychiatry (Hein Goudsmit), while the other had extensive experience of psychotherapy with delinquents in the Van Mesdag Clinic (Koos Reicher).

THE CRIME

The following is taken from the law authorities' records. During a stay in Sweden, when he was twenty-two, the patient, along with a Dutch friend, K, who was a couple of years younger, killed another Dutch boy, F. The patient's friend, K, lured F to the house where the murder took place on the pretext that F's girlfriend, who had been raped shortly before (by someone who plays no further part in this account) would be there. *En route* they talked a little, in the front room, they 'smoked' a bit and after a while F was bound hand and foot with a rope. K took the initiative and the victim allowed it all without protest, even when he was gagged with a scarf. Then they went to the back room, where the victim's hands were briefly untied and he was tied to a post with his hands behind his back. After some hesitation and 'discussion' amongst themselves K started to undress F. Now F began to use his voice. He said he would not take the matter any further if they set him free instantly. This was fatal. Now the patient started to interfere. Probably to shut F up, he hit him on the head several times with the handle of a knife, after which F collapsed and fainted. The patient and K put a rope around his neck and tightened it vigorously. After that K cut one of F's wrists in such a way that his hand was effectively severed. Then the patient stabbed the victim in the neck, back and arm with a knife, penetrating his heart, lungs and carotid artery. According to the autopsy it was highly probable that F had by then already died from strangulation.

CASE HISTORY

The following is derived from biographical notes taken by staff at the Van Mesdag Clinic. The patient is the youngest of six children. His parents' marriage took place in 1932 and was known to be happy. The mother, born in 1906, died in August 1948, just after the patient's fourth birthday. She had the strongest personality in the family and was the binding element in it. She is characterized as a nice, calm woman who was not afraid to assert herself either. She came from a farming family. The patient's father, born in 1889, had worked as a deck-hand on a sand-dredger and after his wife's death took a steady job as a factory worker. His children described him as fanatically religious; he was totally absorbed by his Roman Catholic faith.

After the mother's death he was completely unable to care for the family, especially in an emotional sense. He spent a lot of time with his children, but was more like one of them, and this applies especially to his attitude towards the patient. He allowed himself to be belittled at home and also by official bodies. The children felt themselves to be at the mercy of outsiders. When interviewed, the father was experienced as a friendly but gloomy person who saw himself as having been knocked about by life. That, in a sense, was true: because of his father's alcoholism he was brought up in a foster-home and after the death of his (motherly) wife he was totally at loss. The children appreciated him, but also found him very difficult: for instance when something was bothering him, he would sulk and shut himself off, creating a tense and intolerable atmosphere.

The patient's life history clearly shows the extent to which his mother's illness and the very changeable circumstances of his upbringing, had had a disruptive effect on his emotional development. The very early years were probably adequate, but little is known: in last year of her life the mother was in a hospital far from home for four weeks. A mastectomy took place there. Subsequently she came home for four weeks, after which she had to return for a biopsy. She was at home, ill, for seven months after that, presumably in bed most of the time. Since she was increasingly bedridden, contact between the analysand and his mother took place more and more in her bed. Thus he was involved with her physical decline and – finally – her destruction. Because of the pleuritis carcinomatosa (the spread of cancer to the chest wall), the direct cause of death, she had serious difficulty in breathing. For the child it seemed that his mother was crushed, killed. This did not even happen at home, so it became very mysterious.

At the time of mother's death the family structure was as follows: the father was fifty years old, then came a son of fifteen, then four daughters of fourteen, eleven, ten and eight respectively, and last the patient, who was four years old at the time. From the children's point of view connections within the family were continually disrupted, because the domestic help from the Roman Catholic family-care centre changed so often. Little more is known about the patient as a toddler and during latency except that he had enuresis until he was seven, that he repeated his first year at primary school, probably because he was not yet ready for school, and that he was intensely afraid of the dark. The latter was exacerbated by his solitary confinement in the cellar, where his sisters often put him when they were sick of his provocations. The patient invited punishment a good deal, even more so as he grew older. At thirteen he was put in a Roman Catholic reform school by order of the court because of his behavioural problems. After that some minor offences followed; nothing serious, but enough to result in punishment time and time again.

Before the analysis started one of the research's commentators (Reicher) produced a survey of the existing reports, in which he also wrote down a number of suppositions, a summary of which follows.

The mother left home at twelve to become a housemaid. The father's youth was difficult due to his father's alcoholism and he ended up in a foster-home. The couple had to get married when she was twenty-six and he was thirty-four years of age. The eldest son, the 'reason' for the marriage, got himself into a lot of trouble when he was young, for theft amongst other things. He frequently got a telling-off from his father and often a hiding too in the presence of the analysand. It is said that the mother protected the children from the father time and time again. She was the axis, the driving force of the family. In relation to the mother, the father was not so much a father as a child along with the other children, something which the mother possibly encouraged. In 1944 there was talk of another pregnancy, although this was contra-indicated because of the mother's known kidney trouble. The analysand, the child of this pregnancy, was named after the father's alcohol-addicted father. The mother fell ill when the analysand was not even three. He was seen as mother's favourite. Before her death the mother made father promise to be sure to take care of the analysand.

After mother's death the father was at loss for long spells at a time: very touchy and emotional and rarely at home. He was completely absorbed by his own sorrow and abandoned his children literally as well as emotionally. Despite help from neighbours, social services and so forth, the family was completely disturbed. It seems not impossible that the father had to cover up feelings of hate towards his youngest son – whom he could have seen as a contributory cause of the mother's illness and subsequent death, since the pregnancy was contra-indicated – by depression and feelings of guilt about the death of his wife. He was tied to the defence of his anger particularly, because he was the one responsible for the pregnancy and he had made his vows to the mother. It was the eldest daughter who was really the apple of her father's eye – she was also named after him – but the analysand was the father's link to the deceased. In short, ambivalence in abundance: he was too concerned, could not miss him and often had to try to show his love, all of which made him corruptible and ready for manipulation. The only area in which the father appeared firm was the Roman Catholic faith. It was only here that he set anything of a dependable example. He was, however, always referring to the inimitable figure of Christ, a completely unattainable ideal, an example, surely, of the fanaticism which the father demonstrated and demanded.

Based on the anamnestic data and the material of the first three months of analysis, the study-group arrived at the hypothesis that there was a very close relation between the crime, on the one hand, and the trauma of the experiences surrounding the process of dying of the mother on the other. Unconscious feelings of guilt especially, were seen as having a decisive, motivating role. This I call the central hypothesis central in relation to category (4) (understanding the crime), a crime powered by feelings of guilt, as the title indicates.

THE 'MATERIAL'

In the following review of the research material only one question will be considered: 'In your opinion has anything occurred which clarifies or 'explains' the crime committed by this patient or at least makes it more explicable?' A certain artificiality is inevitable here. It is hard to answer the question satisfactorily without taking into account the whole analytic process. However, this goes far beyond the scope of this chapter, which will have to remain a broad description only of the analysis in all categories, (1), (2), (3) and also (5). And even this restricted review cannot be complete. To include all the material obtained by each commentator on category (4) alone would require more that the total space allotted to me. I have therefore restricted myself to those sessions that were considered most relevant to the crime's 'explicability' by the largest number of commentators. The number of the session is indicated in brackets.

In (5) the analysand casually mentions that as a child he already knew he would murder someone one day. He gives as his motive: I am such a weak boy, I never count as one of the real boys, I am too scared to play soccer. A few days later (7) he recalls a terrifying dream from his past: *he was walking in a corridor while there was a heavy storm outside; large frog-like monsters pressed themselves against the windows and he was scared to death that the windows would give way and the monsters would hurt him.* He believes this was connected with the fact that his guinea-pig had lost so much weight. When it dies, much later in the analysis (532), it becomes clear how much of an unconscious substitute for the mother the guinea-pig was. In (9) he describes how he used to do sadistic things to animals, like throwing frogs in the fire or burying creatures alive and how terribly guilty he felt afterwards. In subsequent sessions he describes in detail his current safeguard against 'such sadistic things': the inexorably strict religion of Jehovah's Witness which enables him 'to fight the seven-headed monster' (18).

In (24) he produces memories of his violent jealousy of Katja, his eldest sister and father's favourite. Father took her to town on Saturdays and the analysand was not allowed to go with them, but he blackmailed his father by following him and being given money to go away. His thieving and general misbehaviour really started when he was six years old. He had bought twenty roosters for five cents each and sold them again for twice the amount. His brother objected to it, but his father said he could keep the money because he had earned it fair and square. However, when the analysand had raised five more young roosters on oat-waste from the flour-mill nearby, his father took them and – in the presence of the analysand, who was aghast – chopped their heads off one by one. They would, after all, be so tasty for Christmas.

Not long after that, the father also smashed the skull of the analysand's rabbit. This is followed by the story of a sheep-dog he looked after but tormented as well. The analysand became furious when the dog was afraid of him. Whenever possible he took the dog inside, near the fire, but his father and his brother made him put it outside again. Finally it caught pneumonia and died. In (26) what has been bothering him all week becomes clear: he has a headache and is irritable and hypersensitive to noise because he masturbated four days ago. 'So punishment does come!' It then becomes evident that his hypersensitivity to sound has to do with his fantasies when masturbating: each sound feels like a whiplash; so whiplashing is what it is all about.

During the following sessions he talks with increasing shame of his masturbation problems. He has masochistic fantasies when he masturbates. He loves to look at a book about Mina, the Goddess of the Whip, while he is at it. He also constructed a box with nails attached and into it so that as he lay on his back the nails would scratch his chest. As he did this, in his fantasy he was split, both actively sadistic and at the same time enjoying along with the passive other, whom he also was. In the same session (43) he recalls that he loved it when his father helped him do a wee-wee and stroked his little penis in doing so. In (56) he describes a terribly frightening event during his detention in the Roman Catholic reform school. He was sexually abused by a much older boy and nearly choked with fear when he was forced. Later on he mutually masturbated with a friend, which was no problem at all. It was a big problem however, to lie in bed with another boy and be affectionate: that is what he finds most shameful of all, being affectionate. In (66) he casually mentions that his father went to Australia for a year to visit his sister Katja, who had emigrated there. 'Strangely enough it was just before I turned twenty-one and left for Sweden. It was a shame for Dad, because when he returned, I had just committed that murder. He had written to me from the ship, telling me that he had bought an expensive bottle of wine for us to drink together.'

In (74) he establishes that he is terribly split; it is like a cycle: after the debauchery of filth, the masturbation, comes a longing for eternal peace, but before long that becomes boring. Then in (75) there is a remark about the murder. The first time he consciously and clearly thought: 'I am going to kill someone', was when he was eighteen. The immediate cause was a poster which said that you always should do what you plan to do. He knew he would go through with it as soon as he became of age, for then he could really be held responsible, then he could really be punished. They could not prove anything in Sweden; after all he did have a watertight alibi, and when that became obvious, he

confessed voluntarily. However, this was on a Saturday so the judge had
to come all the way from his weekend cottage to Stockholm. Fearing the
judge's reproachful eyes, he didn't at first want to admit to his active role
in the murder. He says he has longed for punishment all his life, to be in
a cell and be taken care of, and be especially ascetic as a deliverance from
his atrocious inner fantasies: hence his becoming a Jehovah's Witness.

One memory (89), dating from when he was eleven, begins a period
involving not only much associative material, but also actions during and
outside the analysis, in which magical thought is central. At that time he
had taken his big brother's razor-blade and said to a girl at school: 'How
about me cutting your hand?' She laughed and he cut her. She bled
severely and the patient got a terrible fright. He had not imagined that
such a thing could really have an effect. A complete series of punishments
followed. He continues pushing away reality during the next hour and
tries to scare me with magic: 'The Holy Ghost is a sort of instrument and
could also make you drop dead just like that.' He expresses a similar idea
in (124) when he tells me that at a tin-factory, where he used to work,
he was terribly afraid he would jump into the boiling lead just like that,
as if drawn towards it by an invisible hand in order to prove he was
invulnerable.

He raises the subject of his mother in (130). She had a Swedish name
– the reason he started to learn Swedish as his first foreign language. So
he had good reason to go to Sweden as soon as he became of age. His
mother was so fond of him and she minded so much that she was dying,
leaving him behind when he was so little and so young. He tells me that
after her death he became increasingly troublesome to his sisters; they
had to feed him and he soiled his trousers. Then the idea occurs to him
that, by doing this, he might have been trying to say: I am so young
again that mother will have to return. 'And maybe I went to Sweden to
recover her, or part of her' (131). Shortly after this he admits to me with
shame that he painted blood on his body with red paint, drew wounds
on his arms and torso and subsequently masturbated while looking in
the mirror (143).

Then in (164) he speaks his conviction: 'Fortunately I am
invulnerable; reality does not exist for me and so there are no
consequences; somehow I have always known that the murder I
committed would go unpunished, even before I did it. Committing a
murder is different for me from when other people do it'. The same
magical grandiosity continues, not only in his thoughts, but also in his
behaviour in the clinic, provoking increasingly severe punishment. In
(178) he brings a stamp with the Queen's head on it along to the session
and tears it to pieces. Jokingly he says she will probably die now, or might

die if he were to send her a lot of those torn-up stamps, because she would grow nervous and have a heart-attack, just as his father did. In (184) he explains that his fantasies are really much worse than his actions. He is only really wicked when he masturbates and fantasizes torture and triumph. In (186) he says that he really believes in magic: if he were to make a doll in someone's image and stick pins into it, the person would actually die. 'If I really wanted to, I could do magic, but I don't want to, things might get out of hand.' Then, for the first time, I am able to show him a link with the feeling he might have had as a child, when his mother became ill: it was as if, when he became so angry with mother for being ill, things got out of hand. And the more ill she became, the angrier he grew, and the angrier he grew, the more ill she became: he made her ill by his anger.

In (223) he starts to ask himself why, in a relationship with another person, he absolutely cannot tolerate it if he is not the only one who counts for them and is not absolutely in control. He also says it is very true that he cannot endure jealousy. So he wonders whether or not he felt terribly deprived by his mother's illness and death. Then suddenly he remembers what he was thinking just before he committed the murder: I am going to prison and I want to go to prison. At that moment the idea comes to him: I have killed mother and I want her back, that is why I want to be somewhere where I feel totally secure. But this is also the punishment and penalty for the murder I have committed. In (233) he talks of his experiences with Jack London's book *The Call of the Wild*. He tells the story with a growing intensity of feeling, interrupting himself from time to time in order to laugh it off. The more moved he is, the more he must call it sentimental. The story boils down to this: a man rescues a dog from certain death. After this the dog is absolutely faithful to the man and willing to prove it in the most absurd ways, until one day in spring the mating-call of a wolf is heard. The dog goes to the wolf for one night only and that very night his owner is murdered by Indians. When the dog returns, it is so sad and angry, that it attacks the Indians, savaging two to death, at which the others flee. After that he became the terror of the Indians; he grows to twice the size of a normal dog, but nevertheless every year he returns to the scene of the crime to have a little cry.

In my interpretation I make it clear to the analysand that his own feelings would have been something like this: When strange men – the doctors – took his mother away, his revenge was: I am going to become twice my size and be the terror of the neighbourhood; I have become a dangerous murderer, and I had to do this in order to revenge my mother. After discussing this the analysand becomes so emotional that, for the first time during his analysis, he has to swallow his tears and ten minutes before the end of the session he asks if it is not time yet. We are getting too close to home and that, too, is something for discussion. For the last ten minutes he cries silently, saying nothing.

In (243) it turns out that he feels less and less at home with the Jehovah's Witnesses: increasingly he cannot be a martyr with them and it looks as though in committing murder that was one of his aims. In (293) he voices the feeling that Holland is really a very pleasant country, far more tolerant than others and why not? He goes on to say that he does in a way appreciate analysis. And, regarding the Jehovah's Witnesses, I should not assume that their way of life is terribly orthodox. Sometimes things are very cosy, but...aren't they all a little neurotic if they need such a strict religion? Then he says that he never ever relaxes with a book, it is always the Bible, or the other extreme, comic-books. The last time he could really read a book at ease was in jail in Sweden: 'Raskolnikov,[1] a crime out of guilt and his mother went along to Siberia with him when he was convicted' (his very own words!).

He talks about his masochistic fantasies and actions in more detail in (324). He wants to seduce people to approach him in a sexually sadistic manner. In this way the other person is tied to him by feelings of guilt towards him, and so must pay the penalty by spoiling, cherishing and pampering him. At the same time all this has to remain unreal and so it is done under the influence of hashish. It is really a kind of game, a strange, unreal scenario. I then make the connection with the ultimate goal of it all, the cherishing and spoiling he has to earn by punishment and torture. The unreality seems to indicate that it is about a memory or event from the past, one that must push out the reality of the present: I can only have mother back if I have done to myself as I have done to her. I am able to show him how he also seeks punishment in all sorts of other areas, not just the sexual one, and how he confuses reality and fantasy. So his fantasized murder of his mother is more real than the actual murder of F, his victim.

Surprised, he says that he now understands why he had always consciously known that he would commit murder one day; unconsciously its purpose was to make him the murderer he already was. Only when the real murder had been committed could he be punished for his fantasy murder. To him (and to me) an important part of his masochistic fantasies now becomes understandable. It is like a game of make-believe in which the unbearable reality of his mother's death is

---

1   The protagonist of Dostoievski's (1870) *Crime and Punishment*.

'solved' and 'repaired' by reversing it. The unbearable reality – 'I have destroyed you and so have lost you' – has been made into a reversible game: 'By having you destroy, hurt and punish me, I will have my dear mother back and I'll be cherished and spoiled.'

For the first time without being prompted he says in (344): 'I am really just a very small, angry child, stamping my feet in rage. I cannot even stand it when I do not know my physics book by heart after leafing through it once.' I then suggest to him that his fantasy is that he might always have had his way if his mother had stayed alive. He ends the session by saying that Narcissus must not only have been in love with himself; he must have found himself unendurable as well.

Shortly after this more discoveries come to the surface. Just before the end of one hour (345) he says he has been having very strange fantasies lately. He has created a new sculpture with all sorts of round shapes and he fantasizes that he is small and walks amongst these round shapes as if they were the whole world. In (353) he tells me he has produced a new piece of work in creative therapy. It is a sort of hidden tit, he says, and done so well, that the creative therapist says it is professional. He could go to art school, though he does not want to – having to make all those baroque little objects; what does he want with them anyway? This sounds languid and bored and the way he says it seems to me flat, empty and sad. He is much more open in the next session (354) and talks about his feelings of hopelessness. He firmly believes in the teachings of the Jehovah's Witnesses, but really dislikes their gatherings: he cannot belong any more, he is too wicked: he is being put under more and more pressure, sometimes he can take a little break from his conscience by smoking some hashish, but it does not really help. In fact it is a situation with no possible solution: on the one hand he wants his firm belief in the strict doctrine, but on the other hand, being a murderer, a homosexual and somebody who masturbates, he is bound to be cast aside.

Of course, the more real the murder becomes, the more doomed he is. He says he pondered on it yesterday, but immediately after forgot what it was. It is very hard for him to fall asleep at the moment and most of all he likes to listen to Beethoven's violin concerto. He can follow and retain the part of the violin so well that it is as if his mother is singing to him. He does realize more and more that he committed the murder out of helplessness and a longing for shelter and punishment. Soon he wants to show me his sculptures, but without playing the childish game of me having to admire him; no, he has got something to say with these, he just does not know what. One is a breast in a kind of cover. It is very immaculate and smooth, not even interrupted by a nipple; in contrast the cover is rough. He is saying literally: 'This is my tit, I am looking for something within myself.'

He starts the next session (355) by telling me he is feeling so empty again. I suggest to him that he is looking for an ideal in the perfect breast, something in his own person which ought to be there and which is a substitute, or should be, for the religion of the Jehovah's Witness. It is the only thing that can make him full again. However, this religion is also his death-sentence, making it impossible for him to stay alive. Yet because of his need for punishment it is the only solution to his deep feeling of guilt: by sacrificing himself, he in a sense revives his mother. By creating a perfect breast, he magically repairs the mother's breast he destroyed, and by entrusting himself to the mighty, immaculate and perfect Jehovah, he at least keeps all this secure. He is literally saying: 'The Jehovah's Witness religion is my mother, it is also the perfect tit which is my only salvation'. It is as crystal-clear, logical, smooth, perfect and purified as the breast he has created. His problem is, of course, self-destruction; the necessity to recover repair and maintain the mother-Jehovah-breast: to save himself he has to destroy himself. Because this too is so unbearable, he desperately seeks help in hashish, in art and in the analysis.

When we have discussed this he says it is exactly how he feels and asks how such a thing could have happened. Then we discuss the fact that a three-year-old is almost bound to feel he is the cause of all the bad things that happen to him – the more so because it gives him the feeling that he at least has some influence on events. If he were really to feel how helpless he is, it would be so unbearably frightening that he could only feel panic and that would be unendurable. So it becomes clear to him that the normal process of gradually being disillusioned, yet still feeling safe was badly upset for him, because everything went too far too fast, especially since this was at a time when his mother was the complete source of all perfection, and consequently of all good feelings about the self. Besides that, his father did not prove such a good candidate for this role later on because, even though he loved his father, he did not think him strong.

It is very apparent that when neither analysis, nor sculpting, nor his Jehovah's Witness belief provide him with that perfection, he withdraws into his own perfect make-believe world: hashish, megalomania, not giving a shit about anything, using and ridiculing people – yet it does not really satisfy him. The analysand then says that this is his biggest problem: everything has to be so passionate, so extreme, so total; if only he could stand it when this is not so; what does he have to do to be able to live with the feeling that the perfect breast is nowhere to be found?

In fact, he cannot live without a religion or a faith; every human being has religious feelings and all other religions are inferior to the beliefs of the Jehovah's Witnesses, to him this is the implacable, logical, unavoidable truth. He cannot really abandon this wonderful ideal; he could never become a Catholic again, he sees that as ostentation and fraud. Here I make the connection with his father; after all he was fanatically Catholic, but he was exposed by the analysand, even before the mother's death, as someone with little backbone, who wanted all the attention for himself.

It is a few months later when next he approaches the subject of his crime. Then the father is discussed a little more thoroughly. In (420) he raises the subject of father being suspicious and stingy. Father had been afraid the cashbox would be stolen. The analysand himself advised him to enjoy the money while he still could, to spend it all, not save it. It was he who suggested that father should go to Australia and visit Katja...'and when he came back I was in jail!' He says he thinks he was furious that father actually followed his suggestion; you see, father should have said: no, no way, I am saving all that money for you and furthermore I do not want to go to Australia at all, because I do not want to be away from you for one single day. Could the murder not also have been a revenge for this? He goes onto say that the summer holidays will be coming shortly and that he really does not begrudge me them. I point out that he had said something along those lines to his father too. After a silence, he says ominously that the world will have gone to blazes in a couple of years anyhow, the end is near, but people are blind and do not see that as yet. Here his feelings of revenge towards me surface, and I tell him so.

In (438) he says that he still strongly believes that he can go on living only when he has suffered the death penalty. This is nonsense of course, but only then will he have done penance and be able to continue. He says that now he can understand why he started believing so rigidly and fanatically: the code of the Jehovah's Witness is as tough and inhuman as his own strict conscience. He did feel better for it for some time, rather blameless and 'endearing again', but he could not live with it, because that whole religion was a sort of death-penalty. 'Now I find it hard to believe I did not masturbate in the first one-and-a-half years that I belonged to that group.' In (439) he starts to recall his father's heart-attack. In fact he has always had the fantasy that he was responsible for it because he was always such a handful. 'I must have been a nail in his coffin.' Father was such a strange man, so weak and easily manipulated. He recalls his crying-spell 'which lasted a week' in the Roman Catholic reform school, after his father had written to him that he found it hard to go on living without his mother. It appears he then got the feeling that his father was only interested in his own sorrow and not in his, yet he also felt he should be a replacement for his mother to him. Otherwise his father would be miserable, which in turn made him feel guilty: he had the feeling, after all, it was because of him that mother had died.

In (468) he says: 'I never told you exactly what happened during the murder; it was really a game. Only, it got totally out of hand.' From the start it was an unreal affair to him, something like a game of torture: we are going to play at it, it is not for real. It would not be fun if it were not a game, because then he would not be in charge. K, his fellow offender, and the patient were going to wait for F, the victim. The patient left everything to K, telling him: you think up something. Throughout, K was the active one, except for one moment – more about that later. To lure F, K thought up the story about a girl waiting for him and kept on talking. The patient followed his lead in this very unreal atmosphere. Upstairs in the warehouse the analysand went to stand by the window and looked out. F let himself be tied up by K, after which K asked the analysand for a knife – which he had on him – which he wanted so as to cut F's clothes to undress him. When F protested, K began calling him rude names and using worse and worse threats, for example, we are going to kill you. This made the analysand very scared – after all, this had to remain a game – and he snapped at K to stop for heaven's sake. F started to scream with fear and at that moment the analysand just could not take it any longer and hit F on the head with the handle of the knife. But that was only to silence him, because he could not stand the shouting and F's fear any longer. Then pandemonium broke out. 'However silly this may sound, I can't hurt a fly. I couldn't bear F's fear. Suddenly it wasn't a game anymore and I had to shut him up by hitting him on the head. After that F said groggily: 'I won't report this to the police if you untie me now.' Then we really got scared. It was as though the damage had already been done, could not be reversed and must be brought to a halt.' F was strangled by both of them and when he was already dead, the patient stabbed him in the back. During this account the analysand becomes more and more emotional. Tears of bitter regret run down his cheeks, as he says: 'It all got so terribly out of hand.'

In (532) he describes how his guinea-pig died. It was awful, the animal's breathing became more and more difficult and the analysand felt utterly powerless. At first he was furious with the vet, who could do nothing, but then he realized that it felt like a murder: if you die young, it is like a violent death. Others don't lift a finger, so they are really murderers, because they ought to be able to do something about it! In (537) he starts talking about his masturbation fantasies again. It is nicest when he is tortured by his sisters, all four of them, and sometimes his brother may join in, but his father has no part in it at all. He is eliminated, he says laughingly, but there are always onlookers. After a silence he says that there is something else too. It serves his sisters right that there are onlookers, so others can see what is happening. After another silence he says with shame that there is something else which is also essential: Maria Z (a girl he met and fell in love with at the Jehovah's Witnesses and who has the same Christian name as his mother and his favourite sister) is among the onlookers and watches him being tortured.

In (603) this fantasy changes: now he is nailed to a cross and the last event of his life is that his mother jerks him off and his sisters look on in admiration. There are still many spectators present. Yesterday, he continues, he walked around a jumble-sale (he is allowed to leave the clinic unaccompanied for a short while) and saw a crucifix for sale for thirty-five guilders. He said to the salesman: 'That's far too expensive man, it is not even worth ten guilders.' I suggested to him that Jesus was very important in his family home and that must sometimes have made him furious, because his mother, like his father, was a fanatic follower of Jesus. After all, Jesus was the good, pure favourite who had renounced all sexuality. He, on the other hand, like all little boys, was proud of his penis, and showed it to his mother but, as with his sisters, he always drew a blank. Maybe his masturbation fantasy is reparation for all of these intolerable injuries; he has eliminated father and is also punished by crucifixion for this mortal sin.

During the next session (604) he describes how a woman tried to chat him up in town, but then obviously waited for him to show some interest. Now he finds that unthinkable, intolerable: he cannot be actively masculine as long as he feels women are after his penis, because they do not have one themselves. Then he suddenly remembers how he restlessly wandered to the graveyard and had a strange impulse to pull a dove off a gravestone. Maybe he was a bit jealous of mother's dove: Jesus. Very much ashamed he goes on to tell me his latest masturbation fantasy: yesterday he looked at himself in a mirror, posing this way and that, getting more and more excited, working himself up slowly, for if he came too soon it would not be fun anymore, would it? However, the important thing was that he saw his own erection in the mirror, yes, that his whole body was actually a kind of erection. At that moment he fantasized that he was his mother who was looking at him, while he was being tortured, consequently he was Jesus and at that very moment he came.

DISCUSSION

I will rest the discussion mainly upon the central hypothesis contained in the title: crime resulting from guilt. However, I would like to call attention to a certain artificiality, namely that only material thought of by the commentators and the analyst as relevant to the crime, has been included. Everything relating to the process, structure, transference–countertransference continuum and technique has been purposely omitted. Despite this restriction, a clear development is visible. It is also important to realize that isolating the dependent variable, often desirable in scientific research, can only be an illusion in the field of psychoanalysis. It can clearly be deduced from this material, that feelings of guilt about the actual murder could be a cover for feelings about the fantasized murder of the mother or father. But the reverse could also be true: at any given time remorse, regret and sorrow for this crime suddenly appear intensely from behind feelings of guilt about what had been done to mother or father. So cause and effect cannot be clearly separated here: they are interdependent. Feelings that are a consequence of the crime mingle with feelings that have a causal significance. The two are in interaction and, moreover, can ward one another off, according to where the pain is least unbearable. As long as one is aware that mutual interaction by plural determinants – hence multicausality – is in operation here, one can avoid having expectations which are too great. This chapter is no more than a description of a description which all participants have tried with great care and determination to make objective by exploring different points of view.

I will now briefly summarize the material chronologically in order to show that during the analysis a development has occurred, which clarifies the meaning of the crime and also affects that part of the analytic process which the restrictions permit us to consider.

From the very beginning of the analysis it is clear how intensely a combination of sadism, grandiosity, defective sense of reality and magical thought dominates the analysand's present as well as his past behaviour. The father's behaviour with the young roosters, his own with the frogs and the sheepdog (7, 9, 24), the rapes he suffered at the Roman Catholic reform school (56) explain nothing of course, but they do indicate that danger and seduction were in the air. The wounding of the young girl (89) proves that something was thoroughly wrong at an early stage. Note his genuine surprise that this act had consequences which shows how strongly he already had to deny his own ability voluntarily to do something evil by the age of eleven. He implies something similar when he talks about his inclination to jump into the boiling lead (124).

In the analysis his masturbation fantasies play a large part in falsifying reality. They continue to be about gaining power over others, usually by making them feel guilty, and more intrapsychically, by his double identification during masturbation – by scratching his skin with nails (43), or simulating wounds with red paint (143) for example. In the not directly sexual field this is coupled to magical denial in various areas, the most common element being that fantasies are more real than actions, especially that the fantasized murder is worse than the real one. During the course of treatment the need for martyrdom also emerges as central, later becoming increasingly defined as a crucifixion ritual, in which the mother, especially, plays an important part. Then we gradually gain much clearer insight into the meaning of this fantasy-world, suggesting that this was his only 'solution' to his extreme helplessness during the mother's illness and death.

At the start of the analysis our patient indicates that even as a child he knew that he would murder somebody one day (5). He rationalizes this in various ways:'because he was such a weak boy' or 'because you should always do what you plan to do' (75), but by then the importance of punishment is showing through his bravado: he knew he would do it as soon as he had really come of age and so was truly responsible. Meanwhile he has told me the trigger for the murder at that particular time: the fact that father left him to go to his hated sister in Australia. In (130) and (131) the reason for his stay in Sweden becomes apparent: to recover something of mother. In (164) he announces that there are no consequences for him, he has always known he would not be punished (to him this means not executed) for the murder he has committed. In fact this was an important resistance in the analysis: I am a murderer, I am in paradise being cared for in the clinic and getting psychoanalysis into the bargain; you see, the laws of reality do not apply to me; that is why I need to be a Jehovah's Witness; at least that is real, because it is strict! In (233) the connection is made with feelings he remembers about the doctors who took and destroyed his loved (and hated) mother. In (243) his fantasies of martyrdom appear and his longing to be persecuted for noble reasons. Then in (293) he arrives at the insight that the need to be a Jehovah's Witness is an aspect of his neurosis and he ends with Raskolnikow. After he has been able to understand the function the masochistic fantasies have for him in (342) – the regaining of mother – there is rapid progress (344, 345, 353, 354, 355): insight into the repair function of his impossible ideal, the faith of the Jehovah's Witness and the perfect breast, the magic repair both of mother's breast and of his own world that he destroyed.

After the deep guilt related to his mother has become at least partially conscious and been worked through, the subject of the father is raised. In (420, 438, 439) his fear of having been a nail in his father's coffin, because of his father's heart-attack which he witnessed as a child, comes into focus, and through it he is able to make the connection with his anger about father's egocentricity. Only then, after repressed feelings of guilt about his mother and father have surfaced, do very real experiences connected with the crime appear

(468). This could, of course, only happen after the other meanings he gave to the crime had been 'soaked off'. After this his central masturbation fantasy (which is ideal) surfaces (603, 604): he is his mother, who looks at him and he experiences orgasm at the moment when, as Jesus, he is tortured and his father has been totally put aside. I will leave the dynamic meaning of this fantasy there; for further theoretical understanding I refer to Chasseguet-Smirgel's (1974) work on the relation between idealization and perversion.

EPILOGUE

A little more about what happened to the analysand. After three full years of analysis the government custody order was lifted and he could leave the clinic a free man (except for some ambulant support by rehabilitation officers). As often happens with patients who leave the clinic, he terminated the analysis, probably because, while there, he had found a homosexual partner, with whom he went to live. The analysand had a strong feeling that his partner would not put up with his continuing his analysis. The partner agreed to it only if it could become 'joint therapy'; which was something the analysand absolutely did not want. They did go and live together in a village, managing on the income the analysand made from his drawings and paintings. In 1980, six years after the termination of the analysis, I visited them. The relationship was stable, his work was quite satisfying and provided a regular enough income. In the autumn of 1991 I made contact again and to my shock learned that the analysand had died of a brain-tumor some years earlier. I had a long conversation with the patient's partner about the period after 1980. It emerged during that talk that the theme of guilt had remained important. It was a comfort to the analysand that, in a sense, he did not out-survive his mother, for he died a few days before he reached the age at which she had died. According to the partner they talked a lot about the idea of substitute guilt, which after all was very relevant to Jesus. Even though the analysis was by no means 'finished' at the time of termination, something had changed: before his admission the patient had never had a steady job situation, nor a steady relationship; afterwards he did. Structurally the superego had changed: feelings of guilt were not murderous anymore.

CONCLUSION

Conclusions drawn from a research project like this are bound to be very subjective. It has value for me not only because it is by intersubjectivity that we can take a small step towards objifying the suppositions we have about a patient, but also because it is extremely instructive. This way of describing and discussing the psychoanalytic process has also activated quite another process in all participants: one could call this learning process one of 'relative controversy'. In a contribution to the 'Kohut controversy.' I have described it as follows:

> Ultimately, the only possible realistic answer to these different ways of looking at the situation is a close cooperation on a practical, clinical and technical level between expert members of 'opposing' groups. Frans Verhage developed and implemented such a process in Holland. This method involves a situation where a specialist analyst writes a daily or weekly report on an analysis which is then given to four or five experienced analysts whose theoretical standpoints differ as much as possible and who note down each month their comments and prognoses independently from one another. It would be conceivable that experienced advocates of self-psychology and of classical analysis would thus be able to supervise or instruct one another. (1985, p.939)

It is no coincidence that the 'controversial discussions' between the Kleinians and the Freudians in London during the 1940s (King and Steiner 1991) not only did not cause a break – which alone is extremely rare in the world of psychoanalysis – but also created a 'middle group', with people like Winnicott, Balint, Heimann and Bollas, to name but a few. The continual discourse and teamwork of a study group, which has been busying itself with the same clinical material for a long time, makes it extremely productive.

From Practice to Psychodynamic Theories of Delinquency in Adolescence

Donald Campbell

INTRODUCTION

Anxiety motivates us to develop theory in an effort to understand puzzling and disturbing phenomena. I am using the word 'Theory' in its broadest sense as 'supposition explaining something…' (*The Concise Oxford Dictionary*). In this chapter I will consider those psychodynamic theories which have furthered my understanding of individual delinquent adolescents as I worked with them in youth clubs and in individual and group psychotherapy. I believe these theories can also be applied to work with delinquent adolescents undertaken by youth workers, probation officers, teachers, social workers, education welfare officers, nurses, residential workers, art therapists, psychotherapists, psychologists, and psychiatrists.

Vignette – an encounter with Max
In the early 1960s I ran a youth club for adolescents in Manhattan. One of my regulars was a sixteen-year-old boy I will call Max. Max, a veteran delinquent, was a failure both at school and with his peer group, which is why he played the superior tough guy role around the fourteen-year-old club members. He entertained and intimidated the younger children with tales of petty crime and vivid accounts of his exploits in gang warfare. Then, via the grapevine, I heard that Max had failed his driver's test.

Much to my surprise, Max came to the club that week. Half way through the evening a terrified girl ran over to me shouting that Max had a gun. I didn't move, although my first thought was to get out of the way, duck behind a pillar, or better yet exit unnoticed through a side door. However, a crowd was already cautiously edging up to me while Max flashed a nickel-plated revolver at Mary Lou, a sexually provocative girl who had always brushed him off. Mary Lou put on a brave face as she backed into a corner. I was now embarrassed by my thoughts and angry that these teenagers were expecting me to deal with the situation.

Max then turned and approached me. He was tense and giddy with excitement. His face was flushed as he waved the gun at me and said, 'Hey, Campbell, how do you like my piece?' I paused for a moment, obviously groping for what to say, and then told him that he was frightening the kids with his revolver so why not come to my office and show it to me there. In the heat of the moment, at an intuitive level, I had sensed that Max was also frightened. He wanted to appear in control, while also needing me to contain him without leaving him defenceless and humiliated.

Since delinquent activity always involves a second party it is, as such, antisocial. Whether the delinquent behaviour is aimed at a person's mind (such as lying or trying to deceive), someone's body (as in causing grievous bodily harm, assault or murder) or their property (by burglary, arson, theft or shoplifting), it is always unsettling for the victim. Delinquent actions do not necessarily disturb, at least consciously, the perpetrator. It is the disturbance, or what Winnicott (1956) called the 'nuisance value' in the antisocial symptom which compels the environment to manage the offender.

It was the impact of Max's delinquent behaviour upon me which motivated me to look for theories which would help me make sense of how he made me feel and react. Theories which emphasized the defensive function of delinquent behaviour were most useful in this respect.

THE DEFENSIVE FUNCTION OF DELINQUENT BEHAVIOUR

Williams (1982), following Melanie Klein, draws attention to delinquents who evacuate into others by means of projective identification feelings such as anger, envy, confusion, fear and excitement which have become intolerable. The delinquent act is the vehicle by which the adolescent projects these unwanted states of mind into others (victims, authority figures, parents, professionals, by-standers, accomplices, etc.). Delinquent behaviour also supports other defence mechanisms, such as denial, splitting, reversal, passive into active, and identification with the aggressor. *It is the reliance upon action to project painful thoughts and feelings outside of himself and into the environment that is the fundamental characteristic of the delinquent's psychological defences* (Campbell 1989).

When Max brandished his gun, he succeeded in splitting off his fear of women and his anxiety about being mocked for failing his driving test and projecting these into the crowd. Everyone in the youth club was frightened. I felt tense and backed away from Max. Max turned his passive experience of being failed by the driving instructor into an active one by dominating the group with his gun. In this way, he reversed the trauma of his failed test and Mary Lou's previous rejections. He was not able to handle the car, but he could control an entire crowd. He was no longer looked down upon by the boys of his age who had their driver's licences. Mary Lou could not brush him off. Max was not frightened about being able to cope, but I was.

However, this tendency to project internal conflict into others generates a vicious, self-fulfilling prophecy. As pain builds up inside, the delinquent projects it out and others become disturbed and retaliate in obvious or subtle ways to get back at the delinquent (instead of trying to control or understand him). This confirms the delinquent's expectation that others will relate to him as he did to them; that is, in a delinquent way. The antisocial child now feels persecuted, not by something inside that he feels unable to deal with, but by another person or institution, a tangible something, that he can actively, sado-masochistically engage. I will return to this dynamic later, but first I want to consider theories which seek to understand how the adolescent's past and present may contribute to his delinquent behaviour.

EARLY DEVELOPMENTAL INFLUENCES

The normal infant is unaware of the needs and rights of others. The child is preoccupied with itself and the task of ridding its body of bad feelings and maintaining good ones. In this way the infant achieves a sense of safety and pleasure. When the child feels hungry, or too hot, or too cold, it relies upon actions (e.g. it squirms, screams or cries) to get rid of discomfort and pain. When these involuntary reactions of nerves and muscles are perceived correctly as signals and the mother responds appropriately, the child's needs are met. As these 'dialogues' are repeated with satisfactory results, the child stores the good feelings away in his memory along with the links between discomfort, physical reaction, and disappearance of pain.

However, when the mother is repeatedly unable, for whatever reason, to respond early enough with enough of what is needed, more and more activity is required of the child as the pain persists and his own resources threaten to collapse. There are also insufficient memory traces of good feelings to support fantasies which might postpone his need for gratification. In fact, his inner world is full of memories of pain that wasn't relieved, phantasies that persecute him, and feelings of helplessness. Bad memories, like awful feelings, are expelled by *actions* which are used to project bad memories/conscious fantasies and unconscious phantasies, just as activity was the first reflexive response to physical discomfort.

Later, during the separation and individuation stage of development which we refer to as toddlerhood, the child is involved in negotiating a solution to what Glasser (1979) refers to as the Core Complex. As the child begins to move away from the mother, anxieties about abandonment experienced as threats to survival are aroused. These primitive anxieties about survival revive in the child a wish to return to an earlier fusional state of intimacy with mother which provided safety and relief from fears of abandonment. However, for the toddler who is also individuating itself from the mother, the prospect of fulfilling the wish to merge with mother carries with it another anxiety about survival; anxiety associated with loss of self–object boundaries and loss of one's separate identity by being engulfed or taken over by the mother.

In normal development the good enough mother recognizes when her child needs to be separate and independent and when it needs to be comforted and contained and, thereby, helps the child to separate and move into the world as a unique individual at its own pace and in its own time. However, narcissistic mothers may have difficulty in accurately tuning in to their child and reading its behaviour as cues for an appropriate response. The narcissistic mother is more likely to relate to the child on the basis of her own needs, that is to hold the child when the mother herself needs to be held and to leave the child on its own when she needs to be separate. Consequently, the child of a narcissistic mother often experiences her as providing too much too soon, or too little too late. As a result, the child is left with mounting anxieties about being engulfed or trapped by a mother who is holding the child when it wants to be separate, or terrified of being abandoned when the mother is rejecting or unavailable at a time when the child needs to be fed and comforted.

These twin annihilation anxieties of abandonment and engulfment which make up the Core Complex mobilize self-preservative aggression which aims to negate any threat to physical or psychological survival. Psychological survival includes the child's separate and independent identity, its sense of well being, self-esteem, and is dependent on such factors as safety, biological needs and good enough relationships. For the toddler the threat to its survival and its mother are indistinguishable. Consequently, the child is in a bind. The child cannot afford to eliminate the object which is threatening its survival, because it is the same object upon which it is dependent for its survival.

Glasser (1979) draws attention to a resolution to this dilemma which involves the child changing the aim of its aggression from eliminating the threat, that is, getting rid of mother, to controlling her by sexualizing the aggression. Aggression becomes sexualized (sadism) when pleasure is derived from making the victim suffer and watching the victim. Anxiety about survival is replaced by pleasure in 'torture' and relief that the object can be controlled. The fundamental difference between these two types of aggression is the relation to the object. It is paramount in the use of sadistic aggression that the object not be destroyed but be preserved in order to be seen to suffer. The dangerous mother and the life-sustaining mother, who are experienced as one and the same mother by the child, is not eliminated, but controlled.

Delinquent activity can be characterized by its aim as either self-preservative or sadistic. Adolescents who repeatedly engage in self-preservative delinquent activity are more likely to have weaker controls over their impulses and more unstable personalities than those who perpetrate sadistic delinquent acts. An example of self-preservative delinquency can be found in the following incident which I have described more fully elsewhere (Campbell 1994):

Vignette

One Friday afternoon a handsome, blond seventeen-year-old boy of average height and build who I will call Stan was chatting with some friends. Grummond, an intimidating bully, insinuated that Stan was homosexual. Stan took it all silently but was hurt and fuming. Two days later Grummond again insulted him, and Stan hit him on the head with a hammer, again and again. He was quickly restrained by a number of his friends, although he struggled to inflict more injury on Grummond. Initially, Stan was on a manic high, feeling exhilarated and triumphant. He recognized that he felt absolutely no regret or guilt about what he had done to Grummond but was soon overcome by shame and self-hatred 'for not doing the job properly and finishing him off'. For Stan, the person and the threat were synonymous. While Grummond existed he posed a threat. Stan's violence was essentially self-preservative and, as such, served a defensive function.

Max's use of the gun to threaten and intimidate is an example of sadistic aggression. He controlled the crowd and clearly derived pleasure from Mary Lou's terror. His aim was not to get rid of Mary Lou, but to make her suffer. As the object of a sadistic delinquent act Mary Lou was less at risk than Grummond, who was the object of a self-preservative attack.

Delinquent behaviour does not appear out of the blue when a child reaches adolescence, but is preceded by a pre-delinquent period (A. Freud 1966) which reflects a reliance upon action as a primary mode of dealing with internal conflict. The persistence of a tendency to action-oriented solutions beyond the pre-school years undermines the *capacity to think* about how one might contribute to one's failures and painful feelings.

The potential for delinquent adaptation to conflict can be observed in children who have not achieved an age-appropriate level of social adaptation;

children who behave anti-socially, over-react to stress, viciously attack other children or animals, or damage property. Aichorn (1935) considered such behaviour as evidence of 'latent disasociality'. Another example would be the development of a playful, provoking, self-willed attitude of a toddler into a quarrelsome and acquisitive youngster who tends to make hostile rather than friendly relationships by the time he or she enters school. It is the persistence of a dis-social phase from a time when it was age-appropriate into later phases of development where it is clearly inappropriate (A. Freud 1966) that provides a warning signal for those who are concerned about the development of an antisocial tendency.

The delinquent's body is not only the instrument of its projection but also the medium through which he or she is gratified. We can see signs of pre-delinquent dependence upon bodily excitement in the play of young children. Winnicott (1958) reminds us

> 'that the play of a child is not happy when complicated by body excitement with their physical climaxes…a deprived child with the anti-social tendency, or any child with marked manic defence restlessness, is unable to enjoy play because the body becomes physically involved. Physical climax is needed and every parent knows the moment when nothing brings an exciting game to an end except a smack which provides a false climax but a useful one.' (p.419)

The 'short sharp shock' for delinquents advocated by some politicians is an institutionalization of the parental smack of the child which stops an exciting game while exposing the adult's failure to understand its meaning. Discharge of anxiety through action also by-passes the perpetrator's self-observation and leaves him unaware of the conflicts which produced the need to act out in the first place.

Delinquent behaviour is an enactment of an internal conflict which becomes intolerable and can no longer be dealt with internally. Whatever has precipitated the current emotional crisis for the delinquent, it is likely to be linked to traumatic, perhaps now unconscious, events of childhood over which the child had no control.

Vignette

Helen was referred to the Portman Clinic[1] after her mother discovered she had stolen jewellery from the mother of two children she had been working

---

[1] The Portman Clinic is an out-patient National Health Service Trust facility which offers psychoanalytically-oriented assessment, treatment and management to patients of any age and both sexes who are delinquent or suffer from a sexual deviation.

for as an au pair. Helen had been stealing from her own mother and shops for as long as she could remember.

Helen's father was away on business so much that he felt like a stranger to her. While she was extremely possessive and protective of the older sister, mother handed over the care of Helen to a succession of nannies, some good and some bad, but all, in the end, were found to be inadequate by mother and abruptly sacked. Mother also kept the family isolated from the rest of the village behind the walls of the grandest house in the area. Helen put on a cheery face, and denied the deprivation she had experienced. Her 'solution' was to identify with her mother's possessiveness and, in this way, she managed to feel close to her mother without being smothered by her as she felt her older sister had been. Helen's stealing from other mothers, or taking objects associated with her own mother, appeared to serve at least two functions: it was the means by which Helen displaced her enormous rage toward her mother onto mother substitutes who were, like Helen herself, forced to suffer the loss of something valued; it also enabled her to reverse the experience of deprivation and loss which she couldn't control by actively taking from another mother figure what she could not get from her own mother.

Donald Winnicott (1956) held the view that where an antisocial tendency exists there has been what he called 'a true deprivation'; that is to say, there has been something good and positive in the child's experience up to a certain date that was then withdrawn. The withdrawal extended over a period of time which was really too long for the child to keep alive a memory of the good experience. Winnicott always believed that lack of hope was the basic feature of the deprived child. However, it is during the antisocial time that the child is actually expressing hope because it believes that the environment is there to be contacted and will respond, albeit in a punitive way.

Helen's stealing represented, on one level, her search for something that was good and had been lost. She was trying to take back a mother upon whom she still believed she had a child-like claim. However, Helen's attempt to master the deprivation of her childhood by stealing also served to defend against properly mourning the loss of the good experience that Winnicott referred to. Helen invited her mother to discover her delinquency by leaving the stolen jewellery on top of her chest of drawers in order to provoke containment and restraint. Helen, like other delinquents, unconsciously wishes that her mother (or those authorities who represent mother) would take care of her in an attempt finally to master the relationship that originally she could not control to her satisfaction.

Stan's mother had been depressed and unable to hold him during his early years. He still yearned for his mother and recognized that her early unavailability was somehow linked to his failure to develop a secure masculine identity and stable relationships with women in adolescence. After stomping on the face of a 'yuppie' who insinuated that he was a homosexual, Stan rushed home and bitterly reminded his mother that when he was young she became 'mad, dead, and couldn't leave the house' (Campbell 1994).

ADOLESCENCE

Usually, during the phase of development which precedes puberty, which we refer to as latency, Oedipal wishes to have a sexual relationship with the parent of the opposite sex and get rid of the parent of the same sex are repressed. However, the physiological and hormonal changes which take place during puberty and initiate the adolescent process thrust the sexual and physical body into the forefront of the adolescent's mental life. With the emerging appearance of a man or woman, the adolescent can, for the first time, enact what he or she could only wish for previously. After puberty the adolescent has the capacity to impregnate or bear children and the potential strength to convert into reality any wish to kill the rival parent. The newly developed sexual maturity heightens wishes and anxieties about sexuality and puts pressure on the adolescent's defenses aimed at maintaining the incest barrier. *In this developmental context the boy and girl face the fundamental tasks of adolescence: assuming ownership of a sexually potent body, that is separate from their parents, in the context of heterosexual relationships with non-incestuous objects.*

Delinquency in adolescence represents a developmental breakdown, a failure to complete the tasks of adolescence. It is the pain associated with the awareness of the failure to integrate genital sexuality and heterosexual relationships outside the family that motivates many adolescents to search for excitement in delinquency. The physical excitement experienced by the delinquent is linked to their emerging sexuality. In my view, the adolescent's delinquent act, whether it be motivated by self-preservative or sadistic aims, is the fulfilment of a sexual fantasy and, as such, it generates sexual excitement which momentarily blocks out internal distress. Max's immediate distress grew out of his failure to pass his driving test.

Menzies (1969) has drawn attention to the adolescent's use of inanimate objects (such as motor cycles) to compensate for feelings of inadequacy about their sexual organs and their sexual functioning. The automobile is often a representation of the driver's phallic potency, particularly so for teenagers in car-conscious America. Getting your driver's licence at sixteen is a rite of passage in America; the equivalent of a tribal initiation into manhood. It is a public, even official, recognition of potency. The ability to control this powerful object representing the adolescent's wished for genitality reassures against anxiety that he or she may lose control of his sexual impulses or be unable to satisfy or be satisfied by a sexual partner.

The pain of Max's failure to pass his driver's test, symbolic of the task of adolescence, was wiped out when he dominated the sexually provocative Mary Lou. His gun, flushed complexion, and tense body betrayed the sexual nature of his excitement. Max no longer felt humiliated or weak, but potent and powerful.

While Helen and Stan illustrate the influence of early deprivation on later delinquent behaviour, Roger is an example of a delinquent 'solution' to Oedipal conflicts as they are revived during adolescence.

Vignette

Roger, a diffident, passive sixteen-year-old, had been exposing his genitals to women for six months but had only recently been apprehended by the police for the first time. He said that the excitement and fear associated with risk was the strongest feeling. A smile slipped out when Roger described the 'surprised' look on the woman's face. Roger did not know why he did it. Exhibiting himself did not, in any way, fit the image he had of himself. But, then, he was not sure who he was anyway. He admitted that he would rather not think about exposing himself and thought he would never do it again now that he had been caught.

When he exposed himself Roger explained that he was in a state of mental confusion, at war within himself and cut off from everything around him which was outside a three yard cube. The war inside was described as one part of himself trying to stop another part from exposing himself. He seemed disassociated from both. Only the fear of being caught ever restrained him. However, when his 'defenses were down' or when he was 'a little drunk' he felt out of control and unable to stop himself. At no time did Roger convey any concern for the women he had exposed himself to.

Roger started 'flashing' shortly after his eighteen-year-old brother's girlfriend Caroline moved in to live with the family and share a bed with his brother. Roger told me that the occasion that resulted in his being arrested was unlike all the others because he exposed himself from a window in his parent's bedroom (while his mother was away) to women passing by on the pavement.

His father, a high-ranking police officer, had little time for Roger and appears to have been dominated by his ambitious and unpredictable mother. There were rows and a chronic state of tension between his parents. Mother returned to pursue a high powered career in advertising when Roger was six months old and left him in the care of au pairs. Roger gave me the impression that he grew up with a narcissistic mother who was withdrawn and preoccupied at times and close and intimate at other times. Roger said that she relates to the whole family via 'emotional blackmail'. He would wait for her to come home from work and study her face to see what sort of mood she was in so that he could determine whether she was approachable or not. If he got it wrong or tried to confront her, she would verbally attack him for his insensitivity towards her and then become sullen and withdrawn.

Mother's reaction to Roger telling her about his offence illustrates the intrusive, seductive dimension to their relationship. Mother was lying in bed with the curtains drawn. Roger sat on the bed, told her what he had done, and they 'cuddled'. She then reported that she told Roger that perhaps he had his father's physiology. His father wakes up every morning with an erection. If Roger had the same physiology, his mother said, it must be difficult for him to cope with his erections. After all, his father had herself right there every morning, but Roger had no-one.

Recently, Roger had become more concerned about his inability 'to get beyond friendships with girls'. Roger confirmed my view that his relationship with his mother and the tension between his parents may well have contributed to his difficulties in developing sexual relationships with girls. He agreed that he felt more despairing when he compared himself with his brother who was sleeping with his girlfriend, Caroline, and was particularly upset when she moved in. He felt crowded out of his own house. All this left him feeling depressed and sorry for himself. After all he went through growing up in his family, after all the hassles from stupid and insensitive teachers at school, why should he have to contend with the police and court? All he could think of was, 'Why me?'.

As early as 1916 Freud (S. Freud 1916c) remarked upon children who were naughty on purpose to provoke punishment and were then contented after being punished. He believed that these misdeeds were motivated by an unconscious sense of guilt arising from repressed Oedipal wishes to kill father and have sex with mother. Both the guilt and its source were unconscious. The adolescent who is overwhelmed by guilt arising from the revival of Oedipal fantasies may commit delinquent acts in order to attach the guilt to something conscious and find some temporary relief when he is caught.

Freud's theory is useful in understanding why Roger moved into his parent's bedroom in order to exhibit himself after months of exposing himself on the streets without being apprehended. It would appear that the incestuous excitement aroused by being sexually active in his parent's bedroom also increased his guilt and anxiety about being able to control himself as he moved closer to his parents. Roger's revenge and triumph over his Oedipal rival are evident in his violating the parental bedroom, exposing his father's ineffectual defence of the incest barrier to his police colleagues and the court, and shaming his law enforcement father who raised a son who committed a crime. The sadistic gratification derived from his encounters with women is also evident in Roger's pleasure in the 'surprise' the woman registers in response to the sudden exposure of his penis. Roger unconsciously behaved in such a way as to ensure that law and order would be brought into the parental bedroom and that his Oedipal guilt would be punished.

Roger also brings to mind Freud's (1916c) paper about those characters who feel they are justified in no longer submitting to any disagreeable reality. They feel they are *exceptions* because they have already suffered enough, unjustly so, during their childhoods. I believe Roger sees himself as an exception. The process of taking responsibility for his exhibitionism, acknowledging that he committed an offence and facing up to the reality of that image of himself, and then thinking through, albeit with a professional's help, why he did it, represents a disagreeable reality for which he would like to claim an exemption because he has already suffered enough.

SEXUAL EXCITEMENT AND DELINQUENT BEHAVIOUR

Stoller (1976), identifies three components of both a conscious and an unconscious sexual fantasy which can be applied to the fantasies and phantasies underlying delinquent behaviour: mastery, risk and excitement. Helen and Stan demonstrate the use that can be made of delinquent behaviour to master childhood traumas and compensate for early deprivation. The element of risk is introduced to the sexual fantasy and phantasy and, therefore, to the enactment of it, in order to heighten the excitement between the fear of repetition of the original trauma and the hope of mastering it and achieving a pleasurable outcome. Roger was conscious of the paramount importance of excitement generated by risk in his exhibitionism. Sexual excitement, so evident in Max's behaviour, is the product of an oscillation between the *slight* possibility of failure and the anticipation of *very probable* triumph. When Max pulled out his gun he knew he was holding all the cards.

Limentani (1984-85) builds upon Stoller's observations to distinguish two types of excitement: primary and secondary excitement. In his paper, *Toward a Unified Conception of the Origins of Sexual and Social Deviancy in Young Persons*, Limentani maintains that original primary excitement was stimulated by early phantasies and traumatic experiences which were felt to be entirely outside the individual's control. Later in life, a memory of both the pain and helplessness implicit in these early traumas, fantasies and phantasies has to be avoided at all costs. For this purpose the individual develops a sexual fantasy with an implicit or explicit revenge motif, and the capacity to enact it in a delinquent way, thus generating secondary excitement. Secondary excitement is brought on deliberately by the delinquent himself when he fantasizes about a delinquent act. The fantasy underlying a delinquent act functions in much the same way as a masturbation fantasy. However, the underlying Oedipal and pre-Oedipal aspects of the phantasy motivating the delinquent act are sufficiently repressed so that childhood wishes and anxieties are no longer conscious.

FROM PSYCHODYNAMIC THEORIES TO PRACTICE

Those who have worked with delinquents like Roger will be familiar with the difficulty in perceiving the sexual phantasies fulfilled by delinquent behaviour and the obstacles in the way of enabling the individual to accept these fantasies. Limentani (1984–85) reminds us of the frequency with which

> '...the suggestion of aggression and hostility being inherent in the socially or sexually devient act will be utterly denied. The denial, of course, will be supported by the absence of guilt and of any motivation; in practice most offenders will show little interest in finding why they have acted in a certain way. They will, on the other hand, show readiness to take punishment if necessary so that the episode can be forgotten.'
> (p.396)

The danger for the therapeutically minded is to collude with the delinquent's wish to forget the offence. Preoccupation with punishment not only obscures attempts to understand what motivates the delinquent activity, but may actually gratify the underlying sexual fantasy when, for instance, it has a strong sado-masochistic element.

If the delinquent episode can be 'forgotten', the underlying sexual fantasy can be protected and a recourse to secondary excitement is preserved. Any threat to this capacity to generate secondary excitement must be resisted fiercely because the delinquent fears he will be defenceless against primitive anxieties about his survival. It is the wish for sexual excitement through the delinquent act which accounts for the compulsive and repetitive character of some delinquent activity. The chronic offender is erotically bound to his antisocial behaviour.

The professional's awareness of the existence of an underlying sexual fantasy may alert them to the likelihood that, consciously or unconsciously, a delinquent will see them as playing a role in it. Max clearly wanted me to play a role in the drama he created. I did not know at the time what part he wanted me to play, but I had just enough sense and fear to take Max seriously. I had heard that he had failed his driver's test and knew he would feel humiliated. Somewhere I also realized that what he had in his hand was something which was more than a gun to him. Later, I learned from Max that beneath his conscious fantasy of intimidation was a less conscious homosexual wish to submit to my potency so that he might bolster his flagging masculinity. He gratified this latter wish by acquiescing to my invitation to come into my office.

However, a male adolescent's wish to submit passively to another man may well be accompanied by fears, often unconscious, of losing his masculinity.

The delinquent is likely to draw the practioner into playing a role which will enable the adolescent: (1) to extract revenge for parental failure and, paradoxically, (2) to attract containment or punishment of adolescent sexual impulses which are experienced as dangerous or arouse guilt, and (3) to compel gratification of unconscious unacceptable infantile wishes to be taken over by some person or institution representing a longed-for nuturing and protective mother and supportive, boundary setting father.

Once the environment responds, the delinquent experiences relief, but only momentarily. Soon he becomes anxious again about repeating his or her childhood experience of being abused by his environment. The revival of these primitive anxieties about physical and psychological survival signals the need to generate secondary excitement to block them out. Although this vicious cycle of delinquent behaviour will be repeated by many adolescents, psychodynamic theories which shed light on the meaning of the delinquent act in the context of the adolescent's background and his thoughts and feelings about himself in the present can increase our effectiveness in containing, managing and treating those adolescents who cross our professional paths.

A Group-Analytic Perspective
From the Speech of Hands
to the Language of Words

John Schlapobersky

'Psychotherapy is identical with the process of communication itself.'
(Foulkes 1964 p.112)

'There was speech in their dumbness, language in their very gesture.'
(Shakespeare, *The Winter's Tale*, V.2.13)

'There is a sense of enclosure and division which is engendered by walls of any kind and anywhere, whether physical or invisible. All of us build walls which, though invisible, are nonetheless tangible; for the walls of fear, silence and prejudice, convention and religion are just as impregnable as the great stone walls man has thrown up through the centuries.'
(Walker (1994) *Remember Walls*, p.1)

FORENSIC PARAMETERS IN GROUP ANALYSIS
When More Means Less: A Central Paradox in the Use of Group Methods

Group analysis is a clinical and theoretical discipline that originates in the work of S.H. Foulkes, a psychoanalyst who came to the UK from Germany in the 1930s (Pines 1981b). Over the last 55 years its clinical application – group-analytic psychotherapy – has been developed with different populations and in many settings, including the forensic field (Pines 1981a). My task in this chapter is a discussion of its theory for the light it might shed on the nature of deviance, criminality and violence, and to consider what insights of a general kind we can cull from group analysis that will be of general relevance to the emerging discipline of forensic psychotherapy. Group analysis stands at the interface between sociology and psychology. Within psychology it bridges two traditions, the depth psychologies that begin with Freud, and the positivistic tradition that includes developmental and social psychology (Farr 1990). So the discipline is well-placed by its location to provide a meeting ground for social theorists – whether in criminology, sociology or law – and for practitioners working in the field, including doctors, prison officers, psychologists, therapists and lawyers.

I will make an assumption and then pose a question to open the enquiry. The assumption is that group methods can provide a powerful psychotherapy with beneficial results in a wide range of forensic applications. I make this assumption in order to be spared the task – and, in a brief chapter, the valuable space – of justifying and validating the use of group methods. I want to be able to concentrate here on why group methods work and what we can learn from the fact that they do, that will be of general relevance to the two fields of criminology and psychotherapy that come together in this volume.

For those who question this fact – that group methods 'work' (in any of the different meanings of this word) – I would refer readers to Welldon's chapter on group work (II:6) and to a number of other sources. Caddick's surveys show that 'the Probation Service is the agency most actively involved in the practice of groupwork in Britain today' (1991, p.198), and that 'the use of groups in the Probation Service – particularly in direct work with offenders – is now probably more extensive and more varied than it has ever been' (Brown and Caddick 1993, p.2). A recent report for the Department of Health and Home Office confirms the many studies of therapeutic communities and their small groups which have 'shown the most promising results of any form of treatment for psychopathy' (Department of Health 1994a, p.16). At Special Hospitals such as Broadmoor (Cox 1976, 1990b) and Rampton (Kennard 1993), in prisons such as Grendon (Cullen 1994) and Barlinnie (Boyle 1994), the use of groups in forensic psychotherapy has established credibility for a principle of positive intervention with populations previously thought untreatable, creating movement in both directions across the most impervious boundaries in society.

Most studies indicate that when members of a deviant population are aggregated, their deviant characteristics are aggravated. Research into the dissemination and consolidation of criminality within a prison sub-culture leaves no doubt about this. Therapeutic groups, on the other hand, work in the other direction and what is of general interest is how and why they should do so. Let us imagine eight men with long criminal histories in prison who meet regularly for no directed purpose other than that of talking. How can this exchange hope to make any of them less dishonest? Or, in a Special Hospital, how does the regular exchange amongst eight people with histories of violent offences against others, make any of them less dangerous? The central paradox in the use of group methods in psychotherapy is that *exposure to one's own problem, as it is experienced in the life of someone else, can bring about change of an unforeseen and unexpected kind with far-reaching consequences.* I shall try to consider why this should be so, taking as my reference point the curriculum of a group-analytic training programme and assessing the relevance of its theory to the concerns of a forensic psychotherapist.

The Group-Analytic Frame: The Timeless and the Timed

In therapeutic group analysis a varied or homogeneous group of people with needs or problems of one kind or another, meets on a regular basis with the therapist responsible for the selection. All present will have been chosen by the therapist. They will themselves have chosen to participate and will be expected to justify their continuing presence in the group by reliable attendance. Even within the forensic field there are too many variations in the principles of selection, organization, frequency and pattern of meetings to set them out here. I am concerned with the common principles that will be found in the many different applications. These inform the *setting*; the *therapist* who is referred to as the *conductor* in group analysis; the *therapeutic method*; the *shared experience in the group* referred to as the *matrix* in group analysis; and the *language of the group* (Foulkes and Anthony 1965; Foulkes 1975).

Once a group is assembled no instructions are given to its members beyond the therapist's encouragement that they talk as freely as possible about whatever comes to mind. What ensues is called *free-floating discussion*, the group equivalent of free association (Foulkes 1975; Schlapobersky 1993). Therapy in the group is born out of ordinary language in the free exchange of its members. It occupies the cultural domain of all shared, conversational experience in which people struggle with meaning – in congregational life, in the confessional, in theatre, narrative or poetry – and as such it calls on principles through which:

> 'The depths of the mind are reached and touched by simpler words that speak in images and metaphors…a universal, timeless language, pre-dating contemporary ideas…that touches the heart, the ancient seat of the emotions; (and) that speaks to the soul.' (Pines, in Cox and Theilgaard 1987, p.xxiv)

There are accounts that go back the genesis of story-telling, of people who have found points of renewal in the lower depths and have risen to live in ordinary society, or to flee from it, speaking of the uncomfortable truths of their experience. Theirs is an occasional and exceptional experience. Joseph's prophetic dreams in prison and Jonah's experience in the belly of a whale are some biblical illustrations. Sophocles' *Oedipus*, Gorky's *Lower Depths* and Victor Hugo's *Les Misérables* are three of the many in the literary world.

In group analysis we utilize a set of clinical principles that governs the setting, the therapist, the therapeutic method, the group matrix and its language to take what is occasional and exceptional and turn it into a programme that can open the world of ordinary society to many who would otherwise live and die on its margins. To do so we must move from the timeless to the timed, from universal cultural experiences to an exacting methodology summarized by Cox as the structured use of time, depth and mutuality (Cox 1978b). The method begins with Freud who:

> 'Made it possible for therapists and patients to engage in…forms of transformational dialogue that had never existed before. He showed therapists how to do things with words to help revise radically their patients' hitherto fixed, unconsciously directed constructions of both subjective experience and action in the world…Freud's clinical dialogue alters in crucial ways the analysand's consciously narrated presentation of the self and its history among people by destabilizing, deconstructing, and defamiliarizing it.' (Schaffer 1992, p.156)

These transformational principles are given a group context where, instead of being deployed by one therapist in relation to one patient's monologue, they become the property of the group as a whole. Here they operate through any one of three different forms of speech that arise in the matrix of every group. First, in the most basic form, they are addressed to the monologue of the group's individual members, along the lines Schaffer describes above. Second, in a more advanced form, these transformational principles become part of a dialogue between individuals in the group or between sub-groups representing polarized aspects of the group's life. In the emerging dialogue we begin to see some exchange between these opposites. And third, in the most advanced form, they become part of a discourse in the group as a whole in which each member is a contributing participant. Here there is no single or exclusive narrative line, no individual or polarized contributors and the group's exploration is open and diffuse. It proceeds as a chain reaction of associated experiences that can include words, images, feelings, laughter or tears. To understand a group working in this way we should have to consider the texture of the discourse rather than the text of its narrative. We would need to pay attention to context as well as content; ground as well as figure; and group atmosphere as well as the dynamics of the individual. This is the form Cox and Theilgaard refer to as omniference, in which:

'All-carry-all (including the therapist) temporarily, until each individual can claim responsibility for his own actions, and acknowledge the balance of those internal and external forces which helped to mould him into the person he is.' (Cox and Theilgaard 1994, p.358)

In the process of any well-functioning group there is a steady progression that begins with monologue in the individual's first encounter with themselves. It moves to dialogue in the discovery of the other, and then to discourse as each individual's multiple inner objects are externalized and encountered in the group. The group-analytic approach is distinguished from other group methods in that neither of the two earlier speech forms are disregarded. On the contrary, both monologue and dialogue are encompassed by and integral to group-analytic experience. Free-floating discussion allows a pattern of exchange to move freely between these different speech forms and:

'Through this movement – from monologue through dialogue to discourse and back again – the group-analytic method comes into its own, creating an arena in which the dialectic between the psyche and the social world helps to refashion both.' (Schlapobersky 1993, p.212)

Now, modifying Schaffer's description above to take account of the group context, I shall illustrate in what follows a progression in group development from constructive to deconstructive and finally reconstructive experience, each of which introduces the possibility of change at a different and more fundamental level. In a well-functioning therapy group all three modes are operative and the group moves between them as it does between the different patterns of speech described above. When the struggle with meaning – the timeless – is given a bounded and well-structured clinical framework, language can work to generate mutative metaphors that come in a moment but that can last a lifetime. At such a moment, as Cox and Theilgaard (1987) describe, 'A sense of mystery, astonishment, and uniqueness...transcends any desciptive technicalities' (p.17). Moments of this kind can arise through monologue, dialogue or discourse in which therapeutic transformation is close to its more timeless cultural forms. Monologue is like a soliloquy; dialogue – the resolution of opposites – is like Plato's dialectic; and discourse is like the work of an ancient Greek chorus.

Pure Culture and Extreme Experience

'Offender patients will have been involved in disturbed and disturbing social relations ranging from committing petty offences to such catastrophic out-cropping of violence as the savage dismemberment of a homosexual partner.' (Cox 1978b, p.267)

The index offence usually determines the setting in which treatment takes place and consequently the populations from which groups will be selected are relatively homogeneous (Murphy 1993). In any event, a population that has known extreme experience – as protagonist or as victim – can only realistically be worked with in homogeneous groups (Schlapobersky and Bamber 1989). Group analysis had its very genesis in providing therapy for the 'pure culture' of combat neurosis amongst servicemen during World War II. However, the pooling of experience at the extremities of human deviation might readily be expected to aggravate its aberrant features, as we have already noted. Foulkes (1964) poses the question thus: 'If they all deviate…from what is in any given community considered healthy or normal, how can they possibly be of use to each other therapeutically?' The answer he provides, is that *collectively they constitute the very norm from which, individually, they deviate*' (pp.297–8). This recognition serves as the touchstone for group analysis.

To use it as a touchstone a therapist composes a group in which he fosters a therapeutic culture that is drawn from the personalities and personal resources of the group's membership and it is this that becomes normative and normalizing. 'Deviants agree collectively between them upon the very same basic values held by their own community', Foulkes suggests (Foulkes 1964, pp.297–8), and it is this underlying humanity in any deviant sub-group that becomes its most potent therapeutic resource leading, in due course, to a group culture that is both healing and normalizing. As Pines describes it, the members of a group, to receive help, have to create the structure that provides it and in doing so undergo change (Pines 1985b, p.26). 'Criminal impulses are in everyone…the manifest trio – criminal–society–judge – are the personifications of three elements present in everyone…the id, the ego and the superego.' Criminality 'enacts on an external stage what takes place internally in the mind of everyone' (Foulkes 1990, p.120). The group's therapeutic culture now provides the stage for the personification of these elements in the shared experience of its members. The drama of each individual's inner conflicts is given an audience amongst others who will recognize its different elements and, as the destructive and sometimes bizarre experience of different members is decoded amongst others who not only recognize it but find it in themselves – or find themselves in it – isolation is broken down, new emotional outlets are constructed and a new sense of self can begin to emerge.

CLINICAL PRINCIPLES

The Setting

The therapist supplies, creates and maintains the setting throughout the group's life. This will differ depending on the wider system in which the group is located, calling for one role from the therapist if, for example, it is an out-patients' group where a secretary or receptionist is the only other important person on the boundary; and a much more active liaison role if it is located in a hospital or prison where negotiations with ward and custodial staff are an integral part of the therapist's administrative task (Kennard 1993). This is a continuing and fundamental part of therapy and will involve protection of the group's external boundaries and careful attention to its internal boundaries such as meeting times, including punctual beginnings and endings, the predictable frequency of its meetings and breaks, and the general guarantee of a stable background against which the instability of individual members can become the foreground for the group's attention.

Every aspect of the group's life, including absences, departures, late attendances and extra-group communication in terms of letters, telephone calls and messages, referred to generically as boundary events, are open for discussion and enquiry (Foulkes 1975; Pines, Hearst and Behr 1982). Boundary events are interpreted for the meaning they might hold for the life of the group as a whole. This is a task initiated by but not confined to the therapist and, as the analytic frame and the events that break its boundaries become topics for discussion, the setting itself – to which each member is seen to contribute – acquires a capacity to hold its individual members and contain their anxieties and insecurities. For a forensic population the issue of containment is of great importance, as is the discovery – by people who may have no belief in themselves as responsible members – that they can take responsibility for themselves and expect responsibility from others. The group is thus responsible not only for the nurture, acceptance and security of its members – in a sense for their 'mothering' – but also for their containment, the setting of limits and the maintenance of consistent authority – for their 'fathering'. The therapist will invariably have to lead the way in modelling both roles for the group's members, but the evolution of a therapeutic culture will see individuals taking up these roles and the emergence of some capacity in the group as a whole to develop and maintain its norms from the standpoints of both 'mothering' and 'fathering'. Mark (1993) describes the maintenance of the setting in an applied group-analytic therapeutic community for offenders as follows:

'Tolerating deviant behaviour to a sufficient degree to allow it to be examined in a safe setting was the most difficult aspect of the work. Allowing damaged, often violent men and women to feel safe enough to rage against the boundary and the restrictions, and to internalize an understanding of how better to deal with 'authority' in the outside world was a constant challenge. The principle of reality confrontation was crucial in this task, emphasizing straight and open communication, so difficult with often highly manipulative, boundary-testing clients.' (p.24)

And in a Special Hospital Cox describes the setting as follows:

> 'Within the security of a custodial setting, an offender patient said: "I'm shielded, in here." The defence of a "secure setting" allowed his personal dynamic defences to be slowly and safely relinquished. Changed defences and an opening of latent capacities followed his deepening awareness of corporate life and this was commensurate with enhanced self-esteem.' (Cox 1978b, p.273)

The Therapist

The therapist is referred to as the group conductor, a leadership role in which he is both the group's therapist and one of its members (Foulkes 1964; Foulkes and Anthony 1965). In the former capacity his responsibilities include the selection of its members and the maintenance of its setting as described above. As one of the group's members he participates with some lattitude for free expression of his own, modelling a capacity for open and direct communication whilst – at the same time – maintaining a neutral, analytic stance and withholding personal material (Pines, Hearst and Behr 1982). The question of whether the therapist speaks directly from his own experience of the group at one point or makes an interpretation at another is a matter for clinical judgement but is often determined by the group itself which will call upon him for a varied range of responses to differing situations (Kennard, Roberts and Winter 1993). The importance of the therapist's firmness in his administrative role, and his accessibility and responsiveness in personal terms, allows what Cox calls 'a partial regression in the service of his patient's regression' (1978b, p.265). If 'the executive aspects of the therapist's personality retain a firm hold…on reality', it gives the therapist 'an executive, stabilising autonomy' that then allows him a 'para-regression' in which 'he shares the perceptual perspective and affective thrust of his patient's world', by 'sinking into his patient's social construction of reality' on a controlled and temporary basis (pp.264, 265). If this duality can be developed, the therapist can 'come alongside' individual members in the group and 'be welcomed' in this proximity; members will, at the same, time move towards his therapeutic position as they take an increasingly responsible part in the maintenance of the group's culture and norms.

It is in this area that a profoundly reparative process is engendered as the therapist's emotional proximity earns him members' trust; and their responsibility in the group earns them his trust. This example gives some sense of it:

Vignette

A group with a stable population but still in its early months had recently been joined by two new members. During a session the therapist gave notice of his forthcoming absence – an event which would normally be dealt with by an arrangement for group to meet without him. On this occasion there was some question whether it might be safer if the session were cancelled altogether. Amongst the established membership there was indignation about the imposition of two new members and, in the two new members, there was anxiety about being left to the care of the others who were jealous and resentful about their arrival. The anxiety abated to some extent when the therapist placed himself – in what he said – close to the experience of both sub-groups. People were only able to make a decision to attend in the therapist's absence when he assured the newcomers that he was confident he could entrust them to the others and had every confidence all would be well without him. In the event a constructive meeting took place in which people spent most of their time discussing the therapist! In due course a new-found sense of trust emerged that proved a landmark for the group's progress. People attributed it to the fact that the therapist had entrusted them with one another.

The therapist is trustee for the group; he is entrusted by the group; and, most important, he is there to trust the group so that they can come to trust themselves. This is a subtle and demanding role in any of the applications of group analysis. With a forensic population it is all the more important and is charged with special difficulty. Cox suggests that 'there is no more exacting therapeutic task than that of conducting group psychotherapy with borderline patients (which includes)…many offender patients with histories involving serious crimes of violence' (Cox 1978b, p.271) and he regards trust as the key consideration. In his 1990 S.H. Foulkes Annual Lecture he states:

'There is this pull of the primordial, not as a destiny but as a starting point in the therapy. There is this primordial, shared humanity…only when the trust is there, deep, deep down, then we're able to get up to a level where analysis is tolerable.' (Cox 1993a)

It is for reasons of this kind that a practitioner could not hope to learn the application of the method from its theory. Group analysis makes great demands on its practitioners for whom training and, especially, reliable supervision are absolutely essential. Those interested in its use would gain most by either joining a small group as a member or by enrolling on one of the group-analytic courses that provides an experiential group as part of the training.

Therapeutic Method

Moving up now to the level at which analysis is tolerable, the conductor's first aim is to facilitate members' participation which, as discussed above, often takes the form of serial monologue. Out of this monologue arise the capacities to talk and to listen – capacities which are often undeveloped or even non-existent at the outset of therapy (Pines, Hearst and Behr 1982). From talking and listening comes self-disclosure and from self-disclosure identification which in due course leads to dialogue. So the conductor must give place to monologue whilst, at the same time, cultivating dialogue – the exchange between members or sub-groups – and, ultimately, promoting discourse. In order to do any of this he needs an understanding of the group's dynamics in terms of its structure, process and content (de Maré 1972).

(1) Structure

The notion of structure describes the more enduring aspects of any group's makeup, the 'architecture' of its interpersonal relations, conceptualized first in terms of the setting and its boundaries as described above; and then conceptualized in the triangular bond between each individual, the conductor and the group as a whole. If we imagine a group of eight individuals and consider the bond between each individual, the conductor and the group as a whole, we can see why the breadth and complexity of this network is referred to as a matrix. Each of its members experiences a relationship between themselves and all the other members in a complex *relational field* that will undergo change in terms of alliances, sub-groups and polarizations. Whatever its size or variability, attention to structure will provide a secure and reliable bounded space between the group's principal psychological 'objects' – that is, each individual member, the conductor and the group as a whole.

(2) Process

The notion of process describes the fluid and dynamic fluctuations of emotion and experience based on the key concept of resonance, the unconscious communication of emotion. The group provides its members with a wide field of meaning – *a semantic field* – which is explored as they mirror one another's experience, find their emotions amplified by association with one another and find condensed, in sometimes highly aroused, cathartic experiences, moments charged with meaning and significance.

(3) Content

The group matrix is the 'operational basis of all relationships and communications' (Foulkes 1964, p.118). The matrix has a relational field that is understood through its structural elements, and a semantic field that is understood through its process. These different ways of understanding the matrix are not conflicting but complementary, just as the physics of light supports both wave and the particle theories.

The matrix is analyzed at four different levels, each of which arises through the interplay of its semantic and relational fields. These are: the current or social level; the transference level; the projective level and the primordial or archaic level. The manifest content of a group's life takes place at the current or social level in the course of free-floating discussion which produces an area of mutual exchange and understanding – what Foulkes calls the common zone (1964, p.112) – in which people first come to understand each other. It is dominated by accounts of members' problems, reflections, recollections and feelings, located in the past, the present (in the group) and the outside world. Analysis of this current level – in which everyone participates – sees the emergence of deeper latent content at the second, transference level in which people in the group come to stand for or represent the internalized 'whole objects' of one another's childhoods – their mothers, fathers, siblings and others. The pathology of family failure which is so ubiquitous in a borderline or forensic population emerges as the latent or unconscious content of the group's life. And then, as the group's experience deepens, the transference level is in turn analyzed and beneath it is found a third level comprised of 'part-objects', the more regressed elements which members hold, carry, project or reflect as parts of their own and one another's earliest experience – their rage, need, dependency, sexuality or malice. And finally, at the fourth, primordial level there are the archetypes of primitive experience, the objects and emotions of primary process in dreams, psychotic experience or primitive enactments (Schlapobersky 1993).

Vignette

A man had been in a therapy group for some three years. When he began his marriage had just broken up after he discovered his wife's infidelity. At the time he was sometimes hypomanic and often frightened of his rage. He was now coming to terms with this history, making peace with his ex-wife, doing a good job raising their children who still lived with her and putting his business on its feet. He would often bring the group a clear picture of this emerging sense of resolution, but none was clearer than this dream. He recounted it as he came in one day. He was at sea and there was no way to stay afloat. Eventually he sank to the bottom where a terrifying monster was waiting to attack him. He turned and ran 'til he could go no further. The monster was still pursuing him so he turned to face it and taught it how to sing.

Here, the primordial level provides imagery that records a benevolent transformation. Its redeeming quality needs no interpretation. It arises directly from the fourth level but the work of transformation engaged the group at each level of its experience over a lengthy period of time in which the assurance of its setting and the reliability of its conductor played a crucial part.

THE MATRIX OF SHARED EXPERIENCE

The Language of the Group

Therapists new to the group-analytic method are sometimes at a loss as to how the opening moments of a group should be conducted, particularly if it is composed of a homogeneous population that has known extreme experience of any kind. But the convening frame itself can provide an illuminating point of departure. The group's members may have lost all they hold most precious – their self-respect, their liberty, the lives of their loved ones – but what is still present and available amongst them in the room is the capacity to be of use to others just like themselves. The therapist's language, used in this way, can provide a statement of confidence at the beginning of what may prove to be a long journey. Thereafter, everything that happens in the group, and everything within its purview, is considered a kind of language, a communicative system made up of signs and symbols which will in many cases need decoding. The quest for meaning will discover 'speech in their dumbness, (and) language in their very gesture' (*The Winter's Tale*, V.2.13).

Free-floating discussion proceeds through an interplay between narrative and drama, story and exchange, reconstruction and encounter. As already described, all verbal activity takes the form of monologue, dialogue or discourse. Each of these speech forms will be expressed either as narrative, in which a story is recounted, or as drama in an immediate encounter or event. Cox and Theilgaard describe how:

> 'Repression enables us to forget…so that our memory fails and so does narrative continuity…repressive forces which cause narrative failure, to the extent that a patient is unable to tell that part of his story of which he needs to speak, *can be faced and transformed within therapeutic space.*' (Cox and Theilgaard 1994, pp.24–5)

In their account transformation comes from the prompter who intervenes 'when narrative flow is at the brink of failure' (Cox and Theilgaard 1993, p.8). This is how they describe the key role of the therapist. In group analysis prompting is the prerogative of the group as a whole in which we find 'reciprocal prompters' who might take up an issue in its dramatic form – as it arises in the here and now of the group – and turn it into a narrative reconstruction. This in turn can give rise to other associations that might in due course bring the experience back to something immediate and dramatic in the room. The language of a group, however, is much more complex and varied than the words of its members. It will encompass gesture, behaviour, body-language and other non-verbal communication, and actions that convey feelings when emotions have no words. Here is an example:

Vignette

Christine and Steve are both in their early thirties, the two borderline members of a long-standing group. Their social backgrounds and presenting problems differ but they have related personality problems. She has a boyfriend but, whilst they enjoy trust and affection, she allows virtually no sexual contact and suffers from a disorder of desire. Steve's only sexual experience was a mechanical affair with another man some years ago. He has worked in the group to free himself from long-standing cocaine and alcohol addiction but, despite this progress, hard won over the years, members of the group know nothing about his sexuality or orientation. Christine and Steve often serve each other as reciprocal prompters, drawing each other into more open participation in the group, pulling the enquiry back to early memories of tormenting fathers, and even populating one another's dreams.

One evening Steve had been active during a confrontation with another woman. Christine, too, had played an unusually active part. In the closing minutes of the session she declined the invitation to share a dream – it was something she had referred to but not yet recounted. She was pleased to be saved by the bell. People recognized the contrast between her availability to others and her own defensive secrecy. She entered others' experience, but allowed no-one to enter hers. The therapist took up this language and linked it to her relationship with the boyfriend outside the group. In the group she would not let people in, psychologically, just as at home she would not let her boyfriend in sexually. She found the connection helpful and, with others' assistance struggled to find words common to both areas that would explain how she felt. 'Intrusion; invasion; no room...' Steve interrupted to change the subject and conclude some unfinished business with the woman he had been talking to earlier. The group rounded on him over this and for the first time Christine was distressed at being interrupted. She cried and accused him of selfishness. The therapist suggested that Steve's interruption was a protective act to save Christine from an examination of her own sexuality, which he – Steve – could not tolerate because his own sexuality was still such a secret. Like Christine, he entered others' experience in the group but allowed no-one to enter his.

Steve's interruption represented narrative failure. He broke the thread of a meaningful enquiry and used the act of prompting defensively to protect a collusive alliance. Christine's experience was reversed as she found the therapist helpful and her customary ally destructive. The work of the group illustrates the concepts of *location, translation and interpretation*, each of which has precise clinical significance in group analysis (Foulkes and Anthony 1965). A core conflict – Christine and Steve's borderline defences – is *located* in the group, *translated* from the obscure language of defensive behaviour into a form understandable to all and finally an *interpretation* is constructed drawing on group process that sheds new light on the problem as it arises in the world outside.

There is a correspondence between the form taken by defensive behaviour in the group, the character defence in the individual's personality structure and its manifestation as a sexual problem in their relationships. The defence, the pathology it gives rise to in the outside world and the behaviour it is responsible for in the group are all regarded as analogues of one another. They are isomorphic and consequently change at any level will produce change at every other level. If, at the current or social level of the group, Christine can let people in, the likelihood is that she will find it easier to let her boyfriend in. An exploration of the transference level in the group will help her understand why, until now, she needed to keep people out and this will resolve at least some of her pain about sexual and emotional abuse in her family of origin. An exploration of the projective level will help her understand and resolve the splitting and fragmentation that separate affection from sexuality. And at the primordial level we have a dream – shared with the group – in which she is crushed by an enormous wave at the sea's edge as she asks it whether she can share something beautiful with someone she loves. The many sessions spent exploring the meaning of the dream have provided her – and the other members of the group – with an understanding of the archaic fears that sex might overwhelm love-ties felt to be fragile.

Forensic Applications: Constructive, Deconstructive and Reconstructive Experience

'Offending' or 'offence-related behaviour' is analyzed by its significance in the interpersonal domain. The offence is construed as a a person's attack on, or a perverse affirmation of, their links with others. Our understanding of schizoid and psychopathic personalities provide polarities at opposite extremes of the spectrum of psychopathology, between which the small group does its work. Psychopathic offenders – a group of sexual offenders for example, who rationalize that their victims enjoyed the experience – inhabit a social world of one in which others are not understood to have selves like their own. The group helps to extend subjectivity from the privacy of the self to encompass the lived realities of others. At the other pole, in the case of a borderline offender with a schizoid personality, for example, whose disavowed anger emerges in violent episodes which are then dissociated, periods of quiescence are a disembodiment of the self. The offender might attend the group regularly, but with no access to the emotions of the person who committed the offence. The group can help to locate their violent impulses, uncouple the impulse from the action and thus give access to real emotions which, once contained and expressed in reflective language, can be owned, understood and resolved. The schizoid has no real links with others; the psychopath has no others with whom to have links. In the interchange of a group the self emerges as a social object; and social objects – other people – are recognized as other selves for the first time. In a group, the self, the person, becomes an object in the social world of others and, in the course of interacting with these others, the individual becomes – for the first time – a continuous object to and for themselves. People can begin to recognize the sound of their own voices, uncover the continuing threat of their own aggression and discover the truth about their own inner injuries and needs.

CONCLUSION

Forensic Applications: From the Speech of Hands to the Language of Words

'Speak hands for me!' (*Julius Caesar* III.1.78)

In this quotation from *Julius Caesar* we hear Casca's rage as he leads the assassins in the first strike. The hands that speak tell a story of political intrigue and republican outrage in ancient Rome. The story is followed in all political use of terror. In the case of offender patients with borderline personalities, the dreams that erupt as actions tell stories about different orders of experience. It is primary process rather than political rage that erupts in primitive enactment. As Foulkes (1990) puts it, 'The neurotic acts in his dreams whilst the criminal dreams in his actions' (p.20). The aim of the therapist is to help patients find words that speak rather than hands, so that the dream-like quality of primary process, and the impulses or compulsions through which it has been expressed, can be uncoupled from action and explored in the relative safety of reflective language in a process sometimes referred to as negative elaboration. The elaboration of negative emotions including hostility, anger, despair, loss and envy becomes a major part of the group's work as it provides 'psychic space for perspective, negotiation, recognition, acceptance and verbalization of hurt and anger... Feeling and sharing the past and the present makes it accessible...(as) Internalized, persecutory, vengeful monologues are brought into dialogue.' (Pines 1992, pp.152–153). Cox writes that:

> 'During the early stages of his life in the group the offender patient may hide beneath the label of formal mental illness... Progressive disclosure of hitherto ego-alien material is facilitated... During the affective flow and sequential progression towards deeper disclosure...[we see the] Development of retrospective responsibility [which] is intimately linked with the development of insight and the capacity to sustain emotional disclosure [which] frequently runs parallel to the gradual demisting of focal amnesia for the traumatic episode...' (Cox 1978b, p.272)

Writing about the language of words, Cox and Theilgaard describe how:

> 'Forensic patients, when attempting to relive their offences and to to pluck their rooted sorrows from the memory, use phrases whose poetic purchase on the memory is as embedded as their psychic pain was, until released in language. For example, a patient whose victim's head had been crushed by an immense boulder, said:

> > "His face was squashed like an apple...and terribly disfigured"

> ...forensic group psychotherapy often has the task of enabling patients to come to terms with the sequelae and aftermath of assaults involving massive mutilation. But what tends to hold the group's attention is the "terrible disfigurement" rather than "being squashed like an apple"...

> ...in the presence of such a phrase and such feelings, the paedophile cannot retreat, neither can the arsonist nor the poisoner. All have caused disfigurement of one sort or another. All are kept in the active current of the group matrix, facing their personal homologue of the crushed face that was "squashed like an apple". Yet their painful confrontation with self becomes confluent as their life-streams converge under the bridge of "terrible disfigurement".

> Their lingering distraction persists until psychological work is complete, and they have come to terms with all that happened between the first motion and the acting of a dreadful thing.' (Cox and Theilgaard 1994, pp.357–8)

Acknowledgements

I should like to acknowledge the assistance received in the preparation of this chapter from Murray Cox, co-editor of these volumes; and from David Kennard, Chairman of the Group Work Co-ordinating Committee, Rampton Hospital. I should also like to acknowledge the access allowed me to the theoretical papers of two graduates on the Qualifying Course of the Institute of Group Analysis. They are Peter Mark, Student Unit Supervisor, Inner London Probation Service and Dennis Murphy, Consultant Forensic Psychiatrist, St. Thomas' Hospital.

A Psychodramatic Perspective

Jinnie Jefferies

Psychodrama was conceived by J. L. Moreno whose interest in philosophy and theatre led to the development of a method of group psychotherapy that used theatrical format to incorporate his existential beliefs.

As a therapeutic method it employs action methods to encourage the expression of repressed emotions and to introduce the possibility of change by correcting the maladaptive learning that has taken place. It helps the offender patient, within the context of the group, to find new ways of perceiving and reacting to past and present life experiences and to understand how he has projected negative feelings and transferred his inner world onto other persons and situations.

Vignette
Alan, by his own admission, raped a woman rather than deal with his feelings towards his mother, his childhood and his own inadequacies. Faced with his victim in a psychodrama session he told her, 'I hate myself for what I have done to you. The only person I wanted to hurt was my Mum. God knows what was going through my head that night because I don't.'

A classical psychodrama consists of three stages: the warm up, the enactment and the sharing.

THE WARM UP
This increases a sense of trust and group membership through techniques that encourage interactions between the group members. It stimulates the creativity

and spontaneity of group members and helps them to focus on personal issues. The offender patient whose work will be the focus of the enactment is selected by other group members who feel sympathetic to the issue presented. In this way he works for the group, carrying the group concern, as well as for himself.

THE ENACTMENT

In the enactment stage the offender patient, with the support of group members and the therapist, explores the issues heightened by the warm up process. In psychodrama there is no script; the drama is spontaneous, created in the moment by the protagonist, group members and the director (therapist). Because psychodrama is intrinsically an action method the protagonist is encouraged to move quickly into the drama, creating the space in which events took place and an experience of re-experiencing rather than re-telling. The physical setting of scenes and their portrayal evokes memories and emotions associated with the space and counters the distortions and evasive manoeuvres that may be introduced by verbal disclosure (Meloy 1988, p.310).

The characters the offender patient places on the psychodrama stage are part of his internal world. The choice of certain group members to play these parts, 'auxiliary egos', is determined by complex factors which Moreno defines as 'tele' (the two-way flow between people). I suggest they are also determined by transference reactions towards other group members. Playing the role of an 'auxiliary ego' can in itself be therapeutic, often providing the offender patient with an opportunity to develop roles not hitherto experienced or to discover aspects of himself that he has chosen to deny. The process also helps the offender patient to develop some understanding and empathy for another's position: 'Playing the role of George's Mum made me think of how it must have been like for my Mum', is not an uncommon comment.

Central to the understanding of psychodrama as a method of treatment is the theory of 'role'. Moreno defined role as:

> 'the functioning form the individual assumes in the specific moment he reacts to a specific situation in which other persons or objects are involved. The form is created by past experiences and the cultural patterns of society in which he lives... Every role is a fusion of private and collective elements.' (Moreno 1962 in Fox 1987, p.62)

Whereas the concept of role is usually employed to describe complexes of behaviour limited to a social dimension, psychodramatic role theory carries the concept through all dimensions of life beginning at birth and continuing through the lifetime of the individual. The total of all roles in which a person interacts is his role repetoire, and it is from this complex that the personality develops. Like other role theorists Moreno believed that the self arises out of social interactions with others. Application of psychodrama role theory requires two sets of skills, identification and intervention.

Vignette

Roy presented two scenes in the early part of his psychodrama; in the visiting room where his girlfriend boasted of her sexual exploits with other men and the scene of his offence where the prostitute he had murdered had laughed at his inability to have an erection. The context for him was the same, a situation in which a woman had left him feeling humiliated, and defenceless. His behavioural response was one of anger.

Roy was helped to see how the present situation and his offence held memory traces of past experiences, how his actions were influenced by distorted belief systems and negative feelings associated with these early experiences. Roy's mother had both humiliated and hurt him emotionally as a small child, and he grew up believing that he could not trust women, that they were out to repeat his earlier experiences with mother. They consequently became the object of his angry feelings.

If one is to intervene in the process whereby offender patients redirect their repressed feelings onto others who trigger them again by their attitudes or actions then these emotions need an arena for expression. The psychodrama stage provides just that by creating the 'as if' principle (Vaihinger 1924). George, the offender patient, holds the role of 'rejecting father', for the protagonist; Anna, the probation officer, the role of 'humiliating mother'; as such the action transcends the limitations of reality, allowing repressed emotions to be accessed and expressed. The affectionless character who has learnt to cut off from his emotions is helped through the psychodrama process to contact them again and the psychopath is encouraged to express his feelings verbally rather than move into physical action.

It is as important for the offender patient to understand his own actions and motivation as to understand those of others. Roy needed to differentiate between anger at mother from present anger at self for maintaining patterns developed in the past and transferred onto his victim. 'Self criticism of one's own actions can only follow if these actions are accessible or reportable' (Sarbin 1954, p.236).

Finally, Roy was given an opportunity to explore new ways of dealing with the situation with his girlfriend by bringing together both the affective and cognitive elements of the enactment sequence in order to integrate the work that had taken place.

THE SHARING

In the final stage of the psychodrama process, protagonist and group members come together to share the ways in which they identify with the protagonist's psychodrama. It is not a time for interpretation or comment about what has taken place, for the protagonist will need time fully to internalize and integrate the process. The sharing stage allows the protagonist to feel once again integrated with the group and allows other offender patients to share their own powerful feelings and thoughts, which will have emerged from either participating in the psychodrama or observing the action. Sharing also serves the purpose of focusing on future psychodramatic work.

ROLE REVERSAL AND DOUBLING

Much has been written about the inability of the psychopath to take another's perspective, his lack of empathy (Gough 1948). The psychodramatic techniques of 'role reversal' and 'doubling' develops the ability to see a situation from the other's perspective.

Vignette

John had wanted to take revenge on his own father, whom he described as cold and unapproachable, with little time and energy for him. Having berated him in his psychodrama for all that he had not given, John was asked to reverse roles with his father (a technique requiring the protagonist to experience the interaction from the other pole) whilst another offender patient held John's role. In the role of father, John achieved for himself a clearer understanding of his father's position, struggling for explanations and feelings of which he had hitherto, as son, had little or no awareness. Following this session John told his father of his work in psychodrama and what he had discovered from reversing roles with him. John's willingness to look at the relationship from his father's position opened up an interchange between them that had not previously existed. His father began to talk about his feelings of inadequacy and resentment in his marriage and his job. It also enabled John to share with his father his own angry feelings of past events that had been displaced onto his innocent victim. The technique is frequently used to increase the offender patient's awareness of the consequences of his criminal actions on his victim.

The 'double' expresses thoughts and feelings that the protagonist is repressing or censoring in the psychodrama. These thoughts may be accepted by the protagonist or rejected as incorrect. The process develops an empathetic bond between protagonist and double.

ROLE RECIPROCITY

The offender patient often presents himself as a helpless victim of past experiences and present relationships. He waits for things to change and of course they do not. His way of releasing the frustration and tension of feeling so powerless is to find another kind of power through his antisocial behaviour. The concept of role reciprocity which occupies a key position in psychodrama theory and practice firmly embeds the notion of roles in the arena of interpersonal relations and neatly distributes responsibility for the existence of the interaction. By remaining the passive victim of what he perceived to be true, staying with the relationship in his head rather than confronting the relationship in reality, John had to take part responsibility for the barren years that existed between himself and his father.

If both parties of an interaction bear some responsibility for its maintenance, it follows that both also have some power to halt or alter it. Taking an active part in dealing with his internal and external relationships can be both freeing and empowering for the offender patient.

Vignette

Alan in his psychodrama dealt with his internalized mother–son relationship in which he had previously seen himself as the 'helpless victim' and her as the 'aggressive abuser'. Within the session he was encouraged to express his negative feelings and to find some understanding of her actions. It was a moving moment when he knelt at her psychodramatic grave, placing a flower on the imaginary gravestone, stating 'I love and forgive you'.

In psychodrama, altering the perceptions and challenging the belief component of role is all important. A new way of construing the problem brings its own solutions.

WORK WITH POTENTIALLY VIOLENT PATIENTS

Kernberg (1992) emphasizes the dangerous violence inherent in paronoid attitudes of some offender patients which makes it difficult to work within the ordinary psychotherapeutic approaches. These approaches rely on the therapeutic relationship to represent symbolically the client's internal world – a world full of destructive feelings that places the therapist at considerable risk.

Psychodrama is also concerned with the client's symbolic representation of his external and internal reality but the representation takes a different route through the enactment itself, relying on 'auxiliaries' and 'scene setting' to represent time and place. 'Psychodrama lays out fantasy in three dimensions, and relieves the therapist of the task of becoming everything to the protagonist'

(Williams 1989, p.159). In psychodrama, the re-living of past events is re-enacted on the psychodrama stage. The therapist's interpretations are expressed through the psychodramatic interventions themselves.

The therapist in psychodrama intentionally adopts a more active approach and, when transference reactions do occur, attempts to resolve rather than interpret them.

Vignette

Dave was referred to the psychodrama programme for his violent paranoid behaviour. His mother had suffered from severe schizophrenia and had played with his emotions unmercifully. I was for him his manipulating untrustworthy mother who, in the midst of his emotional vulnerability, would cast my blow. Choosing not to work with Dave's transference reactions, we agreed that he would ask for clarification or share with me and the group when he perceived my actions to be manipulative or potentially harmful. In this way I became a little less like his mother and he less like the helpless son.

Eventually, we explored his relationship with his mother, how the acted out role of mother (held by an 'auxiliary' and not by me) was not only based in history but was part of Dave's reality. The aim was, as in all therapy, to get Dave to reincorporate those aspects he had projected onto mother and others and to see that not only was he vulnerable and helpless, as was his mother in her illness, but also manipulative and potentially harmful. The content of his psychodrama work was full of emotional intensity. In order to create a safe enough environment for all (including myself) it was crucial that I did not encourage transference reactions and resolved those that did exist before we began so that I could work alongside him, as director and facilitator rather than someone who was perceived as out to play 'mind games'.

There is a frequent anxiety amongst offender patients as to whether the group, the protagonist and 'auxiliaries' can survive the emotions that need to be expressed.

Vignette

No one wanted to volunteer to play the role of Jim's violent and abusive uncle, fearful of his own safety in the face of Jim's negative feelings. When Jim came to the psychodrama session stating his need to work, it was obvious that the protagonist and the group were in different places. It took several weeks before there was enough group cohesiveness, trust in the method and myself to consider how his work could be undertaken.

Eventually Jim was provided with a laundry bag of dirty underclothes and an old cupboard which symbolically represented the coffin of his uncle, in reality now dead, but internally very much alive. The auxiliary who had been playing uncle was asked to step aside and Jim was directed to focus his aggressive feelings onto the cupboard.

The psychodramatist relies heavily on psychodramatic techniques to control the action. Should a offender patient be experiencing intense and perhaps violent feelings towards the 'auxiliary' who is playing the role of a significant other, he is asked to reverse roles. Role reversal defuses the intensity of the feelings. Mattresses are used to wrap up and protect 'auxiliaries' from the expression of repressed, hostile feelings; 'batokas' are used instead of fists and the rule that no one is allowed to be hurt in psychodrama is strictly adhered to. When the aggressive feelings seem too much for the protagonist to deal with himself, 'doubles' act as advocates, or the aggressive feelings may be sculpted and explored in a less emotionally provocative manner.

CONCLUSION

More often than not angry outburst are followed by tears. Aggression for many offender patients has been the only form of survival and meaning. To go beyond the despair over what they have done to others to their own personal despair is a journey to be taken cautiously. It is essential to use one's professional judgement as to how much, and at what moment to go further. Not to do so puts all at risk.

Like other psychotherapies, psychodrama (through dramatic representation of self, one's behaviour, beliefs and feelings) is based on the knowledge that a person has the ability to be self-correcting when given accurate information about his behaviour. This is no less so for the offender patient than it is for any human being

The Contributors

Gwen Adshead is Lecturer in Forensic Psychiatry at the Institute of Psychiatry.

Anthony Bateman is Consultant Psychotherapist at the Halliwick Day Unit, St Ann's Hospital.

Arnon Bentovim is Honorary Consultant Child Psychiatrist at Great Ormond Street Hospital for Children and the Tavistock Clinic and Honorary Senior Lecturer at the Institute of Child Health, University of London.

Jacqueline Blatt is Course Co-ordinator for the MA in Dance Movement Therapy at the Laban Centre for Movement and Dance and Associate Professor at Hahnemann University.

Donald Campbell is Principal Psychotherapist and former Chairman of the Portman Clinic, and Member and Training Analyst, The British Psycho-analytic Society.

Jo-anne Carlyle is Clinical Psychologist in Psychoanalytical Psychotherapy at the Tavistock Clinic.

Nick Clark is a Registered Mental Nurse at the Three Bridges Regional Secure Unit, West London Healthcare NHS Trust.

Christopher Cordess is Consultant Forensic Psychiatrist with the North West Thames Forensic Psychiatry Service, London, and Honorary Senior Lecturer in Forensic Psychiatry at Charing Cross and Westminster Medical School. He is a Member of the British Psycho-analytic Society.

Murray Cox has been Consultant Psychotherapist at Broadmoor Hospital since 1970. He is an Honorary Member of the Institute of Group Analysis, the Danish Society for Psychoanalytic Psychotherapy and an Honorary Research Fellow, The Shakespeare Institute, The University of Birmingham.

Richard Davies is Senior Clinical Lecturer in Social Work and Principal Adult Psychotherapist at the Portman Clinic.

Bridget Dolan is Senior Lecturer in Forensic Psychology and an Honorary Lecturer in the Forensic Psychiatry section at St George's Hospital Medical School and Henderson Hospital.

Chris Evans is Lecturer in Psychotherapy at St George's Hospital.

Graeme Farquharson is Co-ordinator of Training at the Institute of Group Analysis.

Elizabeth Flannigan is Head Occupational Therapist at West London Healthcare Trust.

Peter Fonagy is Director of the sub-department of Clinical Health Psychology and Freud Memorial Professor of Psychoanalysis at University College, London, and is Director of the Anna Freud Centre.

Jennifer France is a Speech and Language Therapist at Broadmoor Hospital.

Stephen Freiberg is Consultant Psychiatrist and Psychotherapist at Wycombe Clinic, Sydney, and Visiting Psychiatrist at Long Bay Correction Centre and Prison Medical Service of New South Wales, Sydney.

Patrick Gallwey is a Psychoanalyst in private practice in Exeter and an Associate Member of the British Psycho-analytic Society.

James Gilligan is the Director of the Centre for the Study of Violence, The Cambridge Hospital, and Lecturer in Psychiatry, Harvard Medical School.

Adrian Grounds is Lecturer in Forensic Psychiatry at the Institute of Criminology and the Department of Psychiatry, University of Cambridge.

John Gunn, CBE, is Professor of Forensic Psychiatry at the Institute of Psychiatry.

Robert M. Hardy is the Bishop of Lincoln and the Anglican Bishop to Prisons.

Harriet Haworth is Clinical Psychologist at the Three Bridges Regional Secure Unit, Ealing Hospital.

Maggie Hilton is Consultant Clinical Psychologist at Henderson Outreach Service, Henderson Hospital.

R.D. Hinshelwood is Clinical Director at Cassel Hospital, and a Member of the British Psycho-analytic Society.

Arthur Hyatt Williams, now a Psychoanalyst in private practice in London, was Head of Adolescent Development at the Tavistock Clinic.

Rein Innes is Senior Art Psychotherapist at the Fromeside Clinic.

Barrie Irving is Director of The Police Foundation.

Jinnie Jefferies is a Psychodramatist and Counselling Psychologist at HM Prison Grendon Underwood.

Sue Jennings is an actress and broadcaster, Senior Research Associate at the University of London, Visiting Professor of Dramatherapy at New York University, and Honorary Consultant Dramatherapist at Broadmoor Hospital.

Dilys Jones is Medical Director, The Special Hospitals Service Authority, and an Honorary Lecturer at the Institute of Psychiatry.

Michael Killian is a Registered Mental Nurse at the Three Bridges Regional Secure Unit, West London Healthcare NHS Trust.

Gabriel Kirtchuk is Consultant Psychotherapist at the Regional Secure Unit, St Bernard's Hospital and an Associate Member of the British Psycho-analytic Society.

Peter Lewis is Director of Clinical Services and Director of Therapy at HM Prison Grendon Underwood.

Helen Loth is Head Music Therapist at Henderson Hospital, Haringey Healthcare.

Hjalmer van Marle is Medical Director at the Pieter Baan Centrum, Utrecht.

Clive Meux is Senior Lecturer in Forensic Psychiatry at The Institute of Psychiatry, University of London, and Honorary Consultant Forensic Psychiatrist at Broadmoor Hospital.

Jeannie Milligan is Clinical Lecturer in Social Work at the Tavistock Clinic.

Anton Mooij is a Member of the Directorate of the Forensic Observation Hospital of the Penitentiary, the Pieter Baan Centrum, Utrecht, and Professor of Forensic Psychiatry, State University of Groningen.

Kingsley Norton is Consultant Psychotherapist at Henderson Hospital and Honorary Senior Lecturer in the Section of Forensic Psychiatry at St George's Hospital.

Derek Perkins is Director of Psychological Services at Broadmoor Hospital.

Friedemann Pfäfflin is Senior Consultant in the Department of Psychotherapy at the University of Ulm.

Elaine Player is a Lecturer in Law at King's College, London.

Marie Quayle is Consultant Clinical Psychologist at Broadmoor Hospital.

J.H. Scheffer is a Psychoanalyst in private practice in Utrecht and is a Member of the Directorate of the Forensic Observation Hospital of the Penitentiary, the Pieter Baan Centrum, Utrecht.

John Schlapobersky is a Group Analyst and Psychotherapist at The Group Analytic Practice.

Valerie Sinason is Principal Child Psychotherapist at the Tavistock Clinic.

Ann Stanley is Senior Registrar in Forensic Psyciatry at the Reaside Clinic, Birmingham.

Deirdre Sutton-Smith is in private practice as a group analyst in Bristol, formerly a Probation Officer with the Inner London Probation Service, a group analyst at the Women's Centre, London, and a Member of the Institute of Group Analysis.

Neville Symington is a Psychoanalyst in private practice in Sydney.

Digby Tantam is Professor of Psychotherapy at the University of Warwick.

Mary Target is Lecturer and Senior Research Fellow in Psychology at University College, London and the Anna Freud Centre.

Nicholas Temple is Chairman of the Tavistock Clinic.

Alice Theilgaard is Professor of Medical Psychology at the University of Copenhagen and an Honorary Research Fellow, The Shakespeare Institute, The University of Birmingham.

Nikolaas Treurniet is a Psychoanalyst in private practice in Amsterdam and Training and Supervising Analyst, the Dutch Psychoanalytic Society.

Stephen Tumim is HM Chief Inspector of Prisons.

Cleo van Velsen is Consultant Psychotherapist at The Maudsley Hospital.

Estela V. Welldon is Consultant Psychiatrist at the Portman Clinic and Honorary Senior Lecturer in Forensic Psychotherapy at the University of London.

Richard Wells is Chief Constable of South Yorkshire Police.

Adrian West is Clinical Psychologist at the Personality Disorder Unit, Ashworth Hospital.

J. Stuart Whiteley, now a Consultant Psychotherapist in private practice in Surrey, was Medical Director at Henderson Hospital.

Eric Wilkinson is a Staff Nurse at Broadmoor Hospital.

Peter Wilson is the Director of Young Minds.

Martin Wrench is Senior Social Worker in the Department of Forensic Psychiatry at Shaftsbury Clinic, Springfield Hospital.

John L. Young is Attending Psychiatrist at Yale Medical School and Associate Clinical Professor of Psychiatry at the Whiting Institute.

Felicity de Zulueta is Consultant Psychotherapist at Charing Cross Hospital, Riverside Mental Health Trust, Honorary Senior Lecturer at The University of London, and a qualified Group Analyst.

Subject
Index

abandonment
  infant's fear of **I** 216
  see also attachment
aboriginals, in prisons **II** 156
abstract reasoning, and
    primary identifications
    I 164–5
abuse **I** 10, 14, 59
  anal **II** 374–5
  and animal behaviour
    I 78–9
  'benign' **II** 291
  in care contexts **II** 308–9
  child's survival of **I** 154
  and communication skills
    I 102–3
  and deprivation **I** 150
  differences in male and
    female response
    II 278, 286–9, 296–7
  drug *see* drug abuse
  effects of **I** 3, 14; **II** 362
  expression of **I** 103
  and families *see* family
    violence
  female offenders **II** 64,
    376, 379
  generational pattern
    II 285–8
  growing recognition of
    I 108
  and guilt **II** 381
  and identification with
    aggressor **I** 51
  interlocking roles **II** 297,
    308–9
  internalization of **II** 296–7
  and involuntary orgasm
    II 372

and language disorders
    I 100
  long-term effects **II** 361–2
  maternal **II** 376, 379
  and pathogenic secrecy
    I 10
  and perversion **I** 181;
    II 277–8, 285–8
  police training with mental
    health professionals
    II 23–4
  and post-traumatic stress
    disorder (PTSD)
    II 358–62
  predictors of **II** 292
  prevalence of **II** 368
  of professional power
    II 13, 323
  protection for victims of
    II 300
  pseudo-incest by mothers
    II 377–81
  recovery from **II** 302,
    381–2
  relationship to BPD and
    eating disorders **I** 181
  and removal of children
    II 302
  and repetition compulsion
    I 183–4
  and risk of re-abuse
    II 292, 302, 304–5
  role of statutory agencies
    II 300–1
  and self-deception **I** 19
  and self-mutilation **II** 361
  and sense of loss **I** 100
  social attitudes to victims
    and perpetrators **II** 64
  taking responsibility for
    II 301
  by therapist **II** 323
  transformational dynamics
    II 374–5
  trauma organized systems
    of **II** 294, 295–7
  by victims of abuse **II** 372
  'victimizing process'
    II 295–7
  see also emotional abuse;
    family violence;
    physical abuse; sexual
    abuse

abusers
  characteristics of **II** 292
  group therapy for **II** 73–81
  potential for change
    II 303–5
  as victims of abuse **II** 297
  work with **II** 306, 310
  see also victimzer
abusive acts
  processing of **II** 296
academic interest, as defence
    mechanism **II** 228
accents **I** 104
access to services **II** 536
accountability
  determining level of **II** 42
  see also responsibility
acoustic symbols **I** 96
'acting in' (non verbal
    enactment) **I** 18; **II** 72
acting out **I** 17
  as actualization **I** 18
  in autism and dysmorphia
    I 171
  by professional networks
    II 142
  and countertransference
    I 18–19, 24, 37
  and delinquency **II** 324–8
  eruption into action **I** 17
  of fantasies **II** 479
  in group-analytic
    psychotherapy **II** 70,
    72
  as inimical to
    psychoanalysis **I** 18
  and projection **I** 26, 37
  and premature departure
    from treatment **I** 17
  sexual **II** 368
  and therapeutic
    relationships **I** 18;
    II 129
  in therapy **II** 388
  and transference **I** 17;
    II 123
actions, as substitutes for
    thoughts **II** 478–84
active superego pathology
    I 136–7
actus reus **I** 13
addicts, specialized help for
    II 31

Author Index